D1673930

Financial Inclusion and the Role of Banking System

Sudarshan Maity • Tarak Nath Sahu

Financial Inclusion and the Role of Banking System

palgrave
macmillan

Sudarshan Maity
Directorate of Examination
The Institute of Cost Accountants
of India
Kolkata, West Bengal, India

Tarak Nath Sahu
Department of Commerce
Vidyasagar University
Midnapore, West Bengal, India

ISBN 978-981-16-6084-9   ISBN 978-981-16-6085-6   (eBook)
https://doi.org/10.1007/978-981-16-6085-6

This Palgrave Macmillan imprint is published by the registered company Springer Nature Singapore Pte Ltd.
The registered company address is: 152 Beach Road, #21-01/04 Gateway East, Singapore 189721, Singapore

PREFACE

Financial inclusion is the key to sustain equitable growth. Growth is equitable when all sections, regions, and levels of the economy get the benefit of growth and contribute to the overall growth process through poverty alleviation and equality in the distribution of resources. Without inclusive financial systems, the poor households and small entrepreneurs need to rely only on their own savings and earnings, which are so meager that they do not promote their entrepreneurship or take advantage of growth opportunities. Financial sector policies which provide the right incentives to individuals help them to overcome economic barriers. Also this is significant not only for stability but also for growth, poverty reduction, and equitable distribution of economic resources and capacities.

Based on the need to study the role of financial inclusion in inclusive growth, an exploration of the economic development agenda of the developing nations gives an account that poverty alleviation has been the foremost concern of policymakers all over the world.

Access to finance by the poor, weaker sections, and marginalized group of people is limited due to several reasons. Data at the macro level of the Indian economy show that a large section of the poor and marginalized sections of the Indian economy are not availing the formal financial services. They don't have access to various financial services provided by the institutional setup. This necessitates a good mechanism to operationalize financial inclusion. Financial inclusion of the poor and marginalized class is a necessary step in this regard. This helps to equalize opportunities and reduce inequalities. Therefore, financial sector policies are crucial for equitable growth and broader access to financial services required.

Financial inclusion is important today worldwide. Financial inclusion has become the top priority of the central banks and the Union Government with an objective to achieve inclusive growth. The objective of this book is to study the factors which influence financial inclusion and the role of public sector banks (PSBs) and private sector banks (Pvt. SBs). The study, in addition, looks at the initiatives taken by the Reserve Bank of India (RBI) and the Government of India (GOI) to promote full financial inclusion.

The experiences of major ten PSBs and ten Pvt. SBs toward financial inclusion are analyzed, and it is found that the process of financial inclusion could be facilitated by way of regulation and incentives. These two groups under the Scheduled Commercial Banks are at the center of the mainstream market.

In recent times, much progress of Pvt. SBs in the number of branches and total assets size has been found. It provides access to timely financial services availability and adequate credit to vulnerable groups living in India at an affordable cost. However, their role in financial inclusion largely focuses on payment services and is limited to the urban and metropolitan areas.

Always there is a scope to use more variables and better methodology to ensure the robustness of the results. In earlier studies, the selected banks or selected regions considered as samples are not enough to represent the entire status of the country. The literature on financial inclusion shows that there is a need for research on financial inclusion and determining its effectiveness in India.

Followed by a comprehensive review, it has been observed in this book that to accelerate financial inclusion regulatory initiatives and incentives are not only important but also a major challenge. After a detailed review, the present research suggests that the PSBs have generally made good progress in this regard, while Pvt. SBs still lag behind to achieve financial inclusion.

This book suggests that without enough initiatives by the regulators and incentives, banks can be less motivated in this progress. Thus, such a study is worth doing in the emerging economies like India to provide a good chance to understand more about the factors which influence financial inclusion as well as the role of banks in it among the formal financial institutions.

This study is important for policymakers to frame suitable policies and programs to accelerate the pace of financial inclusion and to create a win-win situation. This study would help RBI along with other financial intermediaries to redesign a financial strategic framework for achieving the long-term vision of financial inclusion drive, that is, inclusive growth.

Kolkata, West Bengal, India   Sudarshan Maity
Midnapore, West Bengal, India   Tarak Nath Sahu

CONTENTS

ABBREVIATIONS

AAEGR	Average Annual Exponential Growth Rate
ACT	Automated Cash Transfer
AFSP	Alternative Financial Services Provider
AGR	Annual Growth Rate
ANOVA	Analysis of Variance
AOTE	Average Overall Technical Efficiency
APPB	Average Population per Branch
APY	Atal Pension Yojana
ATM	Automated Teller Machine
BC	Business Correspondents
BCA	Business Correspondents Agent
BCC	Banker, Charnes, and Cooper
BC-ICT	BCs–Information and Communication Technology
BF	Business Facilitator
BRI	Bank Rakyat Indonesia
BSBDA	Basic Savings Bank Deposit Account
BSR	Basic Statistical Returns
CAGR	Compound Annual Growth Rate
CB	Commercial Bank
CCR	Charnes, Cooper, and Rhodes
C-D Ratio	Credit-Deposit Ratio
CFIP	Comprehensive Financial Inclusion Plan
CR	Central Region
CRA	Community Reinvestment Act
CRISIL	Credit Rating Information Services of India Limited
CRS	Constant Returns to Scale
CSO	Central Statistical Organization

CV	Coefficient of variation
CYFI	Child and Youth Finance International
DBT	Direct Benefit Transfer
DCT	Direct Cash Transfer
DEA	Data Envelopment Analysis
DFID	Department for International Development
DMU	Decision Making Unit
DRS	Decreasing Returns to Scale
ECS	Electronic Clearing Service
ER	Eastern Region
FDIC	Federal Deposit Insurance Corporation
FE	Financial Exclusion
FI	Financial Inclusion
FIP	Financial Inclusion Plan
FITF	Financial Inclusion Task Force
FLCC	Financial Literacy and Credit Counselling Centre
FSDC	Financial Stability and Development Council
GCC	General Credit Card
GDP	Gross Domestic Product
GOI	Government of India
HH	House Hold
ICT	Information and Communication Technology
IDFC	Infrastructure Development Finance Company
IMF	International Monetary Fund
IRS	Increasing Returns to Scale
IT	Information Technology
KCC	Kishan Credit Card
KMO	Kaiser-Meyer-Olkin
KYC	Know Your Customer
LAB	Local Area Bank
MFI	Microfinance Institution
NABARD	National Bank for Agricultural and Rural Development
NACCS	Non-Agricultural Cooperative Credit Society
NAS	National Accounts Statistics
NBFC	Non-Banking Financial Company
NER	North Eastern Region
NGO	Non-Government Organization
NNP	Net National Product
NPA	Non-Performing Assets
NR	Northern Region
NRFIP	National Rural Financial Inclusion Plan
NSO	National Statistics Office

NSSO	National Sample Survey Organization
OGD	Open Government Data
OLS	Ordinary Least Square
OTE	Overall Technical Efficiency
PACS	Primary Agricultural Credit Societies
PAN	Permanent Account Number
PC	Personal Computer
PCA	Principal Component Analysis
PCARDB	Primary Co-operative Agricultural and Rural Development Bank
PMJDY	Pradhan Mantri Jan Dhan Yojana
PMJJBY	Pradhan Mantri Jeevan Jyoti Bima Yojana
PMSBY	Pradhan Mantri Suraksha Bima Yojana
POS	Point-of-Sale
PSB	Public Sector Bank
PTE	Pure Technical Efficiency
Pvt. SB	Private Sector Bank
RBI	Reserve Bank of India
RRB	Regional Rural Bank
RTGS	Real Time Gross Settlement
SAARC	The South Asian Association for Regional Cooperation
SBI	State Bank of India
SCARDB	State Co-operative Agricultural and Rural Development Bank
SCB	Scheduled Commercial Bank
SCF	Surveys of Consumer Finances
SD	Standard Deviation
SDP	State Domestic Product
SHG	Self-Help Group
SMSA	Standard Metropolitan Statistical Areas
SPSS	Statistical Package for Social Sciences
SR	Southern Region
SSA	Sub-Service Areas
TRAI	Telecom Regulatory Authority of India
UCB	Urban Cooperative Bank
VIF	Variance Inflation Factor
WLA	White Label ATM
WR	Western Region

LIST OF FIGURES

LIST OF TABLES

CHAPTER 1

Introduction

1.1   Background of the Study

In recent times financial inclusion has received renewed attention from policymakers and regulators as well as from researchers of both developing and developed countries. Access to finance and also parameters related to finance is essential not only for maintaining and improving their social and economic status but also is essential for meeting all-round needs. An increasing span of financial inclusion reduces economic vulnerability of households, alleviates poverty, promotes economic growth, and enhances quality of life of people. Without having an account in a bank people cannot save for future availability of funds and for future money-related requirements; also in such cases people are compelled for future high-interest payments and fees upon the fund taken as loan for satisfaction of monetary requirement. An account in a formal financial institution can stimulate saving and uncovered access to credit. It can also make it easier to transfer wages, remittances, and various government payments. Banking industry plays a significant role in the development and growth of an economy. It is more essential to the Indian economy, which is a rural-based economy.

The scope of financial inclusion is as deep as the Indian Ocean and has two forms of measurement: business and necessity. About 41 percent of 1.2 billion populations, residing not only in 0.6 million villages but also in slums of towns and metro-cities, still do not have access to banking

© The Author(s), under exclusive license to Springer Nature
Singapore Pte Ltd. 2022
S. Maity, T. N. Sahu, *Financial Inclusion and the Role of Banking System*, https://doi.org/10.1007/978-981-16-6085-6_1

facilities. Most people in these places do not have financial access to formal institutions. In the early 1950s, All-India Rural Credit Survey indicated that unorganized sectors including moneylenders provided 70 percent borrowings to farmers while commercial banks (CBs) had provided less than 1 percent. There are large numbers of branches in metropolitan and in urban areas within a short distance. Even these two areas, where adequate infrastructure and presence of commercial banks are observed, possess a large section of the population who are deprived of facilities from formal banking.

Without the presence of bank branches, there can be no banking access for people. The easiest way to ensure better inclusion is to open more and more branches of financial institutions and remove various obstacles in accessing financial services from banks by very poor people. The larger the presence of bank branches, the more is the access. Without available sources of affordable credit, poor or low-income people may have to borrow from unorganized sectors or sources including money lenders at high costs. Also without having a deposit or savings account facility people will keep their money desiring for saving in unorganized or in an informal financial institution which gives them return at a higher rate of interest initially but uncertain to get back their initial investment amount. People are normally financially excluded, not only because of an absence of bank branches but also rejected or unable to use banking services or products and building societies.

Financial inclusion is the main object of the government as well as of the RBI. Banking services are central to the challenge of financial inclusion, which started from nationalization of banks. The growth of sound commercial banking will lead the nation to the top in the world—equivalent to the status of a developed economy. Commercial banks are entrusted with the responsibility to spread their services in urban, semi-urban, and rural areas to strengthen the economy of the people in general, different types of business organizations, and thereby the nation. The RBI and the GOI had taken initiatives since 1955 by the creation of the State Bank of India (SBI) followed by the nationalization of 14 major private banks (in 1969) and 6 more banks in 1980. In 1982 National Bank for Agricultural and Rural Development (NABARD) was set up mainly to provide refinance facilities to banks for extending agricultural credit.

The lives of people are going to change permanently, as there is a lot of innovation happening across different sectors including banking. Technology has found a prominent place in our everyday banking. It has been the key driver of revolutionary changes in the Indian financial sector with the growing demand for various financial services. Financial inclusion generally focused on the use of information technology (IT) to spread access to banking services. Banking institutions today are undergoing radical electronic transformations with the aim of gaining a competitive advantage. It brings a number of benefits for both financial institution providers and the customers. The government and RBI have issued guidelines and norms for use of IT in the banking sector to offer services through information technology. Technological solutions such as Automated Teller Machines (ATMs), mobile banking, internet banking, and smart cards have contributed a lot toward achieving the goal of financial inclusion (Sahu & Maity, 2021). The new facilities and different delivery channels that banks are giving their customers are not only to attract their customers but also to help reduce servicing cost.

The issue may be of crucial importance in advancing our understanding of financial inclusion. The primary focus of this present research is to study the current status of financial inclusion, measure its determinants, and examine the role of public sector banks (PSBs) and private sector banks (Pvt. SBs) in respect of financial inclusion.

1.2   THEORETICAL BACKDROP

Financial inclusion implies financial services to the needy and the financially excluded people with low cost and improved range of services. Financial institutions located around the world are providing a variety of services including deposits, loans, and so on to individuals and business entities. "The initiative of financial inclusion is important today due to a large part of the population being excluded from formal financial services and waiting for formal credit" (Maity & Sahu, 2021).

Financial inclusion is a global agenda, and due to its importance and impact on the economic growth of the country, large government entities to eminent personalities throughout the world have defined it differently (Sen, 2000; Annan, 2003; United Nations, 2006; Financial Inclusion Task Force, H.M. Treasury, 2007; Committee on Financial Inclusion, GOI, 2008; The Planning Commission, GOI, 2008; Nobel Laureate Dr. Mohammad Yunus, etc.). In broad terms, the authors may define it as providing financial services to all the communities with minimum cost. The financial services include providing deposit accounts, direct benefit transfer facilities, credit accounts for providing credit at low interest rates, and so on.

"To bring financially excluded people under the present financial setup, the regulators have taken a large number of initiatives from the national level to the regional level" (Maity & Sahu, 2021). To achieve holistic inclusive growth especially at the "bottom of the pyramid," it is utmost necessary that financial inclusion programs are given much importance, as a large section of the population from rural and urban areas are excluded and the banking system has failed to reach them (GOI, 2008). "A nation's development largely depends on the upliftment of the people at the lower strata of the pyramid" (Maity & Sahu, 2021).

1.3   FINANCIAL INCLUSION AND INCLUSIVE GROWTH

Beginning from the years 1990 to 2000, the Indian economy was one belonging to a state of fastest registered growth among the developing economies. Its growth rates of about 9 percent registered in those few years are historically unprecedented. With rapid growth rates, however, a question concerned was about the spread of benefits of growth, across society.

Universal financial inclusion may be achieved only with inclusive growth. Growth is inclusive when there is equality of economic opportunities. Financial inclusion accelerates circulation of currency and thereby increases gross domestic product (GDP). To achieve inclusive growth, access and use of financial services are to be ensured to all. With more than 0.6 million villages, the number of branches of bank was only 51,830. Due to low branch penetration, a large percentage of population are excluded from accessing financial services with resulting benefits of high GDP growth not reaching all the population of the country. Therefore, "financial inclusion is the key to sustain equitable growth" (Kelkar, 2009; Chakravarty & Pal, 2013; Anzoategui et al., 2014; Kunt, 2014; Jain, 2015; Unnikrishnan & Jagannathan, 2015; Sharma, 2016; Maity, 2019; Maity & Sahu, 2021).

1.4   PROVIDERS OF FINANCIAL SERVICES

The financial sector in India incorporates a vast network from rural to metropolitan regions. "The institutions that provide banking services include Commercial Banks, Cooperative Banks, Regional Rural Banks

(RRBs), Microfinance Institutions (MFIs), Non-Banking Financial Company (NBFC)" (Savitha, 2014), India Post, and so on. Depending upon the ownership pattern, CBs are classified as Scheduled Commercial Banks (SCBs) and non-SCBs (Fig. 1.1). SCBs are further classified under PSBs, private sector banks, foreign banks, and RRBs. PSBs include SBI (all the associates of SBI were merged with SBI in April 2017) and all nationalized banks. Nationalized banks refer to banks that were nationalized in three phases of 1969, 1980, and 2004.

SCBs are already in the process of reinventing themselves by the process of computerization of their branches, mobile banking, net banking facilities, ATMs (Fig. 1.2), and so on, to improve public service delivery. Now banks are very much interested to open off-site ATMs instead of a

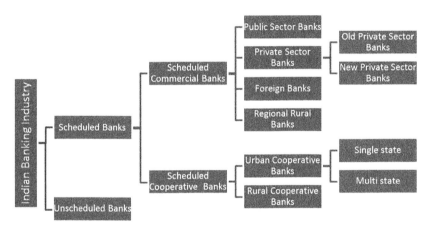

Fig. 1.1 Setup of Indian banking industry. (Source: Prepared by authors)

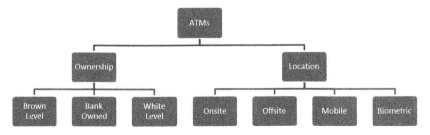

Fig. 1.2 Classification of ATMs. (Source: Prepared by authors)

new branch due to cost-effectiveness. And as a result during the last few years the numbers of ATMs have increased at a higher growth rate than bank branches.

In most cases in India, banks outsource the whole procedure of setting up ATMs to a third party by entering into individual contact arrangements. These ATMs bear the logo of the bank and are responsible for providing the cash. When the machines are operated and owned by third parties in diverse locations and they run in the name of that party, it is known as White Label ATMs. There is a compulsion of operating such banks in specific locations as advised by RBI. The cash is provided by sponsor banks.

Where banks themselves set up the ATMs and take the responsibility of operating they are called bank-owned ATMs. These are on-site ATMs and off-site ATMs. On-site ATMs are set up in the premises of the branch. By opening ATMs in bank premises customers' pressure can be minimized in a branch, and banking services can be improved as most customers are shifting to ATMs for immediate service. On the other side when ATMs are situated in any location other than the bank premises they are called off-site ATMs. Out of around 0.20 million ATMs, 50 percent are on-site ATMs and the rest are off-site ATMs. To reduce the overload of banking service in a branch in semi-urban and rural areas, it is easier to install an ATM either in the same building or in different places.

RBI passed the Regional and Rural Banks Act, 1976, to achieve financial inclusion goals. It plays a greater role in rural and semi-urban areas than SCBs. RRBs are jointly owned by the Government of India, Sponsor Bank, and the concerned State Government in the ratio of 50:35:15. MFIs also played a major role in ensuring financial inclusion. They provide credit and other products with a small interest to reach out to rural and semi-urban poor and underprivileged people. Many of them operate in a limited geographical area and have a better understanding of the issues specific to the people. As a financial intermediary NBFCs are perceived to be playing a complementary role to banks.

Other than scheduled and unscheduled banks, India Post is another formal institution that mostly covers rural areas where banking service is almost absent (Maity & Ganguly 2019a, b). With its vast experience since 1882, it is one of the largest networks in providing financial services especially to the poor, most importantly where the banking sector is ignored. In many developed and developing countries also post office plays a dominant role in achieving the goal of financial inclusion. Approximately one-third of basic accounts operating in Britain were accessible through the post office.

In addition to the above banking system, the Indian financial network consists of insurance companies, Primary Agricultural Credit Society (PACS), State Co-operative Agricultural and Rural Development Bank (SCARDB), Primary Co-operative Agricultural and Rural Development Bank (PCARDB), Self-Help Groups (SHGs), Civil Society Organizations, and Non-government Organizations (NGOs), which are vital financial intermediaries. In the recent past, RBI also issued 11 Payment Banks licenses and 10 Small Bank licenses. "The primary objective of these new entities is to push financial inclusion and promote various government new account opening schemes and insurance schemes" (Maity & Ganguly, 2019a).

Figure 1.3 depicts the various indicators of financial inclusion. With the initiatives and fulfilling all the above intermediaries, the target of financial inclusion can be achieved to sustain economic growth.

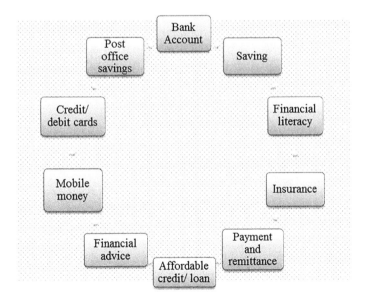

Fig. 1.3 Various financial inclusion indicators. (Source: Prepared by authors)

1.5   Importance of Financial Inclusion

"Bank as a mainstream financial institution has an important role to bring low-income families of both from rural and urban areas into the formal monetary sector, not as a social obligation, but as a clean business proposal" (Maity & Ganguly, 2019a). Having stated the background of access to finance, an examination of the history of the Indian banking industry gives an account of tremendous growth during the last few decades. Bank nationalization, which was directed to shift focus from "Class Banking" to "Mass Banking," has resulted in major positive changes in all areas relating to financial viability, profitability, competitiveness, and so on.

The following may be enumerated to justify why till the present period, even after 70 years of independence, financial inclusion is important. The factors noted below are considered to have a significant influence upon financial inclusion:

- More than 750 million population live in villages.
- Approximately 50 percent of population from rural regions have no bank account.
- 51,830 bank branches in rural regions (March 2016) cater to 0.6 million villages.
- The national average is 9880 population per bank branch (March 2016), with disparities between region to region.
- HHs of 58.70 percent accessing banking services (as of 2011).
- Lack of financial literacy—the biggest hindrance to the country's economic growth.
- Inclusive growth—not possible without outreach to unbanked villages.

1.6   Reasons for Low Inclusion

There are several factors that are considered major reasons for low financial inclusion. These can be summarized into six different categories as follows:

(i) Due to Geographical Location: Under this category, the reasons are remoteness of residence, hilly and sparsely populated areas with poor infrastructure and difficult physical access, long distance from a bank branch and branch timings, and so on.

(ii) Due to Economic Factors: The economic factors are low income and low assets.

(iii) Due to Social Factors: The social factors are ease of availability of informal credit, culture, and gender.

(iv) Due to Low Financial Literacy: Under this fourth category of low financial literacy, illiteracy, no requirement, and lack of awareness are the reasons for low inclusion.

(v) Due to Complex Documentation Process: Under this fifth category, the reasons are classified under two subheads of cumbersome and Know Your Customer (KYC).

(vi) Due to Inefficiency of Financial Institutions: These reasons are high cost of operations, less volume and more number of customers, products not being suitable, local language problem, negative staff attitude, and poor functioning and financial health of some financial institutions (such as financial cooperatives) which limit the effectiveness of their outreach figures, and so on.

1.7   Motivation of the Study

In rural areas, usual reasons for low penetration include absence of bank branches, distance from a branch, travel time and expenses, queuing times, high minimum balance requirements, lack of awareness of advantages of having a bank account, and, above all, low income that made it difficult to save. The picture is different in metropolitan and urban areas. There are lots of banks in urban and metropolitan localities with a short distance between them including two branches of different banks in the same building. But this does not mean that each and everyone in urban and metropolitan areas has deposit and credit accounts in a bank. The urban and metropolitan areas which have adequate infrastructure and good presence of commercial banks also have a large section of the needy population which is deprived of benefits from formal banking.

Data at the macro level of the Indian economy show that a large section of poor and marginalized sections are financially excluded. Most of them don't have access to various financial services. Access to financial services is also not uniform throughout the economy. A large number of studies have been conducted so far on it.

Previous literature surveys show that there is a need for further research on implementing financial inclusion and determining its effectiveness in India. As bank branches are the main formal financial institution for opening a deposit account or a credit account to tackle this problem effectively, much more research is needed to evaluate the role of banks. Therefore, there is a dire need to study the role of banks and measure the determinants and effective programs and policies implemented by regulators in order to achieve inclusive growth.

1.8   Objectives of the Study

From the given background as provided in the above sections, it is observed that the principal objective of this present study is required to inquire the status of financial inclusion, to find its determinants, to identify disparity across regions and states, and to examine the role of PSBs and Pvt. SBs in these respects. Accordingly, the principal objective may be decomposed into the following specific objectives:

1. to analyze the current status of financial inclusion in India;
2. to find out the important determinants of financial inclusion in India;
3. to analyze the disparity in financial inclusion across regions and states on financial inclusion in India;
4. to examine the impact of bank branch network expansion on financial inclusion;
5. to evaluate the technology-based mobile banking solutions for greater financial inclusion; and
6. to examine the comparative role of PSBs and Pvt. SBs in financial inclusion in India.

Considering the above objectives of the study, the authors have formulated the following four hypotheses.

Hypothesis I:
Null Hypothesis (H_0): There is no disparity in financial inclusion across regions and states on financial inclusion in India.
Alternative Hypothesis (H_1): H_0 is not true.

Hypothesis II:
Null Hypothesis (H_0): Bank branch network expansion does not have any significant impact on financial inclusion in India.
Alternative Hypothesis (H_1): H_0 is not true.

Hypothesis III:

Null Hypothesis (H_0): Technology-based mobile banking solutions do not have any significant impact on financial inclusion in India.

Alternative Hypothesis (H_1): H_0 is not true.

Hypothesis IV:

Null Hypothesis (H_0): There is no significant difference between the PSBs and Pvt. SBs on financial inclusion in India.

Alternative Hypothesis (H_1): H_0 is not true.

1.9   SAMPLE DESIGN

This section provides a detailed discussion about sample design of the proposed study to analyze the various objectives and hypotheses. It discusses sample design and selection of banks, study period, and data sources.

This study has been focusing on the services provided by the PSBs and Pvt. SBs under formal financial sector. The study has considered 20 banking companies. Ten banks have been selected from PSBs group and ten banks from Pvt. SB group. All these banks have been considered on the basis of quantum of total income and balance sheet size as of March 2015 which hold 70.83 percent market share of total 91 SCBs operating in India. The term "income" as used is income earned from interest and also from other sources.

The principal focus of this proposed study is to analyze the role of PSBs and Pvt. SBs in the area of financial inclusion. For the purpose of the study, secondary data have been collected from various sources at the national and international levels. At the national level, the relevant data have been sourced from organizations, such as NABARD, RBI, reports of different committees, National Statistics Office (NSO), National Sample Survey Organization (NSSO), National Accounts Statistics (NAS) of Central Statistical Organization (CSO), Open Government Data (OGD), Telecom Regulatory Authority of India (TRAI), Database of Indian Economy, Annual Survey of Industries, and other apex-level organizations. Data of state-wise population and land-area have been collected from the Census of India. Data were also collected from various magazines, journals, research papers, newspapers, and so on. At the international level, the source of data is from the websites and institutions, such as World Bank, International Monetary Fund (IMF), and the Department for International Development (DFID). The required analysis has been done using easily understandable graphs and tables in order to point out the facts of the analysis.

For this study, the authors have selected study period from 2001–2002 to 2015–2016 and it is desired to work on the basis of sufficient data so that the results become reliable. The study considers this period to be long enough to assure the adequacy of data. There have been a lot of policy changes with resulting changes in economic conditions since 1991. The authors have considered the study period from 2001 to 2016 owing to the incorporation of recent trends and major initiatives.

1.10   SCOPE OF THE STUDY

Since the first phase of bank nationalization, governments and regulatory agencies have taken numerous initiatives to bring all the population under the coverage of banking and other formal financial services. "Even after numerous initiatives a large percentage of population are financially excluded and is waiting for the part of economic growth of the country. The macro-level data reveals that poor and marginal sections of the society are mostly excluded as a result disparity in financial inclusion is found across the country" (Maity, 2019). Having a bank account is a primary step toward building a financial identity. This step further leads to development to the account holders and to the nation.

Financial inclusion is essential for ensuring access to timely financial services and providing adequate credit facilities to vulnerable groups living in India at an affordable cost. "While the link of finance and economic development is crucial, financial services to the economy are provided by both formal and informal financial networks" (Siddik et al., 2019).

This study would focus on services provided by PSBs and Pvt. SBs under the formal financial sector. The study has considered 20 banking companies. Ten banks have been chosen from PSB group and the rest ten banks being chosen from Pvt. SB group.

All these banks have been selected based on the quantum of total income and balance sheet size. The study would also focus on the status of financial inclusion. The study, in addition, looks at initiatives taken by GOI and RBI to promote full financial inclusion.

This study is important for policymakers, financial institutions, and technology providers to frame suitable policies and programs to accelerate the pace of financial inclusion and to create a win-win situation.

1.11   STRUCTURE OF THE BOOK

For studying the financial inclusion and role of banking system, the study has been divided into six interrelated chapters. A brief description of each chapter is as follows:

The first chapter is introductory in nature which contains highlights of the study, theoretical backdrop with definition, concept of financial inclusion and inclusive growth, providers of banking services, various financial inclusion indicators, and importance of financial inclusion, and it also explains reasons for low financial inclusion. The motivation of the study, objectives, sample design, and scope of the study have also been discussed in this chapter. Various initiatives by the regulators at global level are summarized in the second chapter. The chapter also contains a brief review of earlier studies based on global region. The studies have been presented starting from 1979.

The third chapter focuses on the financial inclusion status and the role of banks on financial inclusion and its major milestones in India. It also deals with the current scenario in comparison with the global perspective. A brief review of studies based on the Indian region and interrelation of the Indian region with other countries has been presented together yearwise starting from 1997. Research gaps have been identified and a case for the present study has been built in the end.

Determinants of financial inclusion and disparity across regions and states in India are discussed in detail in the fourth chapter. Key findings and their interpretations are also discussed in this chapter. The fifth chapter analyzes the role of banking system in financial inclusion and narrates the findings and their interpretations. The concluding chapter—that is, the sixth chapter—deals with the summary and conclusions derived from the findings of the study. An attempt is also made to put forward recommendations for effective financial inclusion in India and suggestions for future research in the area.

BIBLIOGRAPHY

BOOKS, JOURNALS, WORKING PAPERS ETC.

Annan, K. (2003). *Former UN secretary.* Retrieved from: www.wikipedia.com. Accessed 10 Apr 2016.

Anzoategui, D., Kunt, A. D., & Peria, M. S. M. (2014). Remittances and financial inclusion: Evidence from El Salvador. *World Development, 54,* 338–349.

Chakravarty, S. R., & Pal, R. (2013). Financial inclusion in India: An axiomatic approach. *Journal of Policy Modeling, 35,* 813–837.

Government of India. (2008, January). *Report of the committee on financial inclusion* (pp. 20). Economic Advisory Council to the Prime Minister, under the Chairmanship of C. Rangarajan.

Jain, S. (2015). A study of banking sector's initiatives towards financial inclusion in India. *Journal of Commerce & Management Thought, 6*(1), 55–77.

Kelkar, V. (2009). Financial inclusion for inclusive growth. *ASCI Journal of Management, 39*(1), 55–68.

Kunt, A. D. (2014). Presidential address: Financial inclusion. *Atlantic Economic Journal, 42,* 349–356.

Maity, S. (2019). Financial inclusion status in north eastern region: An evidence of commercial banks. *International Journal of Research in applied Management, Science and Technology, 4*(3), 1–11.

Maity, S., & Ganguly, D. (2019a). SWOT analysis of India post and India post payments Bank and their role in financial inclusion. *The Management Accountant, 54*(1), 68–72.

Maity, S., & Ganguly, D. (2019b). Is demonetization really impact efficiency of banking sector – An empirical study of banks in India. *Asian Journal of Multidimensional Research, 8*(3), 315–327.

Maity, S., & Sahu, T. N. (2021). Financial inclusion in north-eastern region: An investigation in the state of Assam. *VILAKSHAN – XIMB Journal of Management.* https://doi.org/10.1108/XJM-09-2020-0118

Planning Commission. (2008). *Hundred Small Steps: Report of the Committee on Financial Sector Reforms.* SAGE India.

Sahu, T. N., & Maity, S. (2021). Mobile banking a new banking model: An empirical investigation of financial innovation. *International Journal of Business Innovation and Research.* (Accepted for publication). https://doi.org/10.1504/IJBIR.2021.10039945

Savitha, B. (2014). Performance of cooperative banks in the delivery of microcredit in Andhra Pradesh. *Research Journal of Social Science & Management, 4*(8), 92–101.

Sen, A. (2000). *Development as freedom.* Anchor Books.

Sharma, D. (2016). Nexus between financial inclusion and economic growth. *Journal of Financial Economic Policy, 8*(1), 13–36.

Siddik, M. N. A., Ahsan, T., & Kabiraj, S. (2019). Does financial permeation promote economic growth? Some econometric evidence from Asian countries. *SAGE Open, 9*(3). https://doi.org/10.1177/2158244019865811

Treasury, H. M. (2007). *Financial inclusion: The way forward.* The report of the financial inclusion task force. United Kingdom, Retrieved from: www.bris.ac.uk/poverty/downloads/keyofficialdocuments/Financ. Accessed 10 Apr 2016.

United Nations. (2006). *Building inclusive financial sectors for development.* Retrieved from: http://www.un.org/esa/ffd/msc/bluebook/Blue%20Book%20Overview%202005%20-E.pdf. Accessed 26 Apr 2018.

Unnikrishnan, R., & Jagannathan, L. (2015). Unearthing global financial inclusion levels and analysis of financial inclusion as a mediating factor in global human development. *Serbian Journal of Management, 10*(1), 19–32.

CHAPTER 2

Global Initiatives Toward Financial Inclusion

2.1   GLOBAL INITIATIVES

In this chapter, an overall discussion is made about the implementation of effective financial inclusion programs and initiatives in developed and developing countries. The chapter also contains a review of related empirical and theoretical literature based on global regions. The study notices that even the US and the UK have not been successful in providing financial services to all their population. A large percentage of population from developed countries as well are financially excluded and looking for financial services to reach the unreached. Formal financial sectors have taken different initiatives to promote financial inclusion; likewise, regulators have also taken different steps to uplift financial inclusion.

The objective is to ascertain the excluded sections to access various formal financial services. A brief experience by different countries around the globe in promoting financial inclusion is discussed below:

2.1.1   Initiatives by the UK

To promote financial inclusion, the UK, in its pre-budget report in the year 2004, published its strategy for promoting financial inclusion. To monitor financial inclusion development in the UK a Financial Inclusion Task Force (FITF) was founded in 2005. The FITF has discovered three precedence areas for the objective of financial inclusion, namely, banking access, affordable access to credit, and free face-to-face money advice access. To remove financial exclusion a fund has been founded to promote financial inclusion and identify onus to credit unions and banks. A POCA and Savings Gateway has been created for different groups of people unwilling to access and low-income categories.

2.1.2   Initiatives by the US

The US government has taken several measures to deal with the difficulty of financial exclusion. To address concerns about closures of bank branches in low-income and underprivileged areas, in 1977 the federal government introduced the Community Reinvestment Act (CRA). The CRA forbids discrimination by financial service organizations against low- and moderate-income neighborhoods. In 1999 the Treasury Department of the US initiated a program to pay all federal benefits by electronic transfer accounts, such as social security payments.

The Treasury, in 2002, has initiated financial education to help financially excluded adults or community. Wholly owned government corporation within the US Treasury Department, the Community Development Financial Institutions have been servicing the financial needs of unorganized sector in the US to expand financial services.

2.1.3   Initiatives by Germany

Germany also does not much lag behind other countries to expand their basic banking transaction. In 1996 a willful code was introduced in Germany by the German Bankers Association for offering basic facilities of banking.

2.1.4   Initiatives by South Africa

In 1993 Standard Bank set up E-Bank, offering card-only access with simple saving products. In 2004 the country's prime banks introduced a bank account with low cost aimed to enhance banking products to the Black majority. The country's post offices along with four big retail banks introduced Mzansi account with minimum deposits. Standard Bank of South Africa also attempted new ways of meeting the requirement of an unbanked population. With wireless connections, grocery shops in South Africa situated around mines and underprivileged areas provide debit cards to their members for accessing various banking products and services.

2.1.5   Initiatives by Bangladesh

The microcredit approach has diversified into an extensive range of financial services. From vanilla credit products, they moved toward product differentiation by end use and target segments. The three largest MFIs including Grameen Bank serve around 12 million customers.

2.1.6   Initiatives by Mexico

"In Mexico, in a program developed by Nafin, a government development bank, many small suppliers use their receivables from large creditworthy buyers. By transferring the creditworthiness of large to small firms, the program grants them to access more and inexpensive financing" (Klapper, 2006).

2.1.7   Initiatives by Brazil

A new regulation has been attempted in Brazil to achieve universal financial access by enabling partnership between third-party agents and banks.

2.1.8   Initiatives by Kenya

In March 2007, e-money transfer service m-pesa, a small value electronic payment, was launched by Safaricom (mobile operator), which has achieved impressive progress so far. The central bank in Kenya had a major role in supporting mobile phone payment schemes and allowed regulatory space to mobile phone operators. A customer with m-pesa account can transfer funds or pay bills with their phone.

2.1.9   Initiatives by Other Countries

Countries like Brazil, China, Kenya, Mexico, the Philippines, South Africa, and France (which passed a law in 1998) have implemented several technology-based financial inclusion programs. Mobile-based payments are extensively used in Kenya, South Africa, Mexico, and the Philippines.

As a developing country, the Philippines first launched the mobile payment service in 2004.

In Indonesia, being specialized in microfinance, the Bank Rakyat Indonesia (BRI) a government-owned development bank is the provider of most of the financial services in rural areas. Even during the Asian financial crisis, when the banking system in Indonesia collapsed, the microbanking division of BRI remained relatively profitable. Various countries like China and the US also use pre-paid payment cards as an instrument to provide banking services to the unbanked and underprivileged population.

In many countries, for example, Sweden, France, and Canada, banks cannot refuse to open a deposit or saving account. Under Canadian law, everyone has the right to open a personal bank account. A bank cannot refuse to open an account for an individual merely because of them being unemployed or their inability to maintain a minimum deposit or because of them previously being bankrupt—as long as they have the proper identification.

Likewise, in UK, a bank cannot refuse to open a normal deposit account other than it is not feasible for the bank to ascertain the customer in a trustworthy manner or the bank has causes to suspect any misuse of it. Therefore, policymakers and regulators are focusing on a set of appropriate solutions to raise the access of formal financial services to the poorer populace. Notwithstanding the Indian economy has witnessed remarkable prosperity recently and due to diverse socioeconomic factors, enormous sections of the regions are outside India's growth story.

2.2   STUDIES BASED ON GLOBAL PERSPECTIVE

Financial inclusion, of late, has become the buzzword in academic research and is the flaming topic and reinvigorates attention among researchers, financial institutions, and regulators not only in India but across the globe including developed and developing countries. "Apex organizations, including IMF, World Bank, G-20 nations, etc., have undertaken financial inclusion as the key agenda item" (Maity, 2019). Due to its importance, a lot of studies have been conducted previously on various aspects of financial inclusion. Many studies have been conducted on the factors influencing it and influencing the opening of new bank branches.

Always there is a scope to use more variables and better methodology to ensure the robustness of the results. In the previous studies, the sample banks or selected regions were not enough to represent the entire status of the country. This chapter reviews the various empirical studies available and collected from different sources. Review of literature is helpful in gaining a background knowledge of the research topic and identifying the various issues related to it. The literature collected on the present studies has been summarized below.

Evanoff (1988) has investigated the branch impact on accessibility of banking services, measured as proximity of services (facilities) to the customer. He claims both population and per capita income are expected to positively impact accessibility because they directly influence demand for bank services. He uses ordinary least square (OLS) estimates of equation for 1980 to test whether branching affects service accessibility. His findings indicate that accessibility improved when branching was allowed. According to his study in the US, when comparing rural areas in which branching was allowed with those having only unit banks, service improves by 53 percent.

In Greece's banking system, National Bank and Commercial Banks of Greece are two major banks with around 600 branches controlling 70 percent of domestic deposits. Boufounou (1995) has presented a model for the Greece banks in establishing branch goals, planning locations, and evaluating performance. With 62 sample branches, this analysis finds the volume of deposits attracted by each branch. Further, Hirtle (2007) has investigated the impact of increasing branch network on bank performance. For this study, he considers bank and thrift regulatory reports for the years 1995–2003 and regressions are estimated using robust standard errors. The study concludes that the size of a bank branch is not dependent upon the performance, as branch network operations in US are an overall strategy of financial institutions.

In line with that, Seaver and Fraser (1979) have presented evidence on relationship of branching laws and banking offices availability for Standard Metropolitan Statistical Areas (SMSAs) in the US. Their analysis finds significant differences in population per banking office existed for almost all clusters and the public has access to a greater number of banking facilities under branch banking.

Access to financial services is defined as the ability to use new technologies and, awareness is defined as bank charges, interest rates, etc. Following this Worthington (2007) has used binary logistic models to investigate socio-economic, demographic, and financial characteristics in determining access to and awareness of personal banking accounts in Australian adults. A survey of 3548 respondents and eight specific questions have been examined. His results also generally show that consumers with better access also have a better awareness. The study further concludes that consumers develop the skills necessary for managing their bank accounts simultaneously with new ways of access in Australia. In another study, Alama and Ausina (2012) have examined the geographic expansion patterns of financial institutions in Spain during the post-deregulation period. Such an analysis may help develop further insights on relevant topics like access to finance. They focus on socio-economic variables that may have influenced the decisions to expand geographically. In their analysis, they consider that the variables affecting the number of branches in each municipality will not necessarily remain constant along with the conditional distribution of dependent variable. They have added several covariates to the model and also split some of the variables previously analyzed, which enriched the available interpretations. In line with that, Harimaya and Kondo (2012) have investigated the motivations for regional banks in Japan to expand their networks. In this study, they used data on Japanese regional banks for 2002–2006 and used Tobit regression model by employing a two-stage least squares (2SLS) regression. In particular, they focus on the lending behavior of each bank, whether loans are supplied to local markets sufficiently and whether SME finance facilitation occurs. Their analysis suggests that regional banks located in a less competitive lending market cannot help expand their networks geographically to seek out further lending opportunities in new markets.

Collard (2007) has investigated the progress that has been made in tackling financial exclusion in the UK. Of the three policy areas considered, namely, banking, consumer credit, and insurance, he found that availability of basic bank accounts through branch network, including automatic payment system, has resulted in a steady increase in banking inclusion. Russell et al. (2006) have explored the effectiveness of Saver Plus, a savings program in Australia. The program was launched in July 2003 and the first savings period was completed in December 2004. The Saver Plus program is aimed at assisting families on low incomes to reach a savings goal and develop a savings habit. Their studies have found much lower saving rates and saving propensities in lower-income households and households with children. Following this Imboden (2005) has examined the importance of financial inclusion. The empirical results of his study offered several strategies to build inclusive financial sectors. Further, Caskey (2000) has advocated an outreach strategy for banks for effectively bringing unbanked HHs into the banking system. This strategy includes opening special branch offices, called "outlets," for lower-income households. The five elements of his strategy have received wide acceptance from policymakers across the globe. Most financial inclusion policies adopted by developing countries invariably include the five elements of outreach strategy, namely, outlets, starter bank account, accumulation of savings, deposit secured loan, and association with community-based organizations.

Figart (2013) studied that a regulated financial services industry can be integral in meeting the needs of lower-to-moderate income communities. According to the 2011 FDIC survey, almost three-quarters of unbanked households have used an alternative financial services provider (AFSP). Poor households in the US and globally save money but largely outside of mainstream institutions. Figart proposed stricter regulation of AFSPs, which can help lower- to moderate-income HHs to enhance their efficacy in the financial sphere. In another study, Biles (2004) has investigated how globalization and economic liberalization have affected access to informal and formal financial resources in Valladolid, Mexico. In December 2003, a detailed survey of 101 HHs in Valladolid was conducted. According to the survey, informal credit comprised more than two-thirds of the sample HHs. The vast majority of HHs (82 percent) had made use of informal institutions to access financing during the past year. Family and friends that borrow from each other are indeed more likely to lend to each other. The empirical results of his study indicate that, although the transformation of Mexico's financial system may have promoted greater efficiency, it has failed to promote greater accessibility.

In line with the earlier studies, Lyons and Scherpf (2004) have tried to investigate whether financial education transformed from unbanked to bank. Economic theory suggests that an individual will open an account when the marginal benefit of opening an account exceeds the marginal cost. The data were collected from the participants of Federal Deposit Insurance Corporation's (FDIC's) Money Smart program in a pre- and post-evaluation format from 408 participants in Chicago. Two Probit models are estimated and their finding suggests that rather than quantity, that is, the number of accounts opened, qualitative program is important to make sound decisions. Their finding suggests that not all households are in a financial position to manage a healthy bank account regardless of an individual's level of financial education. Likewise, Asaad (2015) has examined confidence and knowledge as two components of financial literacy. Not surprisingly, individuals with both high confidence and knowledge are more likely to make "good" financial decisions than individuals with both low knowledge and confidence.

From an examination of the demographic bank penetration across Austrian districts with the data from 2006, Burgstaller (2013) concluded that mainly credit cooperatives serve the poorer and less developed rural banking markets. Further, he has found that compared with Germany, urban districts are more strongly dominated by commercial banks. In contrast to that, Midgley (2005) has critically focused on universal banking services in Britain.

Black households in the US receiving government assistance are significantly less likely to save, while there is no significant effect of government assistance on saving among White households. Following this Fisher (2010) has presented an exploration of White and Black differences in saving behaviors. The study used the 2007 Surveys of Consumer Finances (SCF) of US households. As shown in the interacted model, the variables for which the two groups' households (Black and White) differ significantly in terms of the effect on dependent variable (saving) are receiving government assistance. His study indicates that households with low-risk tolerance (greater risk aversion) are significantly less likely to save, and this applies to both White and Black households.

Rose (1993) has outlined a pedagogical framework for examining the role of commercial banks and reviewing current trends relating to that role in the US. The proposed framework includes four steps. First, the rationale for existence of banks as financial intermediaries is briefly reviewed. Second, the equilibrium level of financial intermediation is presented. Third, the declining function of large banks as credit intermediaries is documented and discussed. Finally, it examines the response of these banks to their lessened position as commercial credit intermediaries.

The analysis concluded that many major changes occurring in banking today can be tied, at least in part, to improved opportunities for large nonfinancial firms to raise funds through the open financial markets, with a consequent decline in the role of large banks as short-term commercial credit intermediaries. In line with that, Zardkoohi and Fraser (1988) have investigated the effects of geographical deregulation on competition in banking markets from 1964 to 1993.

In line with that, Paul (2001) has undertaken an in-depth study in Liverpool through a survey of 59 people of low-income households on how people on low-income access and use consumer credit. Majority of participants did not use mainstream or bank credit; instead, they went for a range of alternative sources. Factors influencing the choice of source of credit have been found as accessibility, ease and flexibility in repayment, affordability, tradition, and culture. Likewise Hogarth et al. (2003) have explored the reasons for not having an account and whether these reasons have changed over time. Their study is based on the data from 1992 to 1998 of SCF (Federal Reserve Board, 2002).

Arora (2012) has conducted a study of 21 Asian countries to explore the relationship between financial development and human capital. The study observes that the countries which ranked high in educational development did not rank high in financial development. Kumar and Mohanty (2011) have investigated financial inclusion policies and practices in the SAARC nations in general and India in particular. The study has mainly relied upon the data/indices provided in *Financial Access 2010*. Since financial access in SAARC countries is reported to be poor, there is a need for strong financial inclusion strategies and policies. According to them, with growth of IT and allied services, if financial literacy is properly addressed, financial inclusion drive in SAARC countries would definitely progress and show results. Further, Fungacova and Weill (2015) have investigated the level and determinants of financial inclusion and compared the financial inclusion status of China and other BRICS countries with the *Global Findex 2011* database. According to them, higher income, better education, being a man, and being older are associated with greater use of formal accounts and credit in China. Investigations of their findings suggest characteristics of individuals can help explain the use of formal financial services. In line with that, Simkhada (2013) has investigated the role of co-operatives in Nepal in reaching more remote rural communities. In another study, Kim (2016) has examined whether financial inclusion reduces income inequality. To accomplish this, he uses cross-sectional data for 40 OECD countries, the European Union, and Eurozone for the years 2004–2011. The study concludes that financial inclusion is a tool for reducing income inequality which has a very negative effect on GDP growth. The study by Giannetti and Jentzsch (2013) provides a panel dataset on 172 countries for the period 2000–2008. They find that the positive impact on introduction of a mandatory identification system exists independent from other factors that could potentially influence financial access and intermediation.

According to Kunt and Klapper (2012), African countries are lagging behind other developing economies in both usage and access. With more than 130,000 sample firms from 127 countries their analysis shows that cost, distance, and documentation requirements are important obstacles. In a study, Ajide (2017) has examined determinants of 18 sub-Saharan African countries using Generalized Methods of Moments over a period spanning from 2004 to 2010. According to his analysis, financial inclusion is a measure of financial indicators like ATMs and bank branches per 0.1 million adults and ATMs per 1000 sq. km. Variables like inflation, per capita GDP, bank concentration, and z-score constitute the main drivers to measure FI. In line with that, Inoue and Hamori (2016) have analyzed the effects of financial access on economic growth of 37 sub-Saharan African countries with panel data of 2004–2012. In their analysis, they construct proxy measures of accessibility of financial services among users based on the number of CB branches in terms of demographic or geographic measure.

A financially inclusive society is important to help people mobilize more resources to support economic growth and to create better opportunities for poverty reduction. Ansong et al. (2015) have examined branch model banking services in Ghana with demographic data from the 2010 census. Their study utilized spatial analyst tools with geographically weighted Poisson regression. Their study finds evidence of inequality and that not everyone in Ghana has physical access to a bank.

"Also, advanced technologies have been incorporated as a tool towards more financial inclusion. The US data over 14 years period provides an excellent opportunity for analyzing technological change, parental control, and distance effects" (Berger and Deyoung, 2006). Findings reveal that progress in technology has facilitated geographic expansion of banking industry. In another study, Koku (2009) has examined new product innovation and marketing strategies of CBs in Ghana. Other than a literature review, interviews and observational techniques too were used to obtain qualitative data for this study. All the interviewees were married and were between 53 and 70 years of age. His analyses show that the marketing strategies that the banks currently use are consistent with marketing strategies in the literature. The study provides a framework of marketing strategy for access of loans to poor for improving their quality of life.

Alexandre et al. (2011) have examined new banking models to bring financial or banking services to all. There is growing awareness that the absence of retail distribution is the binding constraint in the delivery of financial services to poor people. Their study concludes that mobile communications can bridge distances for people living in remote areas and reduce transaction costs.

In another study Kundu (2015) has tried to find the ways and means to increase demand for financial services among the poor. Lower cost and scalability can be achieved when there is demand. The aim is to see how banks can generate value for the products and services so that low-end customers are willing to avail them and pay for them. Such products and services should be delivered through user-friendly channels leveraging the technology and integrated with financial literacy of the target group. The World Bank Financial Access Survey (2013) has identified that the poor do not feel the requirement for banking because their income is very low which leaves them with little or no savings. In another study, Birochi and Pozzebon (2016) have investigated ICT-based access in the Amazonian municipality of Brazil. The study covers two periods—December 2009 and mid-2010—using semi-structured interviews and field notes. Their results suggest that ICT-supported access might increase financial inclusion. Belas et al. (2015) conducted a study with a questionnaire survey in the Slovak Republic in 2015 with 321 sample respondents. The validity of each hypothesis was verified by them through the Pearson statistics undertaking correlation and reliability test. This method allows them to quantify statistically significant differences within the defined sets of respondents. Their analysis finds that customers with higher education intensively use electronic banking. Further, Nyagilo (2017) has investigated the role of financial technology in rural Kenya. Secondary data on all independent variables were obtained from the Central Bank of Kenya payment system statistics and covered a period between January 2011 and December 2016. The study made use of descriptive statistics, analysis of variance, correlation analysis, univariate regression analysis, and multivariate regression analysis. The result shows positive and significant impact of mobile banking on financial inclusion.

Using data of 2012, Sanz and Lima (2013) have investigated the development of mobile financial services in the Africa region. Their study had three major objectives: first, to analyze country context and environment in each of the selected countries from the point of view of feasibility of deploying mobile financial service in FEMIP (Facility for

Euro-Mediterranean Investment and Partnership) countries; second, to clarify the elements required for successful implementation of mobile financial service and best practices identified in the institutions studied; and third, to outline criteria that will help identify institutions that could fit into follow-up projects. Indeed, thanks to the rapid adoption of mobile phones, in most developing countries more people have mobile phones than bank accounts. Their study concluded that mobile phones can be used as a channel of communication to initiate and execute financial transactions in real time. Not only can they reduce the cost of financial transactions for providers and customers, they can also open the door to new financial industry players using new and more efficient business models for distribution of financial services. Mishra and Bisht (2013) have conducted a study to explore mobile banking services. According to their investigation, there are different types of conjoint analysis techniques, namely, traditional (full profile conjoint analysis), adaptive conjoint analysis, and choice-based conjoint analysis.

Further, Nice and Irvine (2010) have investigated the use of automated banking facilities among low-income people in the UK. Single people, families with children (couples and lone parents), and pensioners were all represented in their study. The study indicates, a relatively low-income group of the population may find it difficult to become or remain comprehensive users of automated payment methods. Their evidence also suggests that financial "cushion" of a slightly higher income allowed people to feel less concerned about the timing of outgoings. Their finding suggests that people on low incomes can make extensive use of automated payment facilities and thus move toward full financial inclusion. According to Hinson (2011) if a traditional financial setup is not allowed to provide financial services to the poor, then it can be provided through mobile technologies. He proposed a model through mobile technologies to banking access for poor people. Moreover, Mitchell (1999) has stated that perceived risk is a critical factor to be focused on by banks and service providers while designing and developing a mobile banking service.

Financial products and services will not support rights of children without effective policy and research. Research and policy will not bear fruit without examples of successful program implementations. All of the players impacting the financial ecosystem of young people as well as young people themselves must work together on constructing a greater ecosystem for economic citizenship. If young people can be empowered and equipped to take charge of their financial futures, we anticipate a much brighter future for all ages. Billimoria et al. (2013) have looked at the effect of education for children and youth on financial inclusion. In their study, they have summarized development of a framework for economic citizenship education and demonstrated the importance of combining this holistic type of education with financial inclusion. Their research has shown that financial services help young people best when these are offered in conjunction with non-financial services such as mentoring and financial education (how to avoid debt, open a bank account, write a check, plan a budget, etc.). Their study suggests positive and wide-ranging correlative effects with financial education programs. Similarly, financial inclusion, or access to savings, has shown positive correlations with variables such as expectations for the future, academic achievement, and even health outcomes (CYFI, 2012). Their studies conclude that economic citizenship education will not have traction without child-friendly products and services.

In a study, Kunt and Klapper (2013) have suggested that financial depth and financial inclusion are related to each other. In another study, Sajuyigbe (2017) has examined the influence of financial and social inclusion on women-owned businesses in Nigeria's Lagos State. The study indicates that social inclusion has a significantly positive relationship with financial inclusion. Using the National Economic Social Survey (SUSENAS) data during 2008–2012 of Indonesia, Gitaharie et al. (2018) investigated household profiles and analyzed factors that determined households' access to loans from banks, non-bank institutions, and individual (informal) sources. By applying the multinomial logistic regression their study investigates the factors that determine the households' loans/credit obtainment. According to them, the biggest constraint to obtaining bank loans is mainly collateral.

Other studies by Claessens (2006); Beck et al. (2007); Honohan (2008); Jones (2008); Sarma and Pais (2008); Chibba (2009); Devlin (2009); Giuliano and Ruiz-Arranz (2009); Ergungor (2010); Manji (2010); Pandey et al. (2010); Aggarwal et al. (2011); Appleyard (2011); Kunt et al. (2011); Diniz et al. (2012); Zhan et al. (2012); Aysan et al. (2013); Koker and Jentzsch (2013); Sinclair (2013); Wentzel et al. (2013); Anzoategui et al. (2014); Evans and Pirchio (2014); Kapoor (2014); Kasekende (2014); Kostov et al. (2014); Koku (2015); Machogu and Okiko (2015); Prina (2015); Sarker et al. (2015); Unnikrishnan and Jagannathan (2015); Yan Yuan (2015); Zins and Weill (2016); Abor et al.

(2017); Chen and Jin (2017); and Musau et al. (2018) on global region also highlighted the importance of financial inclusion in the development of an economy. All over the world many initiatives have been taken to bring financially excluded people into formal financial services. The initiatives may differ from country to country. However, the objective of the initiatives is the same, that is, to bring all the population into a formal banking net. Further, due to its global importance, the study finds that numerous studies have been undertaken by researchers from a global perspective. The enormous financial inclusion initiatives considered globally elucidated in this chapter will influence other countries to be a part of their new agenda to achieve the target of financial inclusion. These various initiatives are also helpful to the researchers who are present across the world for their future research.

BIBLIOGRAPHY

BOOKS, JOURNALS, WORKING PAPERS ETC.

Abor, J. Y., Amidu, M., & Issahaku, H. (2017). Mobile telephony, financial inclusion and inclusive growth. *Journal of African Business*, 1–24.

Aggarwal, R., Kunt, A. D., & Pería, M. S. M. (2011). Do remittances promote financial development? *Journal of Development Economics, 96*, 255–264.

Ajide, K. B. (2017). Determinants of financial inclusion in sub-Saharan Africa countries: Does institutional infrastructure matter? *CBN Journal of Applied Statistics, 8*(2), 69–89.

Alama, L., & Ausina, E. T. (2012). Bank branch geographic location patterns in Spain: Some implications for financial exclusion. *Growth and Change, 43*(3), 505–543.

Alexandre, C., Mas, I., & Radcliffe, D. (2011). Regulating new banking models to bring financial services to all. *Challenge, 54*(3), 116–134.

Ansong, D., Chowa, G., & Adjabeng, B. K. (2015). Spatial analysis of the distribution and determinants of bank branch presence in Ghana. *International Journal of Bank Marketing, 33*(3), 201–222.

Anzoategui, D., Kunt, A. D., & Peria, M. S. M. (2014). Remittances and financial inclusion: Evidence from El Salvador. *World Development, 54*, 338–349.

Appleyard, L. (2011). Community development finance institutions (CDFIs): Geographies of financial inclusion in the US and UK. *Geoforum, 42*, 250–258.

Arora, R. U. (2012). Financial inclusion and human capital in developing Asia: The Australian connection. *Third World Quarterly, 33*(1), 179–199.

Asaad, C. T. (2015). Financial literacy and financial behavior: Assessing knowledge and confidence. *Financial Services Review, 24*, 101–117.

Aysan, A. F., Dolgun, M. H., & Turhan, M. I. (2013). Assessment of the participation banks and their role in financial inclusion in Turkey. *Emerging Markets Finance & Trade, 49*(Supplement 5), 99–111.

Beck, T., Kunt, A. D., & Peria, M. S. M. (2007). Reaching out: Access to and use of banking services across countries. *Journal of Financial Economics, 85*, 234–266.

Belas, J., Koraus, M., & Gabcova, L. (2015). Electronic banking, its use and safety. Are three differences in the access of Bank customers by gender, education and age? *International Journal of Entrepreneurial Knowledge, 3*(2), 16–28.

Berger, A. N., & Deyoung, R. (2006). Technological progress and the geographic expansion of the banking industry. *Journal of Money, Credit, and Banking, 38*(6), 1485–1513.

Biles, J. J. (2004). Globalization of banking and local access to financial resources: A case study from southeastern Mexico. *The Industrial Geographer, 2*(2), 159–173.

Billimoria, J., Penner, J., & Knoote, F. (2013). Developing the next generation of economic citizens: Financial inclusion and education for children and youth. *Enterprise Development and Microfinance, 24*(3), 204–217.

Birochi, R., & Pozzebon, M. (2016). Improving financial inclusion: Towards a critical financial education framework. *Sao Paulo, 56*(3), 266–287.

Boufounou, P. V. (1995). Evaluating bank branch location and performance: A case study. *European Journal of Operational Research, 87*, 389–402.

Burgstaller, J. (2013). Bank office outreach, structure and performance in regional banking markets. *Regional Studies, 47*(7), 1131–1155.

Caskey, P. J. (2000). *Lower income Americans, higher cost financial services.* Retrieved from: http://www.filene.org. Accessed 30 May 2013.

Chen, Z., & Jin, M. (2017). Financial inclusion in China: Use of credit. *Journal of Family and Economic Issues, 38*(4), 528–540.

Chibba, M. (2009). Financial inclusion, poverty reduction and the millennium development goals. *European Journal of Development Research, 21*(2), 213–230.

Claessens, S. (2006). A review of the issues and public policy objectives. *The World Bank Research Observer, 21*(2), 207–240.

Collard, S. (2007). Toward financial inclusion in the UK: Progress and challenges. *Public Money & Management, 27*(1), 13–20.

CYFI. (2012). *Children and youth as economic citizens: Review of research on financial capability, financial inclusion and financial education.* Research working group report, Amsterdam: CYFI. Retrieved from: http://childfinanceinternational.org/index.php?option=com_mtree&task=att_download&link_id=374&cf_id=200. Accessed 19 Aug 2013.

Devlin, J. F. (2009). An analysis of influences on total financial exclusion. *The Service Industries Journal, 29*(8), 1021–1036.

Diniz, E., Birochi, R., & Pozzebon, M. (2012). Triggers and barriers to financial inclusion: The use of ICT-based branchless banking in an Amazon county. *Electronic Commerce Research and Applications, 11*, 484–494.

Ergungor, O. E. (2010). Bank branch presence and access to credit in low- to moderate-income neighborhoods. *Journal of Money, Credit and Banking, 42*(7), 1321–1349.

Evanoff, D. D. (1988). Branch banking and service accessibility. *Journal of Money, Credit, and Banking, 20*(2), 191–202.

Evans, D. S., & Pirchio, A. (2014). An empirical examination of why mobile money schemes ignite in some developing countries but flounder in most. *Review of Network Economics, 13*(4), 397–451.

Federal Reserve Board. (2002). *Survey of consumer finances*. Retrieved from: http://www.federalreserve.gov/pubs/oss/oss2/scfindex.html. Accessed 28 April 2018.

Figart, D. M. (2013). Institutionalist policies for financial inclusion. *Journal of Economic Issues, XLVII*(4), 873–893.

Fisher, P. J. (2010). Black-white differences in saving behaviors. *Financial Services Review, 19*, 1–16.

Fungacova, Z., & Weill, L. (2015). Understanding financial inclusion in China. *China Economic Review, 34*, 196–206.

Giannetti, C., & Jentzsch, N. (2013). Credit reporting, financial intermediation and identification systems: International evidence. *Journal of International Money and Finance, 33*, 60–80.

Gitaharie, B. Y., Soelistianingsih, L., & Djutaharta, T. (2018). Financial inclusion: Household access to credit in Indonesia. In L. Gani, B. Y. Gitaharie, Z. A. Husodo, & A. Kuncoro (Eds.), *Competition and cooperation in economics and business*. Taylor & Francis Group.

Giuliano, P., & Ruiz-Arranz, M. (2009). Remittances, financial development, and growth. *Journal of Development Economics, 90*, 144–152.

Harimaya, K., & Kondo, K. (2012). Determinants of branch expansion by Japanese regional banks. *The IUP Journal of Bank Management, XI*(2), 7–25.

Hinson, R. E. (2011). Banking the poor: The role of mobiles. *Journal of Financial Services Marketing, 15*(4), 320–333.

Hirtle, B. (2007). The impact of network size on bank branch performance. *Journal of Banking & Finance, 31*, 3782–3805.

Hogarth, J. M., Anguelov, C. E., & Lee, J. (2003). Why households don't have checking accounts. *Economic Development Quarterly, 17*(1), 75–94.

Honohan, P. (2008). Cross-country variation in household access to financial services. *Journal of Banking & Finance, 32*, 2493–2500.

Imboden, K. (2005). Building inclusive financial sectors: The road to growth and poverty reduction. *Journal of International Affairs, 58*(2), 65–86.

Inoue, T., & Hamori, S. (2016). Financial access and economic growth: Evidence from sub-Saharan Africa. *Emerging Markets Finance & Trade, 52*, 743–753.

Jones, P. A. (2008). From tackling poverty to achieving financial inclusion – The changing role of British credit unions in low income communities. *The Journal of Socio-Economics, 37*, 2141–2154.

Kapoor, A. (2014). Financial inclusion and the future of the Indian economy. *Futures, 56*, 35–42.

Kasekende, L. (2014). What role does financial inclusion play in the policy agenda for inclusive growth in sub-Saharan Africa? *Development, 57*(3–4), 481–487.

Kim, J. H. (2016). A study on the effect of financial inclusion on the relationship between income inequality and economic growth. *Emerging Markets Finance & Trade, 52*, 498–512.

Klapper, L. (2006). The role of factoring for financing small and medium enterprises. *Journal of Banking & Finance, 30*(11), 3111–3130.

Koker, L. D., & Jentzsch, N. (2013). Financial inclusion and financial integrity: Aligned incentives? *World Development, 44*, 267–280.

Koku, P. S. (2009). Doing well by doing good – Marketing strategy to help the poor: The case of commercial banks in Ghana. *Journal of Financial Services Marketing, 14*(2), 135–151.

Koku, P. S. (2015). Financial exclusion of the poor: A literature review. *International Journal of Bank Marketing, 33*(5), 654–668.

Kostov, P., Arun, T., & Annim, S. (2014). Banking the unbanked: The Mzansi intervention in South Africa. *Indian Growth and Development Review, 7*(2), 118–141.

Kumar, B., & Mohanty, B. (2011). Financial inclusion and inclusive development in SAARC countries with special reference to India. *Vilakshan, XIMB Journal of Management*, (September), 13–22.

Kundu, D. (2015). Addressing the demand side factors of financial inclusion. *Journal of Commerce & Management Thought, 6*(3), 397–417.

Kunt, A. D., Cordova, E. L., Pería, M. S. M., & Woodruff, C. (2011). Remittances and banking sector breadth and depth: Evidence from Mexico. *Journal of Development Economics, 95*, 229–241.

Kunt, A. D., & Klapper, L. (2012, June). *Financial inclusion in Africa an overview* (Policy Research Working Paper, 6088, pp. 1–18). The World Bank Development Research Group Finance and Private Sector Development Team.

Kunt, A. D., & Klapper, L. (2013). Measuring financial inclusion: Explaining variation in use of financial services across and within countries. In *Brookings papers on economic activity* (pp. 279–321). Spring.

Lyons, A. C., & Scherpf, E. (2004). Moving from unbanked to banked: Evidence from the money smart program. *Financial Services Review, 13*, 215–231.

Machogu, A. M., & Okiko, L. (2015). E-banking complexities and the perpetual effect on customer satisfaction in Rwandan commercial banking industry: Gender as a moderating factor. *Journal of Internet Banking & Commerce, 20*(3), 1–8.

Maity, S. (2019). Financial inclusion status in north eastern region: An evidence of commercial banks. *International Journal of Research in applied Management, Science and Technology, 4*(3), 1–11.

Manji, A. (2010). Eliminating poverty? 'Financial Inclusion', access to land, and gender equality in international development. *The Modern Law Review, 73*(6), 985–1004.

Midgley, J. (2005). Financial inclusion, universal banking and post offices in Britain. *Area, 37*(3), 277–285.

Mishra, V., & Bisht, S. S. (2013). Mobile banking in a developing economy: A customer-centric model for policy formulation. *Telecommunications Policy, 37,* 503–514.

Mitchell, V. W. (1999). Consumer perceived risk: Conceptualizations and models. *European Journal of Marketing, 33*(1/2), 163–195.

Musau, S., Muathe, S., & Mwangi, L. (2018). Financial inclusion, GDP and credit risk of commercial banks in Kenya. *International Journal of Economics and Finance, 10*(3), 181–195.

Nice, K., & Irvine, A. (2010). Living on a low income and using banks to pay bills. *Journal of Poverty and Social Justice, 18*(1), 53–67.

Nyagilo, V. (2017). Financial inclusion in rural Kenya: An investigation of the role of financial technology as an instrument. *International Journal of Business Management & Finance, 1*(31), 534–553.

Pandey, T., Krishna, N., Vickers, V., Menezes, A., & Raghavendra, M. (2010). Innovative payment solutions in agricultural value chain as a means for greater financial inclusion. *Agricultural Economics Research Review, 23*(Conference Number), 527–534.

Paul, A. J. (2001). *Access to credit on a low income: A study into how people on low incomes in Liverpool access and use consumer credit.* Retrieved from: http://creditunionresearch.com. Accessed 13 Apr 2017.

Prina, S. (2015). Banking the poor via savings accounts: Evidence from a field experiment. *Journal of Development Economics, 115,* 16–31.

Rose, J. T. (1993). Commercial banks as financial intermediaries and current trends in banking: A pedagogical framework. *Financial Practice and Education – FALL,* 113–118.

Russell, R., Brooks, R., Nair, A., & Fredline, L. (2006). The initial impacts of a matched savings program: The saver plus program. *Economic Papers, 25*(1), 32–40.

Sajuyigbe, A. S. (2017). Influence of financial inclusion and social inclusion on the performance of women owned business in Lagos state, Nigeria. *Scholedge International Journal of Management & Development, 4*(3), 18–27.

Sanz, F. P., & Lima, P. D. (2013). The uptake of mobile financial services in the Middle East and North Africa region. *Enterprise Development and Microfinance, 24*(4), 295–310.

Sarker, S., Ghosh, S. K., & Palit, M. (2015). Role of banking – Sector to inclusive through inclusive finance in Bangladesh. *Studies in Business and Economics, 10*(2), 145–156.

Sarma, M., & Pais, J. (2008, September). *Financial inclusion and development: A cross country analysis* (pp. 1–28). Paper presented at the annual conference of the human development and capability association, New Delhi. Retrieved from: www.icrier.org/pdf/6nov08/Mandira%20Sarma-Paper.pdf. Accessed 20 July 2016.

Seaver, W. L., & Fraser, D. R. (1979). Branch banking and the availability of banking services in metropolitan areas. *Journal of Financial and Quantitative Analysis, XIV*(1), 153–160.

Simkhada, N. R. (2013). Problems and prospects of the cooperative sector in Nepal for promoting financial inclusion. *Enterprise Development and Microfinance, 24*(2), 146–159.

Sinclair, S. (2013). Financial inclusion and social financialisation: Britain in a European context. *International Journal of Sociology and Social Policy, 33*(11/12), 658–676.

Unnikrishnan, R., & Jagannathan, L. (2015). Unearthing global financial inclusion levels and analysis of financial inclusion as a mediating factor in global human development. *Serbian Journal of Management, 10*(1), 19–32.

Wentzel, J. P., Diatha, K. S., & Yadavalli, V. S. S. (2013). An application of the extended technology acceptance model in understanding technology-enabled financial service adoption in South Africa. *Development Southern Africa, 30*(4–5), 659–673.

Worthington, A. C. (2007). Personal bank account access and awareness: An analysis of the technological and informational constraints of Australian consumers. *International Journal of Consumer Studies, 31*, 443–452.

Yan Yuan, L. X. (2015). Are poor able to access the informal credit market? Evidence from rural households in China. *China Economic Review, 33*, 232–246.

Zardkoohi, A., & Fraser, D. R. (1988). Geographical deregulation and competition in U.S. banking markets. *The Financial Review, 33*, 85–98.

Zhan, M., Anderson, S. G., & Zhang, S. (2012). Utilization of formal and informal financial services among immigrants in the United States. *Social Development Issues, 34*(3), 1–17.

Zins, A., & Weill, L. (2016). The determinants of financial inclusion in Africa. *Review of Development Finance, 6*, 46–57.

CHAPTER 3

Financial Inclusion in India: An Assessment

3.1 Introduction

The policy agenda of many developed countries find prominence in the promotion and development of the financial sector. The study of financial inclusion is extremely momentous for the growth of the society and economic development of a nation.

A large percentage of population is excluded from accessing the facilities of banking services. And as such many initiatives have been taken by the regulators being both from the demand side and from the supply side. In regard to the importance of financial inclusion, it is an important topic for researchers. And accordingly, large numbers of research have been conducted on various aspects.

Access to finance, especially to the vulnerable section of the society, has been prerequisite for employment, economic growth, poverty reduction, and social cohesion. Without having an account, people do not save for future purchases and child education, to invest for retirement, or to avoid high-interest payments and fees. CBs have the responsibility to spread their services in urban, semi-urban, and rural areas to strengthen the economy of HHs and thereby the nation.

PSBs started their journey since before nationalization of banks in 1969. Banks started their journey of financial inclusion with the nationalization of 14 CBs in 1969, and 6 more in 1980, and licensing to private banks in 1993. Regulators have taken these initiatives to bring the financially excluded into the banking coverage. The percentage of exclusion is the maximum in rural and semi-urban areas because of long distance or there are no branches in their community. Thousands of banking centers in remote villages started appearing. Largest number of people to cover financial services has become a top priority of RBI.

In this chapter, a detailed study of financial inclusion in the Indian context has been conducted. To overview financial inclusion in India, authors have first studied financial inclusion status according to households and according to states in India with the Census data. Then authors have presented the various financial inclusion dimensions. After that by considering the various dimensions authors present the trend of these dimensions in regard to SCBs, PSBs, and Pvt. SBs. Various initiatives by the regulators in India are also summarized in this chapter. Further, a brief review of studies in the Indian context and research gap have also been discussed in this chapter.

3.2   HOUSEHOLDS AVAILING BANKING SERVICES IN INDIA

Census of India in 2001 and 2011 clearly shows that there is an improvement in the percent of HHs availing banking services during the period, though the improvement is not much satisfactory and is a serious concern among low-income HHs, mainly located in semi-urban and rural areas. Widening the banking net enlarges the opportunity of people to access formal banking facilities. In 1969 when 14 major private banks were nationalized, there were only 89 CBs.

In India alone, 560 million people are excluded from formal sources of finance (NSSO data). In 2011 HHs availing banking services in India were slightly more than 35 percent of the total number of HHs. In rural areas, less than one-third HHs, and in urban areas, less than half HHs availed banking services. The position improved considerably in 2011.

Table 3.1 shows that during 2001–2011, the number of HHs availing banking services overall has increased by 112 percent or a compound annual growth rate (CAGR) of 7.8 percent per annum. In rural areas, CAGR was 8.2 percent per annum, and in urban areas, it was 7.2 percent per annum. As per the 2011 Census, only 58.7 percent of total HHs are availing banking services. Of the urban total HHs 67.77 percent and of rural total HHs 54.44 percent are availing banking services. The country made appreciable progress in availing banking services from 2001 to 2011.

Table 3.1 Position of households availing banking services

House holds	Number of households availing banking services		Total number of households		% of households availing banking services	
	2001	*2011*	*2001*	*2011*	*2001*	*2011*
Rural	41,639,949	91,369,805	138,271,559	167,826,730	30.11	54.44
Urban	26,590,693	53,444,983	53,692,376	78,865,937	49.52	67.77
Total	68,230,642	144,814,788	191,963,935	246,692,667	35.54	58.70

Source: Summarized by authors

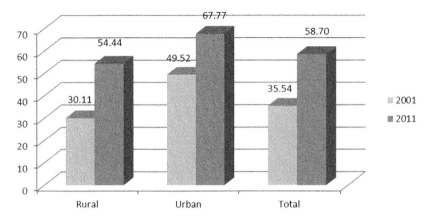

Fig. 3.1 Households availing banking services. (Source: Prepared by Authors)

From Fig. 3.1 it is quite evident that the SCBs have gone for a wide expansion of their branches to their existence in urban and metropolitan areas. While there has been an increase in the number of branches among the entire population group, the increase in rural branches is significantly higher. This indicator is more focused on the objectives of financial inclusion and its successful implementation. It can be observed that there has been a huge upsurge in branches opened in rural and semi-urban areas.

Figure 3.2 shows the HHs availing banking services across the states. According to the figure, it shows that Andaman and Nicobar Islands' HHs were availing maximum formal banking services with 89.3 percent, followed by Himachal Pradesh with 89.1 percent, Goa with 86.8 percent, Lakshadweep with 85.3 percent, Uttarakhand with 80.7 percent, and

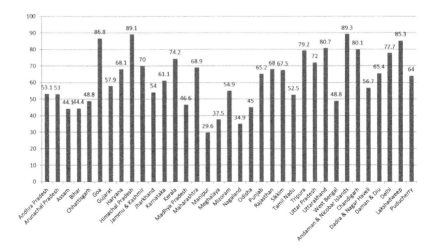

Fig. 3.2 Households availing banking services (percent) across states and union territories. (Source: Prepared by authors)

Chandigarh with 80.1 percent. Contrary in Manipur, only 29.6 percent of HHs had availing banking services, followed by Nagaland with 34.9 percent and Meghalaya with 37.5 percent. Among the total 35 states and union territories, 16 are with below the national average of 58.70 percent and the rest 19 with above the national average. From the presentation of Census data, this study may conclude that still there is a lacuna in India, to provide banking services. From the above, it is quite evident that there has been a massive upsurge in availing banking services by HHs in states and union territories. In the rest of this chapter, the growth of financial inclusion in India is presented by various indicators.

3.3   DIMENSIONS OF FINANCIAL INCLUSION

According to the various definition of financial inclusion by various institutional bodies and academics, this study found that "it is a process which ensures the ease of access, usage and availability of formal financial system for all members of an economy" (Sarma & Pais, 2008). This definition underlines numerous dimensions of financial inclusion, namely, accessibility, availability, and usage of financial system assist in building an inclusive financial system. According to the definition and previous literature, dimensions of financial inclusion have been divided into three heads. "Three basic dimensions of an inclusive financial system include banking availability, accessibility and usage of banking system" (Chattopadhyay, 2011; Kuri & Laha, 2011; Gupta & Singh, 2013; Banerjee & Francis, 2014; Chibango, 2014; Malik & Yadav, 2014; Padmanbhan & Sumam, 2014). Based on various dimensions, the level of an overview of financial inclusion in India can be tested. These dimensions are broadly discussed below.

3.3.1 Availability

"Availability of banking services is an indicator of level of financial inclusion in a country" (Kaur & Abrol, 2018). Unless banking services are available, we cannot expect an inclusive system. There are various parameters of measuring this dimension such as the number of bank branches, number of ATMs, APPB, and number of staff. Now the availability is not only limited to the presence of a physical branch where banking staff will be present to provide the various services. Their presence may be in the form of ATMs, mobile banking, internet banking, or any other technology-based services. "Penetration of bank is measured as bank branches per thousand population" (Singh et al., 2014). Penetration of an ATM is measured as ATMs per 1000 population and per 1000 square kilometers. Due to technology advancement traditional brick-and-mortar branches are shifted into ATMs. Due to many advantages, banks are installing more and more ATMs instead of opening a new brick-and-mortar branch. And as a result number of ATMs exceeds brick-and-mortar branches. So nowadays distribution of ATMs is also an indicator of level of financial inclusion. Like branch penetration and ATM penetration per 1000 population, the number of bank staff is measured as staff per million population.

3.3.2 Accessibility

Accessibility allows either access to or being able to actively use saving products or use of credit. As both saving and credit are important parameters to know banking penetration, deposit and credit accounts have been used as banking penetration. Deposit penetration is measured as the number of deposit accounts per thousand population. The credit accounts consist of loan accounts, small borrower loan accounts, and agriculture advances. The accessibility may be in the form of physical visits to a branch or by using various technology-based banking services.

3.3.3   Usage

Mere measures of availability and penetration cannot give a complete picture of financial inclusion. There is a possibility that a majority of people are actually under-banked or marginally banked. To check the actual availability and accessibility, usage dimension has been incorporated. Usage of banking service is measured by per capita deposit and credit or deposit to GDP and credit to GDP, and so on.

In the Indian context, detailed studies of SCBs with various dimensions are discussed below to obtain an overview of financial inclusion.

3.4   TREND OF BANK AND BRANCH OF SCHEDULED COMMERCIAL BANKS (SCBs)

Table 3.2 illustrates the significant change in number of banks. In the year 1969, there were 89 CBs, of which 73 were SCBs and rest were non-SCBs. RRBs were not started at that time. Total numbers of CBs reached 301 in the Indian Economy in March 2001, of which 296 were SCBs and 5 were non-SCBs. Out of 296 SCBs in 2001, RRBs accounted for 196 banks.

Table 3.2   Trend of commercial banks (as of March)

Year	Number of commercial banks (a + b)	(a) SCBs	Of which: RRBs	(b) Non-SCBs
1969*	89	73	–	16
1991	276	272	196	4
2001	301	296	196	5
2002	298	294	196	4
2003	294	289	196	5
2004	291	286	196	5
2005	288	284	196	4
2006	222	218	133	4
2007	183	179	96	4
2008	175	171	91	4
2009	170	166	86	4
2010	169	165	82	4
2011	169	165	82	4
2012	173	169	82	4
2013	155	151	64	4
2014	151	146	57	5
2015	152	148	56	4
2016	153	149	56	4

Source: Summarized by authors
*As at end June

In 2006, the number of CBs reached 222, of which 218 were SCBs and 4 were non-SCBs. Out of 218 SCBs in 2006, RRBs accounted for 133 banks. But it must be noted that due to mergers and acquisitions of banks to face global challenges, the number of both the SCBs and RRBs decreased (Maity & Sahu, 2021). As a result in 2016 the number of CBs reduced to 153 from 301 in 2001, SCBs from 296 in 2001 to 149 in 2016, and RRBs from 196 in 2001 to 56 in 2016. Commercial banks declined continuously during 2005–2016 primarily because of the introduction of liberalization in the banking sector. The decrease in the number of CBs in 2013 compared to 2006 and 2012 may mainly be due to a sharp decline in RRBs due to amalgamation. But the number of branches and turnover significantly increased to meet the increasing demand.

Table 3.3 shows the number of functioning branches from 2001 to 2016 with 1969 and 1991. The total number of branches of SCBs was 8282 in June 1969 and 65,919 in March 2001 which increased to 132,834 in 2016. The number of branches in March 2001 in rural areas was 32,562 which increased to 50,554 till March 2016. Also, the number of branches increased from 14,597 to 35,959 in semi-urban areas during 2001–2016. In urban areas, the number of branches increased from 10,293 to 24,363 till March 2016. The number of branches has also shown a change in metropolitan areas by increasing from 8467 to 21,958 till March 2016. The number of branches increased at 0.78 percent in 2001 and 5.17 percent in 2016. The lowest rate of growth registered at 0.41 percent during 2001–2002. The maximum percentage increase took place at 10.65 percent during 2013–2014 followed by 8.44 percent during 2011–2012, 8.02 percent during 2012–2013, 7.20 percent during 2014–2015, 6.74 percent during 2010–2011, and 6.63 percent during 2009–2010. However, it registered a growth rate of branch during 2000–2001 at -0.53 percent in rural areas. In rural areas, the maximum percentage of growth took place at 13.91 percent during 2013–2014 followed by 9.07 percent during 2012–2013, 7.87 percent during 2011–2012, and 7.59 percent during 2014–2015. In rural areas, the lowest rate of growth registered at -7.58 percent during 2005–2006. In semi-urban areas, the maximum percentage of growth took place at 11.79 percent during 2011–2012 followed by 10.97 percent during 2010–2011, 10.55 percent during 2013–2014, 10.47 percent during 2012–2013, and 8.98 percent during 2009–2010. In semi-urban areas, the lowest rate of growth registered at 0.76 percent during 2002–2003. In urban areas, the maximum percentage of growth took place at 9.46 percent during

Table 3.3 Number of functioning branches of SCBs according to population group: 1969–2016 (as on March)

Year	Rural Number of branches	AGR	Semi-urban Number of branches	AGR	Urban Number of branches	AGR	Metropolitan Number of branches	AGR	Total Number of branches	AGR
1969*	1833	–	3342	–	1584	–	1503	–	8262	–
1991	35,206	–	11,344	–	8046	–	5624	–	60,220	–
2001	32,562	(0.53)	14,597	1.32	10,293	2.40	8467	3.02	65,919	0.78
2002	32,380	(0.56)	14,747	1.03	10,477	1.79	8586	1.41	66,190	0.41
2003	32,303	(0.24)	14,859	0.76	10,693	2.06	8680	1.09	66,535	0.52
2004	32,121	(0.56)	15,091	1.56	11,000	2.87	8976	3.41	67,188	0.98
2005	32,082	(0.12)	15,403	2.07	11,500	4.55	9370	4.39	68,355	1.74
2006	29,649	(7.58)	15,943	3.51	12,258	6.59	11,728	25.17	69,578	1.79
2007	29,771	0.41	16,716	4.85	13,103	6.89	12,349	5.30	71,939	3.39
2008	30,293	1.75	17,960	7.44	14,343	9.46	13,325	7.90	75,921	5.54
2009	30,943	2.15	19,282	7.36	15,356	7.06	14,288	7.23	79,869	5.20
2010	31,971	3.32	21,013	8.98	16,748	9.06	15,432	8.01	85,164	6.63
2011	33,460	4.66	23,318	10.97	17,681	5.57	16,447	6.58	90,906	6.74
2012	36,093	7.87	26,068	11.79	18,920	7.01	17,493	6.36	98,574	8.44
2013	39,368	9.07	28,798	10.47	19,971	5.55	18,342	4.85	106,479	8.02
2014	44,843	13.91	31,835	10.55	21,584	8.08	19,554	6.61	117,816	10.65
2015	48,247	7.59	34,113	7.16	23,115	7.09	20,824	6.49	126,299	7.20
2016	50,554	4.78	35,959	5.41	24,363	5.41	21,958	5.45	132,834	5.17

Source: Authors' calculation
*As at end June

2007–2008 followed by 9.06 percent during 2009–2010, 8.08 percent during 2013–2014, 7.09 percent during 2014–2015, and 7.06 percent during 2008–2009. In urban areas, the lowest rate of growth registered at 1.79 percent during 2001–2002. In metropolitan areas, the maximum percentage of growth took place at 25.17 percent during 2005–2006 followed by 8.01 percent during 2009–2010, 7.90 percent during 2007–2008, 7.23 percent during 2008–2009, 6.61 percent during 2013–2014, and 6.58 percent during 2010–2011. In metropolitan areas, the lowest rate of growth registered at 1.09 percent during 2002–2003. During 2012–2016, the AGR of bank branches in rural areas is much higher than semi-urban, urban, and metropolitan areas. During 2009–2012, the AGR of bank branch in semi-urban areas is comparatively higher than rural, urban, and metropolitan areas. During the period from 2001–2002 to 2015–2016 authors found that the CAGR of bank branches in rural, semi-urban, urban, and metropolitan areas were at the rate of 3 percent, 6.2 percent, 5.9 percent, and 6.6 percent respectively.

From the table, it is quite evident that the SCBs have gone for a wide expansion of their branches to their existence in metropolitan and urban areas. The same can be observed in Fig. 3.3. This indicator is more focused on the objectives of financial inclusion and its successful implementation. As can be observed, there has been a huge upsurge in branches opened in rural and semi-urban areas.

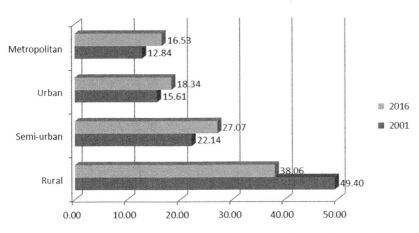

Fig. 3.3 Population group-wise bank branch ratios of SCBs during 2001 and 2016 (as on March). (Source: Prepared by authors)

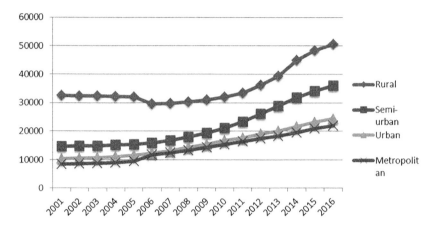

Fig. 3.4 Trend in the number of bank branches of SCBs according to population group over the years. (Source: Prepared by authors)

Figure 3.4 shows the trend in bank branches of SCBs from March 2001 to March 2016. It shows that the growth rate in semi-urban and rural areas is much higher than the other two regions. The total number of bank branches of SCBs in rural areas is also comparatively higher than urban and semi-urban and metropolitan areas. Though the figure is not presented here from March 1969 to 2001, the authors find that there was a slow growth of branches of SCBs. During March 2001 and March 2016 there were a higher growth rate bank branches which increased to 132,834.

Figure 3.4 indicates that more branches are opened in semi-urban and rural areas compared to metropolitan and urban areas. From the figure, it is quite evident that the SCBs have gone for a wide expansion of their branches in rural areas compared to their existence in metropolitan and urban areas. While there has been an increase in the number of branches among the entire population group, the increase in rural branches is significantly higher compared to the rest of population groups. Although, during 1991–2006 the number of branches has declined, still in terms of branch expansion the rural sector still has the top spot.

Figure 3.5 shows that between April 2001 and March 2016, highest growth of branches was found in metropolitan areas at the rate of 25.17 percent in 2005–2006 followed by rural areas at the rate of 13.91 percent in 2013–2014. Highest negative growth was found in rural areas during

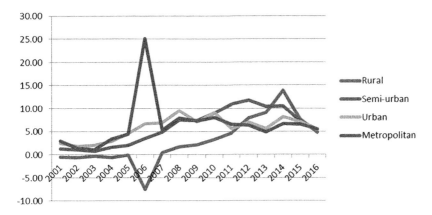

Fig. 3.5   Annual growth rate of branches of SCBs: 2001–2016. (Source: Prepared by authors)

2005–2006 at -7.58 percent. During 2010–2011, 2011–2012, 2012–2013, and 2013–2014 a stable higher growth rate was found in semi-urban areas at 10.97 percent, 11.79 percent, 10.47 percent, and 10.55 percent respectively.

Table 3.4 shows the trend in population per branch of SCBs over the years from 1947 to 2016. Population per branch reduced year by year as the number of branches increased. Increased rate in branches is also much higher than increase in population rate. In 1947 there was a population of 136,000 per branch (SCBs). Following the nationalization of banks, branch networks expanded rapidly with resulting decline in population per branch significantly during 1969–1991. In 1969, there was a population of 64,000 per branch of CB branches which reduced to 14,000 in 1991. In 2015 and 2016 population per branch of CBs was further reduced to 10,225 and 9881 respectively.

One of the indicators for measuring banking access is population per branch. Going by this decrease in population per branch, penetration of banking services is on a consistent increase in India. The branch authorization policy was liberalized in 2009 giving freedom to domestic SCBs to open branches at Tier 3–6 centers (population up to 49,999) without having the need to take permission from RBI. Penetration of banking services is consistently increasing in recent years as depicted in Table 3.4.

Table 3.4 Population per branch of SCBs over the years

Sr. No.	Year	Population per branch
1	1947*	136,000
2	1969*	64,000
3	1991	14,000
4	2001	14,902
5	2002	15,797
6	2003	15,972
7	2004	16,076
8	2005	16,060
9	2006	16,036
10	2007	15,764
11	2008	15,182
12	2009	14,668
13	2010	13,981
14	2011	13,313
15	2012	12,478
16	2013	11,741
17	2014	10,785
18	2015	10,225
19	2016	9881

Source: Authors' calculation
*As at end June

Table 3.4 indicates the decrease in population per branch of CBs rapidly over the years which signifies the growth of bank branches across all regions. In June 1947 the population per branch was 136,000 which was reduced to 64,000 in June 1969.

The movement of population per branch is worsening from 14,902 in 2001 to 16,060 in 2005. The population per branch portrayed an inverted U-shape (Fig. 3.6), with improvement in recent years at 9881 individuals per branch being served in 2016.

The data show that population per branch has declined rapidly, due to branch expansion policies. The population per bank branch has declined in rural areas, but when compared to urban areas and to the overall population range, the number is still high which is indicative of the fact that there is still a need for further expansion of branches as lower the population allocation per branch, the higher is the penetration level in that region.

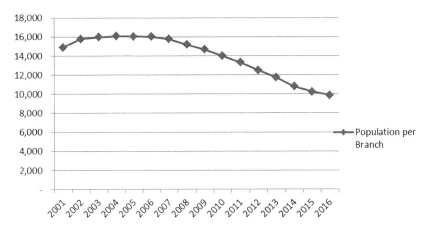

Fig. 3.6 Trend of population per branch of SCBs over the years. (Source: Prepared by authors)

3.5   ATM TREND OF SCBs

Wide acceptance of ATMs will help maintain growth in the banking industry. Increased numbers of people are using ATMs for their banking needs. The increased use of ATMs by foreign and private banks has helped them to compete with PSBs by enabling them to expand their reach. Due to relaxed norms by RBI in 2014, the number of ATMs has increased considerably. According to availability, data have been presented here from March 2005.

Due to the increase of ATMs steadily, the usage of ATMs has gone up substantially in the last few years. Table 3.5 shows the expansion of ATMs from March 2005 to 2016. The total numbers of functioning ATMs of SCBs were 17,642 in March 2005 which increased to 198,952 in 2016 with CAGR of 24.6 percent.

3.5.1   Trend of Off-Site and On-Site ATMs

Figure 3.7 shows the expansion of on-site and off-site ATMs from March 2005 to 2016. The numbers of off-site ATMs were 7654 in March 2005 which increased to 97,078 in 2016, with CAGR of 25.98 percent. In on-site, it was 9988 in March 2005 which increased to 101,874 in 2016, with CAGR of 23.50 percent. From the presentation of data, this study found

Table 3.5   Number of off-site and on-site ATMs of SCBs

As on March	Off-site			On-site			Total	AGR (%)
	ATMs	%	AGR (%)	ATMs	%	AGR (%)		
2005	7654	43	–	9988	57	–	17,642	–
2006	10,128	48	32.3	11,019	52	10.3	21,147	19.9
2007	14,796	55	46.1	12,292	45	11.6	27,088	28.1
2008	18,486	53	24.9	16,303	47	32.6	34,789	28.4
2009	24,645	56	33.3	19,006	44	16.6	43,651	25.5
2010	32,679	54	32.6	27,474	46	44.6	60,153	37.8
2011	40,729	55	24.6	33,776	45	22.9	74,505	23.9
2012	48,141	50	18.2	47,545	50	40.8	95,686	28.4
2013	58,254	51	21.0	55,760	49	17.3	114,014	19.2
2014	76,676	48	31.6	83,379	52	49.5	160,055	40.4
2015	92,263	51	20.3	88,989	49	6.7	181,252	13.2
2016	97,078	49	5.2	101,874	51	14.5	198,952	9.8
CAGR	25.98			23.50			24.64	

Source: Authors' calculation

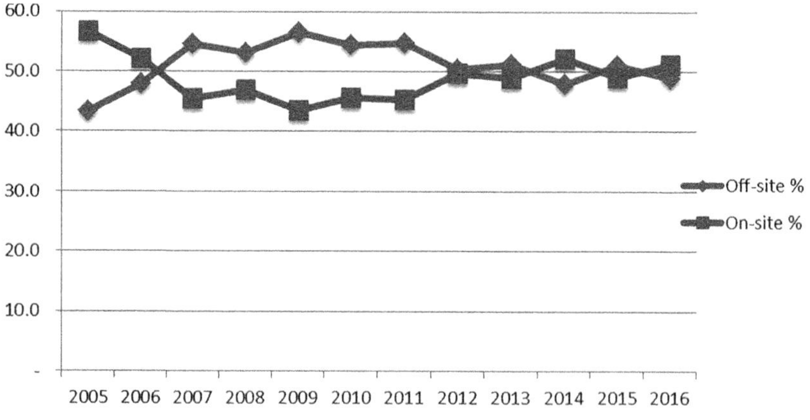

Fig. 3.7   Share of off-site and on-site ATMs. (Source: Prepared by uthors)

almost the same CAGR between off-site, on-site, and in total at a rate of 25.98 percent, 23.50 percent, and 24.64 percent respectively. So the banks have maintained a balance of opening ATMs in on-site and off-site locations. The share of off-site ATMs increased to 48.8 percent as of 2016 from 43.4 percent in 2005. The share of on-site ATMs in total increased to 51.2 percent as of 2016 from 49.1 percent in the previous year.

Without existence of full-fledged brick-and-mortar branches, off-site ATMs can play an important role by providing basic banking services. Looking at the cost-effectiveness and efficiency, non-bank entities were also allowed by the regulator in 2012 to own and operate ATMs called White Label ATMs (WLAs). As of 2016, 12,962 WLAs have been installed, of which there were 1724 each in metropolitan and urban areas, 4326 in semi-urban areas, and 5188 in rural areas. Figure 3.7 shows the share of off-site and on-site ATMs during 2005–2016.

3.5.2   Population Group-Wise Distribution of ATMs

Though in recent years metropolitan and urban centers still dominate, shares of ATMs in semi-urban and rural areas have been rising gradually.

Table 3.6 shows population group-wise expansion of ATMs from March 2005 to 2016. The total numbers of functioning ATMs of SCBs were 17,642 in March 2005 which increased to 198,952 in 2016, with CAGR of 24.6 percent. The numbers of rural ATMs were 512 in March 2005 which increased to 34,384 in 2016, with CAGR of 46.6 percent. In semi-urban areas, it was 3017 in March 2005 which increased to 53,476 in 2016, with CAGR of 29.9 percent. In urban areas, it was 6686 in March 2005 which increased to 57,569 in 2016, with CAGR of 21.6 percent. In metropolitan areas, it was 7427 in March 2005 which increased to 53,523 in 2016, with CAGR of 19.7 percent during 2005–2016. Overall highest AGR was found at 40.4 percent during 2013–2014 followed by 37.8 percent during 2009–2010. The lowest growth rate was found during the last year of study (2015–2016) at 9.8 percent. In a nutshell, ATMs of SCBs have increased to almost 67.2-fold in rural areas, 17.7-fold in semi-urban areas, 8.6-fold in urban areas, 7.2-fold in metropolitan areas, and overall a total of 11.3-fold of all SCBs during 2005–2016. During 2015–2016, ATMs installed by banks grew by 9.8 percent and the number of ATMs reached 198,952 in 2016. Figure 3.8 also shows the trend of ATMs of SCBs according to population group which displays an upward direction throughout the study period.

There was a greater concentration of ATMs in urban areas. In both number and percentage, ATMs in rural areas have been rising steadily in recent years. The share of ATMs located at various centers is portrayed in Fig. 3.9, indicating a rising trend in semi-urban and rural centers due to

Table 3.6 Population group-wise ATMs of SCBs (as on March)

Year	Rural Number of ATMs	AGR	Semi-urban Number of ATMs	AGR	Urban Number of ATMs	AGR	Metropolitan Number of ATMs	AGR	Total Number of ATMs	AGR
2005	512	–	3017	–	6686	–	7427	–	17,642	–
2006	782	52.9	3891	29.0	7761	16.1	8713	17.3	21,147	19.9
2007	1300	66.2	5391	38.5	9616	23.9	10,781	23.7	27,088	28.1
2008	1879	44.5	7445	38.1	12,107	25.9	13,359	23.9	34,789	28.4
2009	2750	46.4	9647	29.6	14,798	22.2	16,456	23.2	43,651	25.5
2010	5196	88.9	14,478	50.1	19,763	33.6	20,716	25.9	60,153	37.8
2011	7155	37.7	18,082	24.9	24,062	21.8	25,206	21.7	74,505	23.9
2012	8639	20.7	22,677	25.4	31,006	28.9	33,364	32.4	95,686	28.4
2013	11,564	33.9	27,710	22.2	36,111	16.5	38,629	15.8	114,014	19.2
2014	23,334	101.8	43,200	55.9	47,641	31.9	45,880	18.8	160,055	40.4
2015	31,652	35.6	48,201	11.6	51,115	7.3	50,284	9.6	181,252	13.2
2016	34,384	8.6	53,476	10.9	57,569	12.6	53,523	6.4	198,952	9.8
CAGR	46.6		29.9		21.6		19.7		24.6	

Source: Authors' calculation

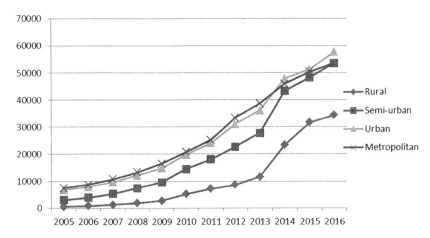

Fig. 3.8 ATM trend of SCBs according to population group. (Source: Prepared by authors)

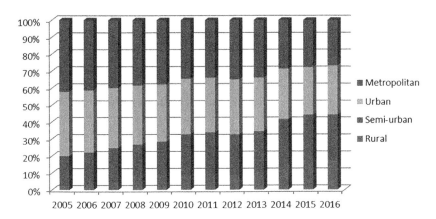

Fig. 3.9 Percentage share of SCBs ATMs located at various centers. (Source: Prepared by authors)

untapped market, and stagnant in metropolitan and urban centers due to saturation. Share percentage of ATMs located in rural areas accounted for 2.9 percent in March 2005, which increased to 17.3 percent in 2016. The growing penetration of ATMs in rural areas could also be seen from population per ATM. The percentage of ATMs located in semi-urban areas accounted for 17.1 percent in March 2005, which increased to 26.9 percent in March 2016. Though the percentage of ATMs located in semi-urban and rural areas increased during March 2005–2016, in the case of metropolitan and urban areas the percentage of ATMs located decreases. The share percentage of ATMs located in urban areas accounted for 37.9 percent in March 2005, which decreased to 28.9 percent in 2016. The percentage of ATMs located in metropolitan areas accounted for 42.1 percent in March 2005, which decreased to 26.9 percent in March 2016. This indicates that ATMs in semi-urban and rural locations are rising gradually.

In terms of ATM penetration, the State Bank group has been the most successful of institutions compared with other banks in rural areas. The private and foreign banks are emphasizing their operations in metropolitan and urban centers. The inclusion of foreign banks in semi-urban and rural centers is minimal; even the performance of private banks is not satisfactory. They need to extend their coverage in these areas so that objectives laid down in policy agenda of financial incision could be achieved in future. The study found that ATM penetration in rural and semi-urban centers has been increasing though it is decreasing in urban and metropolitan centers due to saturation.

3.6   TREND OF DEPOSITS AND CREDITS OF SCBs

In line with the positive trend of bank branches and ATMs, the authors also found a positive trend in other financial inclusion parameters of deposit and credit accounts. Tables 3.7, 3.8, and 3.9 present the trend of deposit accounts, deposits outstanding, credit accounts, and credit outstanding according to population groups and overall trend respectively.

Aggregate deposits amounted to ₹95,995 billion, registering a growth of 7.6 percent in 2016 as against 12.1 percent in 2015. The number of deposit accounts increased by 14.3 percent in 2016 to 1646 million from about 1440 million in 2015. Semi-urban and rural centers registered higher growth in deposits in 2016 at 12.1 percent and 10.2 percent respectively compared with urban and metropolitan centers at 9.4 percent and 5.0 percent respectively.

In March 2016, gross outstanding credit amounted to ₹75,226 billion, registering an increase of 9.4 percent as against an increase of 9.5 percent in 2015. Numbers of borrowed accounts have increased by 12.6 percent to 162 million in 2016 from 144 million in 2015. Rural centers registered

Table 3.7 Deposits of SCBs—according to population group (number of accounts in thousand, amount in ₹ billion)

Year	Number of accounts	AGR (%)	Amount	AGR (%)	Number of accounts	AGR (%)	Amount	AGR (%)
	Rural				Semi-urban			
2001	131,723	–	1394.3	–	116,400	–	1861.9	–
2002	133,000	1.0	1594.2	14.3	117,394	0.9	2149.9	15.5
2003	136,733	2.8	1765.0	10.7	117,537	0.1	2417.6	12.5
2004	138,760	1.5	1950.8	10.5	120,651	2.6	2682.2	10.9
2005	141,908	2.3	2131.0	9.2	125,198	3.8	2956.9	10.2
2006	139,570	-1.6	2260.6	6.1	121,664	-2.8	3022.1	2.2
2007	149,663	7.2	2530.1	11.9	132,808	9.2	3574.0	18.3
2008	168,034	12.3	3034.2	19.9	148,361	11.7	4302.8	20.4
2009	199,695	18.8	3639.1	19.9	169,725	14.4	5297.6	23.1
2010	224,155	12.2	4203.4	15.5	189,457	11.6	6140.5	15.9
2011	250,254	11.6	4932.7	17.3	212,043	11.9	7168.3	16.7
2012	283,072	13.1	5731.9	16.2	239,951	13.2	8425.5	17.5
2013	335,347	18.5	6698.9	16.9	283,990	18.4	9791.9	16.2
2014	406,624	21.3	7871.5	17.5	340,522	19.9	11,410.8	16.5
2015	493,970	21.5	9156.8	16.3	404,661	18.8	13,172.5	15.4
2016	576,171	16.6	10,089.4	10.2	470,711	16.3	14,772.1	12.1
	Urban				Metropolitan			
2001	92,769		2178.3		87,137		4059.8	
2002	94,622	2.0	2554.8	17.3	94,975	9.0	4935.0	21.6
2003	96,099	1.6	2905.0	13.7	95,711	0.8	5674.3	15.0
2004	99,571	3.6	3303.0	13.7	98,176	2.6	7176.8	26.5
2005	101,376	1.8	3748.9	13.5	98,310	0.1	8631.3	20.3
2006	106,172	4.7	4308.1	14.9	117,692	19.7	11,320.9	31.2
2007	113,422	6.8	5325.9	23.6	123,306	4.8	14,540.4	28.4
2008	128,021	12.9	6577.0	23.5	137,241	11.3	18,585.4	27.8
2009	142,272	11.1	8229.1	25.1	150,611	9.7	22,054.0	18.7
2010	152,323	7.1	9449.9	14.8	168,934	12.2	25,816.5	17.1
2011	168,037	10.3	11,105.1	17.5	179,796	6.4	30,689.4	18.9
2012	180,626	7.5	12,725.9	14.6	199,551	11.0	33,899.2	10.5
2013	203,091	12.4	14,970.1	17.6	222,677	11.6	38,665.3	14.1
2014	231,521	14.0	17,140.1	14.5	248,043	11.4	43,134.8	11.6
2015	266,228	15.0	19,649.0	14.6	275,033	10.9	47,242.8	9.5
2016	297,715	11.8	21,505.8	9.4	301,519	9.6	49,628.0	5.0

Source: Authors' calculation

Table 3.8   Credits of SCBs—according to population group (number of accounts in thousand, amount in ₹ billion)

Year	Number of accounts	AGR (%)	Amount outs.	AGR (%)	Number of accounts	AGR (%)	Amount outs.	AGR (%)
		Rural				Semi-urban		
2001	22,511	–	688.8	–	14,047	–	711.1	–
2002	25,163	11.8	877.1	27.3	15,037	7.0	901.6	26.8
2003	25,637	1.9	1064.8	21.4	15,434	2.6	1041.5	15.5
2004	25,565	-0.3	1099.1	3.2	16,108	4.4	1148.7	10.3
2005	29,357	14.8	1604.8	46.0	18,226	13.1	1428.4	24.3
2006	29,054	-1.0	1994.2	24.3	21,475	17.8	1747.9	22.4
2007	31,029	6.8	2357.0	18.2	22,099	2.9	2127.5	21.7
2008	33,546	8.1	3231.3	37.1	24,021	8.7	2560.0	20.3
2009	33,823	0.8	3096.3	-4.2	24,793	3.2	3110.9	21.5
2010	37,074	9.6	3851.5	24.4	27,047	9.1	3678.6	18.2
2011	40,018	7.9	3924.5	1.9	28,772	6.4	4519.9	22.9
2012	41,749	4.3	4422.1	12.7	31,292	8.8	5282.9	16.9
2013	45,703	9.5	5239.7	18.5	34,621	10.6	6756.5	27.9
2014	48,343	5.8	5667.1	8.2	39,094	12.9	7177.6	6.2
2015	49,928	3.3	5983.5	5.6	40,470	3.5	7591.9	5.8
2016	54,161	8.5	6746.7	12.8	45,736	13.0	8519.9	12.2
		Urban				Metropolitan		
2001	7934	–	953.0	–	7873	–	3031.4	–
2002	7661	-3.4	1237.6	29.9	8528	8.3	3543.7	16.9
2003	7972	4.1	1428.7	15.4	10,448	22.5	4024.7	13.6
2004	8931	12.0	1699.7	19.0	15,786	51.1	4855.6	20.6
2005	10,177	14.0	2123.0	24.9	19,391	22.8	6368.5	31.2
2006	12,919	26.9	2763.7	30.2	21,988	13.4	8632.6	35.6
2007	13,254	2.6	3501.9	26.7	28,060	27.6	11,484.5	33.0
2008	14,194	7.1	4305.9	23.0	35,230	25.6	14,072.8	22.5
2009	14,750	3.9	4985.7	15.8	36,690	4.1	17,284.3	22.8
2010	16,242	10.1	5936.2	19.1	38,285	4.3	19,985.5	15.6
2011	16,896	4.0	7795.2	31.3	35,038	-8.5	24,516.9	22.7
2012	17,740	5.0	8548.7	9.7	40,099	14.4	29,779.0	21.5
2013	20,924	17.9	9877.6	15.5	27,038	-32.6	33,379.3	12.1
2014	25,379	21.3	10,614.7	7.5	25,934	-4.1	39,361.4	17.9
2015	21,154	-16.6	11,039.2	4.0	32,688	26.0	44,170.2	12.2
2016	24,581	16.2	11957.7	8.3	37,895	15.9	48002.1	8.7

Source: Authors' calculation

Table 3.9 Total deposits and credits of SCBs—according to population group (number of accounts in thousand, amount in ₹ billion)

Year	Deposits				Credits			
	Number of accounts	AGR (%)	Amount outs.	AGR (%)	Number of accounts	AGR (%)	Amount outs.	AGR (%)
2001	428,029	–	9494.3	–	52,365	–	5384.3	–
2002	439,991	2.8	11,233.9	18.3	56,389	7.7	6559.9	21.8
2003	446,080	1.4	12,762.0	13.6	59,491	5.5	7559.7	15.2
2004	457,158	2.5	15,112.7	18.4	66,390	11.6	8803.1	16.4
2005	466,792	2.1	17,468.1	15.6	77,151	16.2	11,524.7	30.9
2006	485,098	3.9	20,911.7	19.7	85,436	10.7	15,138.4	31.4
2007	519,199	7.0	25,970.4	24.2	94,442	10.5	19,471.0	28.6
2008	581,657	12.0	32,499.5	25.1	106,991	13.3	24,170.1	24.1
2009	662,303	13.9	39,219.8	20.7	110,056	2.9	28,477.1	17.8
2010	734,869	11.0	45,610.3	16.3	118,648	7.8	33,451.7	17.5
2011	810,130	10.2	53,895.5	18.2	120,724	1.7	40,756.5	21.8
2012	903,200	11.5	60,782.4	12.8	130,880	8.4	48,032.7	17.9
2013	1,045,105	15.7	70,126.2	15.4	128,286	-2.0	55,253.2	15.0
2014	1,226,710	17.4	79,557.2	13.4	138,750	8.2	62,820.8	13.7
2015	1,439,892	17.4	89,221.1	12.1	144,240	4.0	68,784.7	9.5
2016	1,646,116	14.3	95,995.3	7.6	162,374	12.6	75,226.4	9.4

Source: Authors' calculation

higher growth of credit in 2016 at 12.8 percent compared with semi-urban, metropolitan, and urban centers at 12.2 percent, 8.7 percent, and 8.3 percent, respectively.

As per Table 3.9, highest AGR in deposit accounts has been found at 17.4 percent during 2013–2014 and 2014–2015, followed by 15.7 percent during 2012–2013, 14.3 percent during 2015–2016, 13.9 percent during 2008–2009, 12.0 percent during 2007–2008, 11.5 percent during 2011–2012, and 11.0 percent during 2009–2010. Though there is a highest growth rate of deposit accounts during 2013–2014 and 2014–2015, growth in terms of deposit balances was only 13.4 percent and 12.1 percent respectively. Highest growth in deposit has been found during 2007–2008 and 2006–2007 at 25.1 percent and 24.2 percent respectively. CAGR of deposit accounts is highest with 11.04 percent in rural areas, followed by semi-urban areas with 10.43 percent which is higher than all-India CAGR of 9.88 percent during April 2001–March 2016. The CAGR of urban areas is 8.53 percent, whereas in metropolitan areas it is 8.60 percent which is lower than all-India average during April 2001–March 2016. It proves that initiatives have been taken in semi-urban and rural areas to enhance deposit accounts. The AGR of deposit in value was highest during 2007–2008 with 25.1 percent, followed by 24.2 percent during 2006–2007 and 20.7 percent during 2008–2009. Though the AGR of deposit in value was highest during 2007–2008, the AGR in the number of accounts was only 12.0 percent.

As per Table 3.9, the highest annual growth in credit accounts has been found at 16.2 percent during 2004–2005, followed by 13.3 percent during 2007–2008, 12.6 percent during 2015–2016, 11.6 percent during 2003–2004, 10.7 percent during 2005–2006, 10.5 percent during 2006–2007, and 8.4 percent during 2011–2012. Though there was a growth rate of credit accounts at 16.2 percent during 2004–2005, growth of credit outstanding was much impressive at 30.9 percent. The AGR of credit outstanding was highest during 2005–2006 at 31.4 percent, followed by 30.9 percent during 2004–2005, 28.6 percent during 2006–2007, and 24.1 percent during 2007–2008. During 2015–2016 lower growth rates in deposits and credit outstanding have been found at 7.6 percent and 9.4 percent respectively.

Table 3.10 shows population group-wise growth of deposits in SCBs from 2001–2002 to 2015–2016. The deposit accounts were 440 million in 2002 which increased to 1646 million in 2016 with CAGR of 9.88 percent. The CAGR of deposit accounts in rural and semi-urban during 2001–2016 is higher than the overall CAGR at 11.04 percent and 10.43 percent respectively, whereas the CAGR of deposit accounts in urban and metropolitan during 2001–2016 is lower than the overall CAGR at 8.53 percent and 8.60 percent respectively.

The amount outstanding in deposit accounts was ₹11,234 billion in March 2002 which increased to ₹95,995 billion in 2016 with CAGR of 16.56 percent. The CAGR of rural, semi-urban, and urban areas are 14.09 percent, 14.76 percent, and 16.44 percent respectively which are lower than the overall CAGR of 16.56 percent. Only in metropolitan areas the CAGR of deposits outstanding is 17.92 percent during April 2001 and March 2016 which is higher than the overall CAGR of 16.56 percent.

Rural and semi-urban centers registered higher growth in deposit accounts from 2001–2002 to 2015–2016 with CAGR of 11.04 percent and 10.43 percent respectively compared with urban and metropolitan centers with CAGR of 8.53 percent and 8.60 percent respectively. Urban and metropolitan centers registered higher growth in deposits from

Table 3.10   Population group-wise deposits growth of SCBs from 2002 to 2016 (as on March) (number of accounts in thousand, amount in ₹ billion)

Population group	Deposits					
	Number of accounts			Amount		
	2002	2016	Trend (CAGR)	2002	2016	Trend (CAGR)
Rural	133,000	576,171	11.04	1594	10,089	14.09
Semi-urban	117,394	470,711	10.43	2150	14,772	14.76
Urban	94,622	297,715	8.53	2555	21,506	16.44
Metropolitan	94,975	301,519	8.60	4935	49,628	17.92
Total	439,991	1,646,116	9.88	11,234	95,995	16.56

Source: Authors' calculation

Table 3.11   Population group-wise credits growth of SCBs during 2002–2016 (as on March) (number of accounts in thousand, amount in ₹ billion)

Population group	Credits					
	Number of accounts			Amount outstanding		
	2002	2016	Trend (CAGR)	2002	2016	Trend (CAGR)
Rural	25,163	54,161	5.63	877	6747	15.69
Semi-urban	15,037	45,737	8.27	902	8520	17.40
Urban	7661	24,581	8.68	1238	11,958	17.59
Metropolitan	8528	37,895	11.24	3544	48,002	20.46
Total	56,389	162,374	7.85	6561	75,227	19.04

Source: Authors' calculation

2001–2002 to 2015–2016 with CAGR of 16.44 percent and 17.92 percent respectively compared with rural and urban centers with CAGR of 14.09 percent and 14.76 percent respectively.

Table 3.11 shows population group-wise growth of credits in SCBs during 2001–2002 and 2015–2016. The number of credit accounts was 56 million in 2002 which increased to 162 million in 2016 with CAGR of 7.85 percent. CAGR of credit accounts in rural areas during 2001–2016 is lower than the overall CAGR. The CAGR of semi-urban, urban, and metropolitan areas during April 2001 and March 2016 in number of accounts is higher than the overall CAGR.

Credit outstanding in the credit accounts was ₹6561 billion in March 2002 which increased to ₹75,227 billion in 2016 with CAGR of 19.04 percent. CAGR of rural, semi-urban, and urban areas are 15.69 percent, 17.40 percent, and 17.59 percent respectively which are lower than the overall CAGR of 19.04 percent. Only in metropolitan areas the CAGR of credit outstanding in the credits accounts is 20.46 percent during 2001–2016 which is higher than the overall CAGR of 19.04 percent.

Urban and metropolitan centers registered higher growth in credit accounts from 2001–2002 to 2015–2016 with CAGR of 8.68 percent and 11.24 percent respectively compared with rural and semi-urban centers with CAGR of 5.63 percent and 8.27 percent respectively. Urban and metropolitan centers registered higher growth in credit outstanding from 2001–2002 to 2015–2016 with CAGR of 17.59 percent and 20.46 percent respectively compared with rural and semi-urban centers with CAGR of 15.69 percent and 17.40 percent respectively.

Tables 3.10 and 3.11 show that there is much growth in credit or deposit accounts in rural, semi-urban, and urban areas. But in respect of credit outstanding the growth rate is not up to the mark in rural, semi-urban, and urban areas. Only in metropolitan areas the CAGR of both deposit amount and credit outstanding is higher than the overall CAGR during the period from 2001–2002 to 2015–2016.

If we look at Table 3.12, it can be seen that the bulk of the deposits received and credit allocated were to urban and metropolitan areas. The picture is same throughout the years from 1969 to 2016. Deposits mobilized in 1969 were 3 percent from rural areas, 22 percent from semi-urban areas, 26 percent from urban areas, and 49 percent from metropolitan areas. In the case of credit allocated in 1969 it was 2 percent only to rural areas, 11 percent to semi-urban areas, 20 percent to urban areas, and 67 percent to metropolitan areas. In 2001 deposit mobilization were 15 percent from rural areas, 20 percent from semi-urban areas, 23 percent from urban areas, and 43 percent from metropolitan areas. During the same year credit allocated was 10 percent to rural areas, 11 percent to semi-urban areas, 17 percent to urban areas, and 62 percent to metropolitan areas. In 2005 deposit mobilization was 12 percent from rural areas, 17 percent from semi-urban areas, 22 percent from urban areas, and 49 percent from metropolitan areas. During the same year credit allocated was 10 percent to rural areas, 11 percent to semi-urban areas, 16 percent to urban areas, and 63 percent to metropolitan areas. In 2010 deposit mobilized was 9 percent from rural areas, 14 percent from semi-urban areas, 21

Table 3.12 Source of deposits and credits (%) according to population group

Population group	Source of deposits (%)					Source of credits (%)				
	1969	2001	2005	2010	2016	1969	2001	2005	2010	2016
Rural	3	15	12	9	11	2	10	10	8	9
Semi-urban	22	20	17	14	15	11	11	11	10	11
Urban	26	23	22	21	22	20	17	16	17	16
Metropolitan	49	43	49	57	52	67	62	63	66	64
Total	100	100	100	100	100	100	100	100	100	100

Source: Authors' calculation

percent from urban areas, and 57 percent from metropolitan areas. During the same year credit allocated was 8 percent to rural areas, 10 percent to semi-urban areas, 17 percent to urban areas, and 66 percent to metropolitan areas. In March 2016 deposit mobilized was 11 percent from rural areas, 15 percent from semi-urban areas, 22 percent from urban areas, and 52 percent from metropolitan areas. In the case of credit allocated it was 9 percent to rural areas, 11 percent to semi-urban areas, 16 percent to urban areas, and 64 percent to metropolitan areas in 2016. It has been observed that the share of deposits and credit in rural and semi-urban areas is on a declining trend. In contrast, the share of metropolitan areas is in a rising trend. Further, the share of credit is lower than deposits in all regions, except metropolitan, implying that resources get intermediated in metropolitan areas.

Figure 3.3 shows that rural and semi-urban areas constitute a majority of CBs branches in India. However, that is just one part of the story. If we look at Figs. 3.10 and 3.11, it can be seen that the bulk of the credit allocated and deposits collected are to the urban and metropolitan areas. In fact the share of deposits and credit in rural and semi-urban areas has been declining.

C-D ratio is the ratio that indicates lending share out of the mobilized deposits. A higher ratio indicates more flow of credit from deposits mobilized and vice versa. Table 3.13 shows the growth of credit to aggregate deposits and credit to GDP from 2001–2002 to 2015–2016. Credit to aggregate deposits was 53.4 percent in 2001–2002 which increased to 77.7 percent in 2015–2016. Deposit to GDP was 47.0 percent in 2001–2002 which increased to 68.7 in 2015–2016. Again, credit to GDP was 25.1 in 2001–2002 which increased to 53.4 in 2015–2016. The same

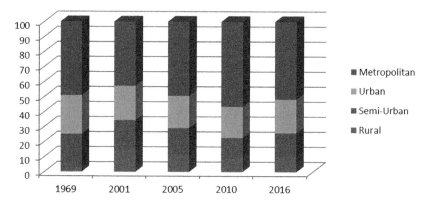

Fig. 3.10 Source of deposits in India (%). (Source: Prepared by authors)

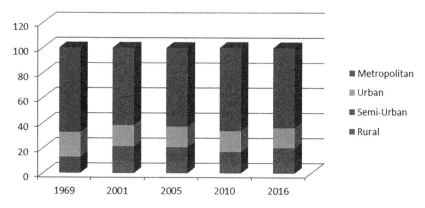

Fig. 3.11 Source of credits in India (%). (Source: Prepared by authors)

is also depicted in Fig. 3.12. It shows that from 2001–2002 to 2015–2016 deposit to GDP was higher than the credit to GDP. This is due to the disbursement of credit being lower than the collection of deposits.

The progress of credit to aggregate deposits and credit to GDP is presented in Fig. 3.12 with deposit to GDP. As credit to GDP is approximately 50 percent and credit to aggregate deposit is around 75 percent, so banks are definitely mobilizing deposits, but credit offtake is less as compared to deposits mobilized which may be a hindrance to inclusive growth.

Table 3.13 Scheduled commercial banks ratios

Year	Credit as percent to aggregate deposits	Deposits as percent to GDP	Credit as percent to GDP
2001–2002	53.4	47.0	25.1
2002–2003	56.9	50.6	28.8
2003–2004	55.9	53.0	29.6
2004–2005	64.7	52.4	33.9
2005–2006	71.5	57.1	40.8
2006–2007	73.9	60.8	45.0
2007–2008	73.9	64.1	47.4
2008–2009	72.4	68.1	49.3
2009–2010	72.2	69.4	50.1
2010–2011	75.7	66.9	50.6
2011–2012	78.0	66.9	52.2
2012–2013	77.9	67.8	52.9
2013–2014	77.8	68.4	53.2
2014–2015	76.6	68.3	52.3
2015–2016	77.7	68.7	53.4

Source: Summarized by authors

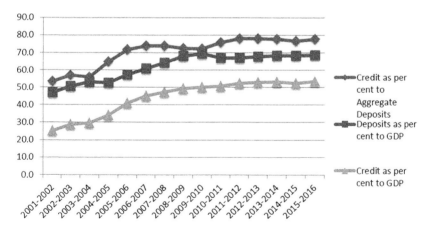

Fig. 3.12 Scheduled commercial banks ratios. (Source: Prepared by authors)

Table 3.14 shows the trend of various indicators of deposit and credit during 1969–2016. During the study period, the trend in demand deposit grew from ₹1691.03 billion in March 2002 to ₹8618.67 billion in 2016 and time deposit grew from ₹9620.85 billion to ₹87376.64 billion. Deposits per office grew from ₹170.9 million to ₹711.8 million and per capita deposits grew from ₹10,994 to ₹73,134. The trend in bank credit has grown steadily from ₹6090.53 billion in March 2002 to ₹75226.45 billion in 2016. Credit per office has also grown from ₹92.0 million to ₹557.8 million and per capita credit grew from ₹5919 to ₹57,311. In June 1969 demand deposit was ₹21.04 billion and time deposit was ₹25.42 billion. Also, deposits per office were ₹5.6 million with per capita deposits of ₹88 only and credit per office was ₹4.4 million with credit per capita of ₹68 only.

Figure 3.13 shows the trend of per capita deposit and credit of SCBs. From 2001–2002 to 2015–2016, per capita deposit was higher than per capita credit of SCBs. It is evident that per capita deposits and credit are rising enormously. The data of the 15 years revealed that per capita deposits and per capita credit are piercing at a good speed, which has risen to 6.7 times and 9.7 times respectively in 2016 from 2002.

Figure 3.14 shows both deposits per office and credit per office are increasing year-on-year. From the above graph, while the authors compare the deposits per office and credit per office, it is observed that credit per office is increasing at a higher rate than in deposits per office. The data of the 15 years have shown that the deposits per office increased at 4.2 times and credit per office increased at 6.1 times in 2016 from March 2002.

The employee of bank is also an availability dimension, because people will come to banks if they get services on time. Due to the absence of banks' employee data previous literature has not been considered in their studies as a financial inclusion dimension. Table 3.15 shows the trend of employees of SCBs with number of SCBs employees per 0.1 million population, number of SCBs employees per 1000 km^2, and business per employee of SCBs. The more the employees employed in banking sector, the more the employees per 0.10 million population or per 1000 km^2 which indicates more services to customers. The various trends show that there has been a positive trend from April 2001 to March 2016. The number of SCBs employees has been rising from 0.90 million in 2002 to 1.26 million in 2016. The number of SCBs employees per 0.10 million population has risen from 86 to 96, though in March 2015 it has been 100. The

Table 3.14 Progress of deposit and credit mobilization by SCBs (as on March)

Year	Deposits (Indicators)					Credit (indicators)		
	(a) Demand	(b) Time	Total	Deposits per office (₹ in million)	Per capita deposit (₹)	Bank credit of SCBs in India (₹ in billion)	Credit per office (₹ in million)	Per capita credit (₹)
1	2	3	4	5	6	7	8	9
1969*	21.04	25.42	46.46	5.6	88	36.00	4.4	68
2001	1594.07	8297.34	9891.41	150.1	9758	5292.72	80.3	5221
2002	1691.03	9620.85	1,1311.87	170.9	10,994	6090.53	92.0	5919
2003	1878.37	11,239.24	13,117.61	197.2	12,554	7464.32	112.2	7143
2004	2459.43	12,963.42	15,422.84	229.5	14,550	8655.94	128.8	8166
2005	2650.33	14,678.24	17,328.58	253.5	16,091	11,243.00	164.5	10,440
2006	3646.40	17,444.09	21,090.49	303.6	19,276	15,070.77	216.9	13,774
2007	4297.31	21,822.03	26,119.33	363.1	23,468	19,311.89	268.5	17,355
2008	5243.10	26,726.30	31,969.39	420.4	28,327	23,619.14	310.6	20,928
2009	5230.85	33,110.25	38,341.10	476.0	33,471	27,755.49	344.6	24,230
2010	6456.10	38,472.16	44,928.26	526.1	38,062	32,447.88	380.0	27,489
2011	6417.05	45,662.64	52,079.69	577.0	43,034	39,420.82	436.7	32,574
2012	6253.30	52,837.52	59,090.82	600.9	48,732	46,118.52	469.0	38,033
2013	7671.61	61,671.19	69,342.80	657.7	55,445	53,931.58	511.5	43,123
2014	8272.11	70,862.32	79,134.43	674.7	62,252	61,390.45	523.5	48,294
2015	7800.53	81,188.48	88,989.01	708.1	68,576	64,998.29	517.2	50,089
2016	8618.67	87,376.64	95,995.31	711.8	73,134	75,226.45	557.8	57,311

Source: Summarized by authors

*As at end June

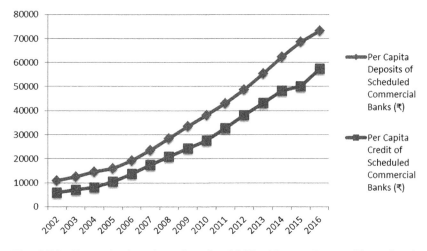

Fig. 3.13   Per capita deposits and credit of SCBs. (Source: Prepared by authors)

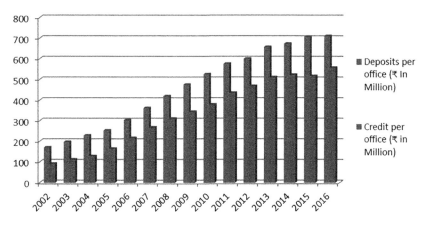

Fig. 3.14   Deposits and credit per office of SCBs. (Source: Prepared by authors)

number of SCBs employees per 1000 km² has risen from 274 to 383, though in March 2015 it has been 393. During the period, business per employee of SCBs has risen from ₹19.74 million in 2002 to ₹135.94 million in 2016.

Table 3.15 Employees of SCBs (as on March)

Year	Number of employees of SCBs (includes officers, clerks and sub-staff)	Number of SCBs employees per 1 lac population	Number of SCBs employees per 1000 km²	Business per employee of SCBs (₹ in million)
2002	901,288	86	274	19.74
2003	901,149	85	274	22.55
2004	881,722	82	268	27.12
2005	900,433	82	274	32.20
2006	900,124	81	274	40.05
2007	899,407	79	274	50.52
2008	838,769	73	255	67.56
2009	824,659	70	251	82.09
2010	926,028	78	282	85.38
2011	1,050,885	87	320	90.07
2012	1,175,149	96	357	92.60
2013	1,220,731	98	371	102.71
2014	1,253,955	99	381	113.54
2015	1,291,542	100	393	122.34
2016	1,259,510	96	383	135.94

Source: Summarized by authors

3.7   BANKING OUTLETS IN VILLAGES

Table 3.16 and Fig. 3.15 show that total banking outlets have increased over the years from 2009–2010 to 2015–2016 by about 766.11 percent. Total numbers of outlets have increased from 67,694 in 2009–2010 to 586,307 during 2015–2016. Of the total outlets in villages, 33,378 outlets are in branch mode during 2009–2010 which increased to 51,830 during 2015–2016. Moreover, in branchless mode, total outlets increased from 34,316 in 2009–2010 to 534,477 in 2015–2016. It expresses that banks are interested in opening outlets more in branchless mode (CAGR 58.03 percent) than in branch mode (CAGR 7.61 percent) due to higher cost in establishing brick-and-mortar branches in villages.

3.8   COMPARISON OF DIFFERENT FINANCIAL INCLUSION DIMENSIONS OF PUBLIC AND PRIVATE SECTOR BANKS

In this part of the study comparative statistics of different financial inclusion dimensions of PSBs and Pvt. SBs are presented to get a status of the two groups and to compare between them.

Table 3.16 Banking outlets in villages

Year	Banking outlets in villages—branches	Banking outlets in villages—branchless mode	Banking outlets in villages—total
2009–2010	33,378	34,316	67,694
2010–2011	34,811	81,397	116,208
2011–2012	37,471	144,282	181,753
2012–2013	40,837	227,617	268,454
2013–2014	46,126	337,678	383,804
2014–2015	49,571	504,142	553,713
2015–2016	51,830	534,477	586,307
CAGR	7.61	58.03	43.31

Source: Authors' calculation

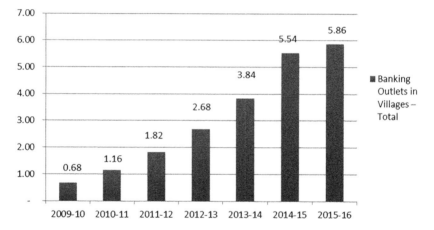

Fig. 3.15 Banking outlets in villages. (Source: Prepared by authors)

A strong positive upward direction of the number of branches is an indication of improvement of financial inclusion. Table 3.17 shows that numbers of branches of PSBs grew from 47,483 in 2002 to 91,304 in 2016 and bank branches of Pvt. SBs grew from 5549 in 2002 to 22,511 in 2016. The study brought out that for branch penetration when compounded annually, a growth of 4.78 percent for PSBs was reported which is lower than the compound growth calculated for Pvt. SBs of 10.52 percent. As revealed by the analysis, for Pvt. SBs though number of branches

Table 3.17 Branches, ATMs, and employees of PSBs and Pvt. SBs from 2002 to 2016 (as on March)

Year (as on March)	Branches		ATMs		Employees	
	PSBs	Pvt. SBs	PSBs	Pvt. SBs	PSBs	Pvt. SB₃
2002	47,483	5549	N/A	N/A	755,052	68,796
2003	47,679	5531	3473	N/A	752,860	71,071
2004	47,919	5855	6748	N/A	727,817	77,099
2005	48,698	6400	9992	6853	748,805	92,419
2006	49,241	6683	12,608	7659	744,333	110,505
2007	51,061	7228	16,329	9799	728,878	139,039
2008	54,542	8068	21,788	11,967	715,408	158,823
2009	57,146	9112	27,277	15,320	731,524	176,339
2010	60,826	10,291	40,680	18,447	739,646	182,520
2011	64,154	11,764	49,487	23,651	755,102	187,913
2012	70,027	13,825	58,193	36,079	774,329	248,284
2013	75,501	15,962	69,652	43,101	798,535	273,070
2014	83,718	18,393	110,424	48,467	830,487	294,968
2015	89,711	20,434	128,665	51,490	844,454	310,043
2016	91,304	22,511	142,312	55,581	859,877	374,419
CAGR	4.78	10.52	27.31	20.96	0.93	12.86

Source: Authors' calculation

is less than the PSBs, the compound annual growth has been shown higher than PSBs during 2001–2016. Further, employees of PSBs have been growing from 755,052 to 859,877 with CAGR of 0.93 percent only and employees of Pvt. SBs have been growing from 68,796 to 374,419 with CAGR of 12.86 percent.

As far as the ATMs of PSBs and Pvt. SBs are concerned, CAGR is 27.31 percent and 20.96 percent respectively during 2004–2016. The number of ATMs of PSBs grew from 3473 in 2003 to 142,312 in 2016 and of Pvt. SBs grew from 6853 in 2005 to 55,581 in 2016.

In a nutshell, branches and employees of PSBs have increased to almost 1.92- and 1.14-fold respectively in comparison to 4.06- and 5.44-fold respectively in the case of Pvt. SBs during 2001–2016. ATMs of PSBs have increased to 14.24-fold, whereas in the case of Pvt. SBs, ATMs increased to 8.11-fold during 2004–2016. Given the fact that PSBs are in the process of rationalization of staff strength, introduction of ATMs would help them to facilitate improved customer service. Figures 3.16, 3.17, and 3.18

also show the trend of branches, ATMs, and employees of both PSBs and Pvt. SBs respectively.

Table 3.18 shows the trend in deposit accounts (in million) and deposits (₹ in billion) of PSBs and Pvt. SBs from 2001 to 2016 with CAGR. A significant increasing trend in deposit accounts of PSBs has been found from 344.87 million in 2002 to 1240.29 million in 2016 with CAGR of 9.57 percent. The trends of deposit accounts of Pvt. SBs grew from 42.32 million in 2002 to 194.98 million in 2016 with CAGR of 11.53 percent. Deposits accounts of PSBs have increased to almost 3.60–fold, whereas in the case of Pvt. SBs it increased to 4.61-fold during April 2001–2016. Figures 3.19 and 3.20 present the trend of deposit accounts and deposits respectively of PSBs and Pvt. SBs.

Table 3.18 also shows deposits of PSBs are ₹67,810 billion in 2016, as against ₹8432 billion in 2002, registering CAGR of 16.06 percent from April 2001 to 2016. The CAGR in deposits of Pvt. SBs from 2001 to 2016 has been reported at 19.05 percent which was higher as compared to PSBs. Deposits of Pvt. SBs have been growing from ₹1801 in 2002 to ₹20,681 in 2016. The results show that the pace of deposit penetration by PSBs has been found to be slow as compared to Pvt. SBs. Figure 3.21

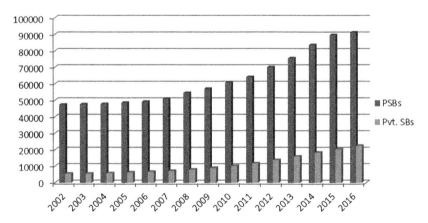

Fig. 3.16   Trend of branches of PSBs and Pvt. SBs from 2002 to 2016 (as on March). (Source: Prepared by authors)

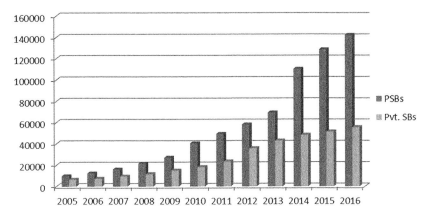

Fig. 3.17 Trend of ATMs of PSBs and Pvt. SBs from 2002 to 2016 (as on March). (Source: Prepared by authors)

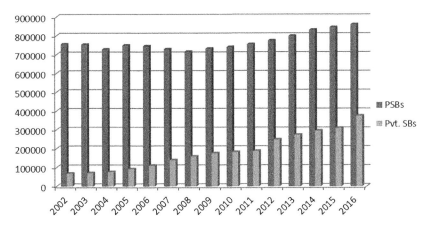

Fig. 3.18 Trend of employees of PSBs and Pvt. SBs from 2002 to 2016 (as on March). (Source: Prepared by authors)

presents the trend of credit accounts and Fig. 3.22 presents the trend of credit outstanding of PSBs and Pvt. SBs.

Table 3.19 shows the trend in credit accounts and credits outstanding of PSBs and Pvt. SBs from 2001 to 2016. The trend of credit accounts of PSBs has grown from 37.08 million in 2002 to 83.25 million in 2016 with

Table 3.18   Deposit accounts and deposits of PSBs and Pvt. SBs from 2002 to 2016 (as on March)

Year	Number of deposit accounts (in million)		Deposits (amount ₹ in billion)	
	PSBs	Pvt. SBs	PSBs	Pvt. SBs
2002	344.87	42.32	8432.31	1801.30
2003	344.61	45.07	9528.53	2162.21
2004	348.72	48.27	11,132.50	2694.09
2005	356.69	48.49	12,959.78	3128.56
2006	369.65	52.33	15,031.52	4061.26
2007	395.55	54.80	18,337.63	5357.70
2008	437.33	63.92	23,155.29	6572.99
2009	496.03	70.92	28,844.58	7144.79
2010	555.27	74.24	33,842.63	8065.69
2011	609.91	87.82	40,189.45	9721.52
2012	678.53	104.31	45,280.69	10,978.49
2013	787.57	123.22	52,131.54	13,134.93
2014	931.32	141.17	58,802.19	14,967.94
2015	1096.32	158.15	65,025.01	17,573.15
2016	1240.29	194.98	67,809.60	20,680.69
CAGR	9.57	11.53	16.06	19.05

Source: Authors' calculation

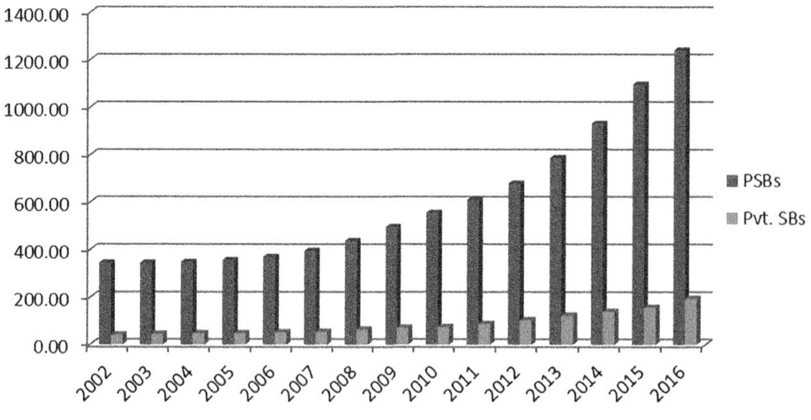

Fig. 3.19   Trend of deposit accounts of PSBs and Pvt. SBs from 2002 to 2016 (as on March). (Source: Prepared by authors)

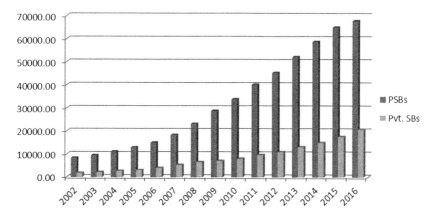

Fig. 3.20 Trend of deposits of PSBs and Pvt. SBs from 2002 to 2016 (as on March). (Source: Prepared by authors)

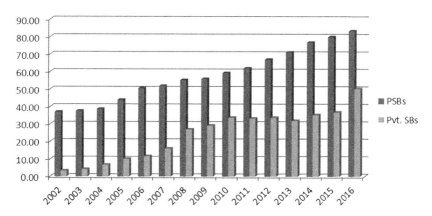

Fig. 3.21 Trend of credit accounts of PSBs and Pvt. SBs from 2002 to 2016 (as on March). (Source: Prepared by authors)

CAGR of 5.95 percent. Credit accounts of PSBs have increased to almost 2.24-fold during the period. So far as Pvt. SBs are concerned they were 3.37 million in 2002 which increased to 50.26 million with CAGR of 21.28 percent. Credit accounts of Pvt. SBs have increased to almost 14.91-fold during the period.

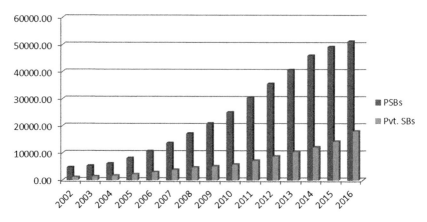

Fig. 3.22   Trend of credit outstanding of PSBs and Pvt. SBs from 2002 to 2016 (as on March). (Source: Prepared by authors)

Table 3.19   Credit accounts and credit outstanding of PSBs and Pvt. SBs from 2002 to 2016 (as on March)

Year	Credits (number of accounts in million)		Credits outstanding (amount ₹ in billion)	
	PSBs	Pvt. SBs	PSBs	Pvt. SBs
2002	37.08	3.37	4739.51	1150.20
2003	37.65	4.22	5364.29	1432.91
2004	38.73	6.66	6165.70	1741.07
2005	43.92	10.13	8173.44	2269.44
2006	50.59	11.73	10,750.73	3029.41
2007	51.86	16.04	13,743.27	3900.64
2008	55.19	26.98	17,220.68	4758.13
2009	55.83	29.20	20,940.25	5191.38
2010	59.26	33.83	25,114.54	5859.98
2011	61.87	33.30	30,520.63	7259.11
2012	66.91	33.83	35,617.59	8865.43
2013	71.05	32.02	40,711.01	10,537.68
2014	76.78	35.38	45,980.76	12,213.34
2015	79.85	36.86	49,283.11	14,334.22
2016	83.25	50.26	51,259.17	18,129.21
CAGR	5.95	21.28	18.54	21.77

Source: Authors' calculation

Table 3.19 also shows credit outstanding of PSBs in 2002 was ₹4740 billion which increased to ₹51,259 billion in 2016 registering CAGR of 18.54 percent from 2001 to 2016. Credit outstanding of Pvt. SBs has been grown from ₹1150 billion in 2002 to ₹18,129 billion in 2016 with CAGR of 21.77 percent. Credits of PSBs have increased to 10.82-fold compared to 15.76-fold in Pvt. SBs. The results show that the pace of credit penetration by PSBs has been found to be slow as compared to Pvt. SBs.

C-D ratio gives the idea of how much amount is given by the bank to the people and how much money is deposited by the people in the banks. Higher C-D ratio indicates a better financial inclusion position. How efficiently the deposits are mobilized and are utilized to carry out investment and capital formation activities can be measured through the C-D ratio.

A high C-D ratio is usually associated with higher investment and growth. Table 3.20 and Fig. 3.23 depict the C-D ratio of two different bank groups of PSBs and Pvt. SBs during the time period of 2001–2016.

The C-D ratio of all selected PSBs in 2002 was 56.21 percent which increased slightly to 56.30 percent in March 2003 and further kept of increasing at 63.07 percent in 2005, 74.95 percent in 2007, 75.94 percent in 2011, 78.09 percent in 2013, 78.20 percent in 2014, and further downward to 75.79 percent in 2015 and 75.59 percent in 2016. So far as Pvt. SBs are concerned, there was a significant increasing trend found in the C-D ratio. It was 63.85 percent in March 2002, 66.27 percent in 2003, 72.54 percent in 2005, 72.80 percent in 2007, 74.67 percent in 2011, 80.23 percent in 2013, 81.60 percent in 2014, 81.57 percent in 2015, and 87.66 percent in 2016. The Pvt. SBs have been able to achieve 87.66 percent compared to PSBs at 75.59 percent, which is a clear indication of better performance of Pvt. SBs than PSBs.

3.9   FINANCIAL INCLUSION INITIATIVES AT NATIONAL LEVEL

3.9.1   *Major Movements During 1935–1990*

During 1947–1969, the maharajas, or kings of the princely states of India, owned maximum of the banks, which used to serve rich families and industrial houses. This notion of class banking narrowed the aggrandizement of the banking system. The social banking policy remained effective

Table 3.20   C-D ratio of PSBs and Pvt. SBs from 2002 to 2016

Year	C-D ratio	
	PSBs	Pvt. SBs
2002	56.21	63.85
2003	56.30	66.27
2004	55.38	64.63
2005	63.07	72.54
2006	71.52	74.59
2007	74.95	72.80
2008	74.37	72.39
2009	72.60	72.66
2010	74.21	72.65
2011	75.94	74.67
2012	78.66	80.75
2013	78.09	80.23
2014	78.20	81.60
2015	75.79	81.57
2016	75.59	87.66

Source: Authors' calculation

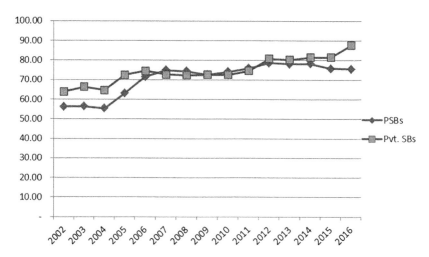

Fig. 3.23   Trend of C-D ratio of PSBs and Pvt. SBs from 2002 to 2016. (Source: Prepared by authors)

for a little more than one decade in India. The rapid development, which followed from 1969 till 1991, included enhancement of the number of bank branches, deposits, advances, priority sectors lending, decreased APPB, and so on. Availability of formal financial service at an affordable cost to low-income and underprivileged groups is the prime objective of financial inclusion. In reality other than bank accounts and accounts in the post office, financial inclusion in India includes loans, insurance services, and much more. And that is the main reason that the regulator has directed banks to open 25 percent of new branches in rural areas only. To provide banking services to rural population the regulator also established RRBs.

Though the individual bank has the authority to decide whether the account should have zero or minimum balance, banks have been offering zero balance with various names. As directed by RBI, every bank—be they PSBs or Pvt. SBs—has incorporated various initiatives to promote financial inclusion. The distribution of bank branches was highly concentrated in urban and metropolitan areas and the trend continued until the 2000s when RBI adopted a financial inclusion growth model. In order to spread deposit, credit, and other services to wider sections of population, a wide network of financial institutions has been established over the years. Accordingly, several initiatives have been taken over time to raise financial inclusion. Major attempts during 1935–1990 to provide financial access to the masses have been summarized in Table 3.21.

3.9.2   Major Movements After 1990

In 1998 Kishan Credit Card (KCC), in 2005 General Credit Card (GCC), and no-frills accounts have been launched to develop financial inclusion. "Financial inclusion has been pursued with a regulated bank-led model" (Sharma & Sharma, 2014). In addition, NBFCs engaged in financial inclusion promotion were regulated along with MFIs after the 2010 Andhra Pradesh crisis. From 1993 to 2015, a total of 15 new private bank licenses have been issued to minimize population per branch. Among other major schemes, simplification of KYC norms in 2011 and PMJDY in 2014 played a major role. Major attempts after 1990 are summarized in Table 3.22.

Over the last few years, rural branches have exhibited a falling trend and it gradually moved away from rural to urban areas. In response, "RBI has introduced Financial Literacy and Credit Counseling Center (FLCC) to provide consumers with the tools to make better credit choices" (GOI,

Table 3.21   Major list of movements during 1935–1990

Year	Initiatives
1935	Creation of RBI
1949	Nationalization of RBI
1949	Enactment of Banking Regulation Act
1955	Nationalization of SBI
1959	Nationalization of SBI subsidiaries
1969	Nationalization of 14 major private banks
1970	Initiating the Lead Bank Scheme was a big step to expand financial inclusion
1971	Creation of Credit Guarantee Corporation
1975	Establishment of RRBs to encourage branch expansion in rural area
1980	Nationalization of six more private banks with deposits over ₹20 million
1982	NABARD was set up

Source: Summarized by authors

2008). The focus of monitoring is now more on usage of these accounts through issue of many credit products through the channel.

Many times opening of accounts only not fulfill the purposes other than its usage regularly. In order to raise transactions, there should be clear communication to customers about the mission and banks should be incentivized to provide appropriate products that increase usage. With the increased intensity of operation, there is a possibility of reduction of cost of loans especially on account of adoption of better technology. Coverage inclusion of less creditworthy investors may lead to an increased default rate.

The government told RRBs to expand their respective branch network by 10 percent between March 2011 and 2013, as using technology becomes more profitable when size increases. RRBs are expected to quickly roll out a massive ATM and business correspondent's network, besides setting up ultra-small branches. Banks have also been asked to provide all documents related to banking activities in regional languages to the customer, which will make it easier for the local people to understand the guidelines.

To provide banking service to common men KYC requirement has been simplified with the objective of preventing money laundering. As per the recent guidelines, wages, subsidies, social security pensions, scholarships, and other schemes have been directly credited to beneficiaries' accounts through Direct Cash Transfer (DCT) or Direct Benefit Transfer (DBT) to plug leakages, avoid delay, and for more transparency. The Rajan

Table 3.22 Major list of movements after 1990

Year	Initiatives
1992	Launching of SHGs' linkage programmed by NABARD also major steps taken for financially excluded people
1998	KCC has been launched
2005	GCC has been launched
2005	Introduction of "no-frills" account with "nil" or very low minimum balance
2006	Engaging BFs and BCs as intermediaries for providing financial and banking services
2009	Simplification of branch authorization to freely open branches in tiers 3–6 centers
1993 to 2010	Total 12 bank licenses issued to minimize population per bank branch
2011	Simplification of KYC norms
2013	RBI gave license to the Bharatiya Mahila Bank Ltd. with a vision of economic empowerment for women (merged with SBI in April 2017)
2014	RBI has given in-principle approval to microfinance lender Bandhan Financial Services Ltd. and infrastructure lending company IDFC
2014	PMJDY has been launched with the objectives of providing universal access to banking facilities
2015	Payment bank license issued to 11 applicants out of the 41 companies and individuals that applied for licenses.
2015	Small bank licenses have been issued to 10 applicants out of the 72 companies and individuals that applied for licenses.

Source: Summarized by authors

Committee in its report entitled "A Hundred Small Steps" has given thrust on the broadening of access to finance or financial inclusion (GOI, 2008). All the stakeholders need to join hands and make it possible. "The government has estimated that the DBT scheme that it has expanded significantly has helped save around ₹ 82.985 billion" (The Economic Times, Kolkata, 23 March 2018).

Initiatives of BCs Model
One of the principal moves by the RBI is to spread the banking networks to reach the unreached people, particularly in rural and semi-urban areas to assist the underprivileged and poor to avail benefits through banking. As a result, efforts are being made to open more bank branches, ATMs, and other modes in the form of Business Correspondents (BCs), Business Facilitators (BFs), and customer service points to facilitate deposit mobilization and credit penetration.

Possibly the most important initiative of the RBI has been the BC model. Under the BC model, agents are used to delivering services on a commission basis to increase banking penetration. To make the BC model more viable, more innovative products are to be introduced for the benefit of the rural people.

Initiatives of No-Frills or Zero Balance Accounts Model
Under financial inclusion, banking coverage is spreading day by day. "To promote financial inclusion no-frills accounts have been initiated" (Thyagarajan & Venkatesan, 2008). The principal objective of opening accounts with no or minimal balances by those who would have been not served in backward and rural areas is to extend the basic banking facility to an immense section of the population. The UK, the US, Germany, and numerous other countries use basic savings accounts as entry products. The basic accounts, if well designed, can be valuable in encouraging the use of accounts.

Since the introduction of "no-frills" accounts, the experience highlights the fact that banks had taken this initiative more to achieve their targets on compliance. The RBI has given direction to banks that made available this account through their branches and business correspondences. Table 3.23 illustrates the significant change in Basic Savings Bank Deposit Accounts (BSBDAs) opened by branches and BCs both in number and in amount. It shows the steady growth of BSBDAs since 2010. In 2010, there were 73 million BSBDAs in India, of which 60 million were opened by branches and the rest 13 million by BCs. At the same period, there have been ₹55 billion outstanding savings balance, of which ₹44 billion was by branches and ₹11 billion by BCs. A phenomenal growth in BSBDA and outstanding saving balance was found in the case of both branches and BCs. In 2016, there were 469 million BSBDAs in India, of which 238 million were opened by branches and the rest 231 million by BCs. Further, there has been ₹638 billion outstanding savings balance, of which ₹474 billion balances are by branches and ₹164 billion balances by BCs. Reaching small villages through the BC model is more economically viable than by opening brick-and-mortar branches. The growth of BSBDA indicates the enhanced reach of banking in the economy.

Table 3.23 Progress of BSBD accounts (as on March)

Year	BSBDA through (no. in million)			BSBDA through (₹ in billion)		
	BCs	Branches	Total	BCs	Branches	Total
2010	13	60	73	11	44	55
2011	32	73	105	18	58	76
2012	57	81	138	11	110	121
2013	81	101	182	18	165	183
2014	117	126	243	39	273	312
2015	188	210	398	75	365	440
2016	231	238	469	164	474	638

Source: Summarized by authors

Formation of Financial Inclusion Funds, Plans, and Council/ Committee

Other than the above, regulators have also taken many initiatives from both the demand side and the supply side. GOI constituted a "Committee on Financial Inclusion" to address issues of financial inclusion. The committee has advised setting up the Financial Inclusion Fund and FITF and these two funds are situated with NABARD. Financial Inclusion Department is the nodal department and NABARD is the coordinating agency of financial inclusion initiatives. In 2004, RBI also set up the Khan Commission to promote financial inclusion.

Various modes and plans have been adopted to by banks to provide banking services in villages as allotted under a time-bound plan. The most important initiative of RBI is the creation of a Financial Inclusion Plan (FIP) that banks are asked to develop and integrate into their operations. Banks have been encouraged by RBI to pursue Board-approved three-year FIP since 2010. RBI had adopted financial inclusion as one of its major projects in January 2010. The first FIP ended in 2013 (2010–2013) and the second one in 2016 (2013–2016).

Subsequently, the financial inclusion initiative is being led by a technical group on financial literacy, and financial inclusion under the Financial Stability and Development Council (FSDC) sub-committee, involving all financial sector regulators and other government and non-government agencies. The FSDC is the inter-institutional body for financial inclusion and is active in policy implementation. Financial inclusion reports by the

World Bank (Global Financial Inclusion Database, Findex) and CRISIL have been released in 2013.

A National Rural Financial Inclusion Plan (NRFIP) has been launched with a target to access of at least 50 percent of the financially excluded HHs (approximately 55.77 million) by 2012 through commercial and RRBs and remaining HHs by 2015. GOI constituted a National Mission on Financial Inclusion comprising delegates from all stakeholders and responsible for deciding on policy issues.

All State Level Bankers' Committee/Union Territory Level Bankers' Committees were advised in May 2007 to set up, on a pilot basis, an FLCC in any one district in the state/union territory falling under their jurisdiction to provide financial counseling services. At the district level, District Consultative Committee and District Level Review Committee meetings are conducted by District Commissioner to monitor the progress of financial inclusion. At the block level, Block Level Consultative Committees are working to identify financially excluded people and to bring them into the mainstream economy. Recently metropolitan areas are also included in Lead Banks Scheme. In 2011, the GOI launched the Swabhimaan campaign program with aims to bring banking services to large rural areas. In 2014, Sampoorn Vitteeyea Samaveshan, or Comprehensive Financial Inclusion Plan (CFIP), was launched with hopes to extend basic financial services to all excluded HHs. Each Sub-Service Areas (SSAs) has been serviced by a Business Correspondents Agent (BCA) to facilitate opening accounts and smooth operation. In July 2015, RBI constituted an Expert Committee on Medium-Term Path to plan long-term and medium-term roadmap for financial inclusion.

Recent Indian Initiatives

We face several challenges in implementation of financial inclusion policies. In 2014 RBI gave in-principle approval to Bandhan Financial Services Ltd. and Infrastructure Development Finance Co. (IDFC) to drive financial inclusion. Both the new banks started their journey in 2015. To acquire the target of financial inclusion the PMJDY was initiated on August 28, 2014. Further to raise penetration of banking, pension, and insurance coverage in the country, GOI launched some social security and insurance schemes, that is, PMJJBY, PMSBY, and Atal Pension Yojana (APY), in May 2015. Prior to the above pension schemes, Swavalamban, a co-contributory pension scheme, had been launched on September 26, 2010, for workers of the unorganized sector.

Table 3.24   Progress of PMJDY

Bank type	Number of accounts (in million)			Number of Rupay debit cards (in million)	Balance in accounts (₹ billion)
	Rural/ semi-urban center	Urban metro center	Total		
PSBs	94.3	74.2	168.5	143.2	281.4
Pvt. SBs	4.8	3.0	7.9	7.4	13.5
RRBs	32.6	5.4	37.9	26.9	61.8
Grand Total	131.7	82.6	214.3	177.5	356.7

Source: Summarized by authors

Table 3.24 shows that as on March 30, 2016, 214.3 million accounts have been opened, of which 131.7 million in rural and 82.6 million in urban areas with ₹356.7 billion balances in the account. Further, 177.5 million Rupay debit cards have been issued under PMJDY, of which 143.2 million by PSBs. In all respect, PSBs dominate in the PMJDY scheme (Maity & Sahu, 2020). As of 2017, the number of accounts reached 307.3 million, of which 180.7 million in rural/semi-urban centers and 126.7 million in urban metro centers with a total of ₹704 billion deposits in the accounts and 231.4 million Rupay debit cards issued to beneficiaries.

3.10   ACCESSIBILITY AND AVAILABILITY OF BANKING SERVICES

Financial access is essential not only for maintaining and improving socio-economic status of a person but also for meeting all needs of a country as a whole and its different functional areas like industries, trade and commerce, and agriculture. Adequate fund at a reasonable cost is important for socio-economic and other necessary development of a country. A well-settled and evenly distributed financial sector is first needed for financial inclusion. "Financial inclusion is the key to inclusive growth with its motto of empowerment of poor, underprivileged and low income, unskilled, rural or urban households" (Khan, 2011).

The distribution of branches during 1969 was highly skewed. Financial inclusion includes accessing savings and facilities of checks, financial advice, debit and credit card facilities, overdrafts facilities, micro-credit, insurance, commercial loans, electronic fund transfer, and so on. In the Indian context, the main pillars of financial inclusion are SCBs.

3.10.1   Accessibility and Availability of Banking Services of SCBs

In this first part of the study, to describe the current status of financial inclusion in India toward accessibility and availability of banking services, the authors have presented the position of different financial inclusion indicators as on March 2002 and as on March 2016 to reflect the trend. In India, a bank-led model is effectively adopted to achieve financial inclusion. The reason for this is that banks are well regulated and highly trusted institutions doing banking operations in a fair and transparent way. Muhammad Yunus, Noble laureate of Bangladesh, considers financial inclusion as the social business by banks to solve financial problems. "Bank the unbanked" is the slogan of financial inclusion. By providing small, simple, and affordable banking products and services banks can bring poor people into the banking purview. Table 3.25 indicates the summary of financial access and use of banking services related to India. It specifies financial inclusion position of the Indian economy by considering different related parameters.

3.10.2   Progress Made Under Financial Inclusion Plans

To achieve the target of financial inclusion, FIPs have been initiated from March 2010. With the conclusion of FIP phase I (2010–2013) in 2013 and FIP Phase II (2013–2016) in 2016 the regulator advised all SCBs to set new targets for the ensuing three years of 2016–2019. To monitor the bank's financial inclusion initiatives, banks were advised to submit district-level data on progress made under FIPs. Table 3.26 shows the progress of FIPs as of 2015–2016. In rural areas banking outlets have been increased from 67,694 in 2009–2010 to 586,307 in 2015–2016. Of this, banking outlets in villages have 51,380 branches, while the villages have 534,477 branchless banking outlets.

Urban locations covered through BCs have been increased from 447 in 2009–2010 to 102,552 in 2015–2016. Total number of BSBDAs increased to 469.0 million in 2015–2016 from 73.5 million in 2009–2010.

Table 3.25   Accessibility and availability of banking services of SCBs

Indicators	Position as on March 2002	Position as on March 2016
SCB branches per 1000 km²	20.1	40.4
SCB branches per 100,000 population	6.33	10.12
ATMs per 1000 km²	5.4*	60.5
ATMs per 100,000 population	1.6*	15.2
SCB employees per 100,000 population	86.20	95.96
Employee of SCBs per branch	13.62	9.48
Number of deposit accounts of SCBs per thousand of population	420.8	1254.1
Number of credit accounts of SCBs per thousand of population	53.9	123.7
Bank deposits as a percent of GDP	47.0	68.7
Bank credit as a percent of GDP	25.1	53.4

Source: Summarized by authors

*Data related to March 2005

The development of BSBDAs can be attributed to the push given by the government under the PMJDY. Total number of KCCs issued has been increased from 24.3 million, with an outstanding balance of ₹1240.1 billion in 2009–2010 to 47.3 million, with an outstanding balance of ₹5130.7 billion in 2015–2016. GCCs issued have been increased from 1.4 million with an outstanding balance of ₹35.1 billion in 2009–2010 to 11.3 million with an outstanding balance of ₹1493.3 billion in 2015–2016. BCs–Information and Communication Technology (BC-ICT) transactions recorded a considerable increase from 26.5 million for the year 2009–2010 to 826.8 million on 2015–2016. From the above various tables and figures, the authors find that there is a positive sign of various financial inclusion parameters in India. Progress status under FIPs also shows significant growth.

From the above discussion and presented data, authors conclude that though in global perspective status of financial inclusion in India much lags behind developed countries or world financial inclusion status. However, growth rate toward expansion of bank branch, expansion of ATM, positive trend of employees, expansion of deposit (both in volume and in value), expansion of credit (both in volume and in value), C-D

Table 3.26 Progress made under FIPs, all SCBs including RRBs

Sr. No.	Variable	March 2010	March 2014	March 2015	March 2016	Absolute change (2015–2016)
1	Banking outlets in villages—branches	33,378	46,126	49,571	51,830	2259
2	Banking outlets in villages—branchless mode	34,316	337,678	504,142	534,477	30,335
3	Banking outlets in villages—total	67,694	383,804	553,713	586,307	32,594
4	Urban locations covered through BCs	447	60,730	96,847	102,552	5705
5	Basic Savings Bank Deposit Account (BSBDA) through branches (no. in million)	60.2	126.0	210.3	238.2	27.9
6	Basic Savings Bank Deposit Account (BSBDA) through branches (amt. in ₹ billion)	44.3	273.3	365.0	474.1	109.1
7	Basic Savings Bank Deposit Account (BSBDA) through BCs (no. in million)	13.3	116.9	187.8	230.8	43.0
8	Basic Savings Bank Deposit Account (BSBDA) through BCs (amt. in ₹ billion)	10.7	39.0	74.6	164.0	89.4
9	BSBDA total (in million)	73.5	243.0	398.1	469.0	70.9
10	BSBDA total (amt. in ₹ billion)	55.0	312.3	439.5	638.1	198.6
11	OD facility availed in Basic Savings Bank Deposit Account (no. in million)	0.2	5.9	7.6	8	0.4
12	OD facility availed in Basic Savings Bank Deposit Account (amt. in ₹ billion)	0.1	16.0	19.9	14.8	(5.1)
13	KCCs (no. in million)	24.3	39.9	42.5	47.3	4.8
14	KCCs (amount in ₹ billion)	1240.1	3684.5	4382.3	5130.7	748.4
15	GCC (no. in million)	1.4	7.4	9.2	11.3	2.1
16	GCC (amount in ₹ billion)	35.1	1096.9	1301.6	1493.3	191.7
17	ICT a/cs-BC transactions (no. in million) during the year	26.5	328.6	477.0	826.8	349.8
18	ICT a/cs-BC total transactions (amt. in ₹ billion) during the year	6.9	524.4	859.8	1686.9	827.1

Source: Summarized by authors

ratio, and other parameters have been much impressive in India to achieve financial inclusion. The regulators have been circulating different guidelines for expansion of branches in unbanked rural and semi-urban areas; closure of branches in rural, semi-urban, or unbanked areas; and restriction of branches in urban and metropolitan areas. As per direction from the regulators, banks may also open an account for poor and underprivileged people with zero balance and low or very minimal cost to bring them under the umbrella of banking net. To achieve financial inclusion, various government subsidies, scholarships, and wages are being directly paid to the beneficiary accounts.

3.11   Banking Access: Comparison of India with the World

As per the various table and figures presented in previous sections, we found that there is a positive sign of various financial inclusion parameters of number of branches and number of ATMs, number of employees, deposit accounts, credit accounts, C-D ratio, and so on in India.

Through the various dimensions of financial inclusion toward a positive direction, India does not fare well compared to developed countries in respect of geographic and demographic penetration. In respect of various financial inclusion parameters, this study found that there is an upward trend. These indicators enable us to get a glimpse of the financial inclusion over several years.

"Between April-June 2011 a financial inclusion survey was conducted in India by World Bank team and the survey results suggest that India lags behind developing countries in using a formal account" (Kunt & Klapper, 2012). But when it comes to borrowing from financial institutions the Indian average is much closer to the global average.

India does not fare well compared to developed countries in the aspects of geographic and demographic penetration. In respect of other parameters also there is an upward trend. Table 3.27 depicts the comparative position of banking-related indicators like accounts in formal financial institutions, saving percentage of adults, and loans from formal financial institutions which clearly indicate that India lags behind as compared to the world level in 2014.

In this chapter with the presentation of financial inclusion data collected from different sources presented in the various tables and figures,

Table 3.27 Key statistics of financial inclusion in India with the world

		India	World
Share with an account at a formal financial institution	All adults	53	62
	Poorest income quintile	44	53
	Men	63	64
	Women	43	58
Borrowed any money in the past year	All borrowing	46	42
	From formal financial institution	6	11
	From family and friends	32	26
	From a private informal lender	13	5
Saved at a financial institution using formal accounts		14	27
Adults with an outstanding mortgage		4	10
Adults with a credit cards		4	18
Adults with a debit cards		22	40
Adults with a mobile accounts		2	2
Transaction using a mobile phone through an accounts		6	16
Used the internet to pay bills or buy things		1	17

Source: Summarized by authors

authors found a significant growth of different factors. Expansion of branches, ATMs, bank employees, deposit penetration, credit penetration, and so on found a significantly higher growth during the period. To check the growth rate, both AGR and CAGR have been presented and to compare year to year and between different bank groups.

While comparing the financial inclusion data of two groups, PSBs and Pvt. SBs, the study also found the same results with a higher growth in both the groups. Though in volume and numbers PSBs hold a major percentage due to their long presence in the market, the growth rate of Pvt. SBs compared to PSBs is much superior throughout the study period.

While the study compares the different financial inclusion dimensions of India with the global status, authors have found India is much behind than the global status, except share with an account of men at a formal financial institution and adults with a mobile account (Table 3.27). The results of higher growth found may be due to various initiatives considered in the recent past. Notwithstanding, the growth rate of financial inclusion dimensions is not up to the mark to reach the world average level. So from the study and presentation of data of different financial inclusion factors the authors conclude that to reach the world position much more initiatives need to be taken by the regulators and by the financial institutions.

3.12   Studies Based on Indian Perspective

In this part of the chapter, a brief review in both segments of studies based on the Indian region and interrelation of the Indian region with other countries is presented. A large number of studies have been conducted previously on various aspects of financial inclusion.

In a study Swamy (2013) has offered specific suggestions on institutional reforms. Structural reforms, coupled with new vigor in the governance of rural financial institutions, will aid in heralding a new growth momentum in the hinterland of the Indian economy. In line with that, Joshi (1998) looks at banking sector reforms that have created grave problems in rural credit. The study concluded that underprivileged people are outside the orbit of organized institutions and they are in clutches of moneylenders.

Stephen and Tom (2015) have examined the role of Puthuppally and Manganam Cooperative Banks, the apex bank being the Kottayam District Cooperative Bank, during June 2014 and August 2014. They used ANOVA tools to analyze sample data and found a significant relationship between gender of respondents and level of preference of financial services, preference of small personal loans, the income of respondents, and reasons for not having an account in a bank. Further, Basak (2015) has examined the role of Urban Cooperative Banks (UCBs) and Non-Agricultural Cooperative Credit Societies (NACCSs) of Howrah in West Bengal (India) on financial inclusion. This study covers 6 UCBs and 21 NACCSs out of a total of 8 UCBs and 29 NACCSs, and it also covers the period from 2006–2007 to 2010–2011. Using binomial test and Z-test, results of his study indicate that UCBs and NACCSs did not play any significant role in providing banking services to the larger portion of population of the area under operation of UCBs and Credit Societies of the district. These UCBs/NACCSs could not play any recordable role in financial inclusion as such.

Rural households adopt different types of strategies to avoid severe income and consumption shortfalls caused by risk. A survey was conducted by Kar and Dash (2009) to assess the impact of microfinance on the economic position of poor in Baripada district of Orissa. It was observed that the sample respondents were more interested in informal saving like saving cash or in kinds like livestock, utensils, or land which is not able to meet their demand in event of risk. Following this Ramji (2009) looks at how HHs and banks influence the process of becoming "banked." The study finds that the proliferation of new accounts to excluded households has been quite small. In January 2007, RBI formally declared Gulbarga to be 100 percent financially included, though close to 70 percent sample remains without a bank account. Singh et al. (2014) has focused on some important aspects which are necessary for financial literacy for effective financial and economic stability in the Indian context. He also determines whether financial education helps low- and moderate-income individuals to achieve their financial stability. He has also discussed the role of RBI in improving financial knowledge of individuals. He also investigates some important content, namely, transaction of money, risk and returns analysis, financial landscape, and so on, of financial literacy which play a major role to develop sound financial stability in the country.

As highlighted in various national and international deliberations, there are three dimensions, that is, simple access (penetration), availability, and usage. Pathania et al. (2016), in their study, take the quality dimension into consideration for exhaustive and accurate analytical purposes and a true picture of financial inclusion. Four banks, that is, SBI, J&K Bank, PNB, and Jammu Kashmir Grameen Bank in J&K, were approached and their employees were interviewed regarding various initiatives. The proposed approach of adding the quality dimension to existing index can be of immense use and very useful for exhaustive and accurate analytical purposes. Their study reveals that the concept of financial inclusion is incomplete without incorporating quality dimensions.

In a study, Joshi (2014) has analyzed the penetration and awareness of various financial services offered by banks to the urban unorganized sector workers in Nagpur, India. The study found that if awareness increases among urban poor to average, there is a high probability to have an account in a bank for the non-holder. Further, Bruntha and Indirapriyadharshini (2015) have analyzed the banking habits of street hawkers in Pollachi, Tamil Nadu, with a sample of 300 street hawkers residing in and around Pollachi taluk considered through an interview scheduled in 2012. Their study reveals that most street hawkers do not have a bank account or even have basic knowledge regarding banks. In another study, Chakraborty and Barman (2013) have studied the opportunities and challenges of financial inclusion in Tripura based on 20 questionnaires. Due to various challenges, a huge number of cases of non-recovery of loans and financial assistance are being dragged into various forums including Public Demand Recovery and Debt Recovery Tribunal. Their study concludes that a lot of people take money but they don't want to return them and are ready to receive services but they are less interested to pay for it.

Shafi and Medabesh (2012) have investigated the financial exclusion problem in J&K and impact of initiatives taken by RBI. The study finds that although many banks in J&K have failed, J&K Bank through its large branch network has helped the state to achieve financial inclusion to a satisfactory level. As such their study suggests that banks in a state would need to pay equal attention, rather more attention, to this aspect of financial inclusion. Further, Cnaan et al. (2012) have investigated whether financial inclusion has been successfully implemented in Kerala, Andhra Pradesh, Tamil Nadu, and Karnataka of Southern India. These states have relatively well-developed banking in comparison to northern India and it was found that without banking access monetary services will be far more expensive.

Jones et al. (2007) have examined the development of training program, its implementation, and the results of its evaluation in two districts, Hoshangabad and Dhar, in Madhya Pradesh. They concluded that training in banks can affect positively on poverty alleviation and financial exclusion. Further, Kodan and Chhikara (2011) have analyzed the status in Haryana and also compare it with aggregate India. They analyzed data for 2001–2009, based on deposit accounts, credit accounts, bank offices, and uses ratio. The statistical techniques of Average, Average Compound Growth Rate, and Kruskal-Wallis Test have been used to analyze various dimensions of financial inclusion. They find that there is no difference between Haryana and India significantly, but the status of Haryana is somewhat better than aggregate India.

Following this Das and Guha (2015) have investigated the regional disparity in India. Their study also seeks to understand district-level banking coverage in village areas of Assam. Descriptive statistics have been calculated for understanding the pattern of disparity in banking sector at the regional level. CAGR has been estimated for an overall period (1996–2010) and two sub-periods (1996–2004 and 2005–2010). In estimating the CAGR, the following semi-log-linear trend equation has been used. OLS technique is used to determine respective coefficient value. The ANOVA has been fitted with a time dummy for understanding whether banking sector has undergone a change during the period. According to their analysis, they concluded that compared to other regions in India, NE region is much lag behind. Likewise, Kodan et al. (2011) have examined the status of seven NE Indian states and policy adopted by RBI. In their analysis, they found that according to different parameters like GDP, population, deposit, and credit, the position of financial inclusion was found to be poor in comparison to the all-India level.

In a study Gupta (2014) has evaluated the scope of financial inclusion in India vis-à-vis other developing and developed nations. Compared to other countries, India fares well in regulatory framework. Additionally, the study suggests various measures to make financial inclusion more effective and far-reaching so that even disadvantaged low-income groups can have access to banking services. Following this Dangi (2012) has made an investigation to explore diffusion of financial inclusion in the Indian context. He emphasized the in-depth study of inclusion of CBs, cooperative banks, RRBs, and microfinance institutions from 2004–2005 to 2009–2010. The study covers 27 PSBs, 22 Pvt. SBs, and 27 foreign banks. PSBs include all 19 nationalized banks, the SBI and its associates, and IDBI Ltd. The banking sector is dominated by PSBs, followed by Pvt. SBs. He finds that CBs, cooperative banks, RRBs, and microfinance programs have been playing a vital role in removing financial exclusion in India. In line with that, Jain (2015) has investigated financial inclusion progress in India. The empirical study also focuses on work done and products offered by four private banks, namely, ICICI, HDFC, Kotak, and AXIS. In another study, Barot (2017) has attempted to focus on approaches adopted by different banks for inclusive growth and examine the progress and achievements during the past years. This study also focuses on the role of financial inclusion and strengthening India's position in relation to other countries. The study concluded with opportunities available and challenges in India.

A bank account is a primary requirement which enables access to any banking service or product. In many parts of the world, social security benefits are administered through bank accounts. According to Mahadeva (2008), financial institutions play their own role in increasing access to households, especially in rural locations. He considers a number of alternative initiatives to increase access for under-served population. In a study, Burgess and Pande (2005) have evaluated how bank branch expansion programs affect rural poverty. Specifically, private banks favor opening a new branch in richer areas, while state-led banks favor poorer areas. Their dataset covers 16 Indian states, spans the years 1961–2000, and comprises different types of variables. They used state-level panel data and applied OLS regression model. According to their analysis, they found a negative linkage between branch expansion and rural poverty. In line with the same Jalaludeen (2014) has investigated how branch expansion policies influenced. The study uses balanced panel data of 14 districts of Kerala during 2007–2012. Panel data analysis shows that banks have not considered economic activities of the districts while deciding on the districts where the new branches are to be opened rather than the business of existing branches.

With secondary data of 2007–2008, Iqbal and Sami (2017) have examined the impact of financial inclusion on growth. The study considers GDP as an endogenous variable and financial inclusion variables as independent variables like branches, ATMs, and C-D ratio. Their study reveals that among the three independent variables two variables of branch and C-D ratio have a significant and positive impact on GDP and the other variables of ATMs growth have no significant impact. Bhat and Bhat (2013) have investigated the comparative growth of ATMs and made a comparative analysis of on-site and off-site ATMs of different bank groups. They used exponential growth model using the 2005–2011 data period. Their study concludes that the ATM network is expanding at a rapid pace, as this mode of delivery channel is becoming widely accepted for accessing banking services. Thus, ATMs would be the "future of banking" and the traditional branches may not grow as fast as the ATM networks. Their result indicates that a day may come when traditional branches would be a thing of the past. Further, Kumar (2012a) has analyzed how the relationship between operating branches varies according to population categories, bank groups, and income. Regression has been carried out using pooled dataset from 1990 to 2008 with dependent variables as the number of branches opened and functioning branches and a set of control variables included by him to disentangle the role of various institutional and demographic factors. Evidence of conditional convergence has been found, which implies higher growth in regions having less density of branches initially. The result implies that higher-income regions are experiencing a higher branch growth.

Recently, due to technology innovation, there are a lot of changes in banking habits as well as banking penetration rather than the branch banking mode. In this regard a large number of studies have been undertaken on ICT-based banking.

In a study, Bansal (2014) has attempted to investigate the contribution of ICT toward financial inclusion. According to him, the main reason for slow inclusion is the absence of an appropriate delivery model and products which satisfy the financial need of low-income families. The study concluded that modern ICT would support in achieving financial inclusion. In line with that, Boro (2015) has investigated the challenges and prospects of different ICT-based banking services like debit and credit cards, ATMs, Electronic Clearing Service (ECS), Real Time Gross Settlement (RTGS), mobile banking, internet banking, and mobile wallet in NE India. The main purpose was to know issues related to IT innovation in the banking sector in NE India from a bank's perspective. The findings of his study show that, due to limited trading in NER, IT innovations have so far not highly penetrated. In another study, Chauhan (2015) provides insights on how different factors affect the acceptance and use of m-money with survey data collected from 225 users of m-money by using partial least square technique to test hypotheses empirically. The study found strong support for most hypotheses in the proposed research model. This information may be used to leverage promotion of m-money.

Kulkarni and Warke (2015) have put an effort to examine ICT-based financial inclusion in Marathwada Region of Maharashtra. Their study finds most beneficiaries use only deposit and withdrawal services under FI-based banking services. FI is useful in improving cost efficiency. Non-availability of network connection is a major hurdle in ICT-based FI. The majority of financial inclusion-based bank account beneficiaries have more benefits than traditional savings account. Maximum beneficiaries use FI bank account for saving their time. Most beneficiaries are fully satisfied with debit card facility offered by FI bank account. BCA promotes fixed or recurring deposit accounts to the villagers covered under FI. FI Department provides training to all BCA on a regular basis with some changes in FI schemes. No-frills account facility has attracted villagers for using banking services. The contribution of Women SHG has helped banks in attracting more number of villagers for banking. Fast enrolment process has helped in increased satisfaction of stakeholders. The use of ICT in FI has improved the quality of planning and control. High-level awareness among villagers is created because of financial inclusion. BCAs are trusted mediators between villagers and banks. Banks covered untapped market at a low operating cost. Further, Gautam and Garg (2014) have conducted a study to highlight various IT-enabled measures and various schemes launched by the Union Bank of India toward financial inclusion. The study finds that banks considered have achieved tremendous success in the implementation of FI initiatives, although banks had to face certain challenges while implementing the project, namely, reaching doorsteps of unprivileged customers and providing banking services awareness.

Dhar (2012) has made an attempt to examine the performance for the period ending March 2011 of five banks, namely, SBI, Syndicate Bank, UCO Bank, ICICI Bank, and HDFC Bank. To find out performance on the financial inclusion front as reported by the sample banks, a detailed study was done with the help of their annual reports. His analysis reveals that PSBs have been showing better performance compared to Pvt. SBs from their own reports. Further, he has found that among PSBs, achievement of SBI is comparatively better. Finally, he concluded that in the Indian experience mitigating supply-side issues is not enough and that demand-side effects need to be considered including improving human and physical resource endowments. In another study, Kumar and Gulati (2008) have investigated the efficiency of 27 PSBs by using DEA with the financial data of 2004–2005 sourced from RBI. In their analysis, they considered net-interest income and non-interest income as output variables and physical capital, number of employees, and loanable funds as input variables. The results found that 7 banks have Overall Technical Efficiency (OTE) scores equal to 1 and 12 banks have Pure Technical Efficiency (PTE) scores equal to 1. OTE scores among inefficient banks range from 0.632 to 0.974, with Average Overall Technical Efficiency (AOTE) score of 0.885. Their study also carried out slacks and target-setting exercises to assess directions for improvement in the operations of inefficient banks and logistic regression to work out the relationship between OTE and environmental factors. Likewise Bhattacharyya et al. (1997) have examined the efficiency of Indian public-owned, private-owned, and foreign-owned banks during 1986–1991 by applying DEA and Stochastic Frontier Analysis. They observe that PSBs have been most efficient and private-owned banks least efficient in utilizing resources. Foreign banks have improved their efficiency level from least efficient during the beginning of the study period, but later they were marginally inefficient as the publicly owned banks, which exhibited a temporal decline in performance.

Other studies by Mahajan and Ramola (1996); Burgess et al. (2005); Dev (2006); Sachan and Ali (2006); Rao (2007); Goyal (2008); Mahadeva (2009); Ang (2010); Lokhande (2011); Swamy (2011a, 2011b); Bhanot et al. (2012); Ghosh (2012); Gupte et al. (2012); Kozhikode and Li (2012); Singh (2012); Stephens (2012); Chakravarty and Pal (2013); Dangi and Kumar (2013); Kumar (2013); Sakaria (2013); Gwalani and Parkhi (2014); Raina (2014); Swamy (2014); Agarwal et al. (2015); Maity (2015); Ranjani and Bapat (2015); Maity (2016a); Maity (2016b); Sehrawat and Giri (2016); Sharma (2016); Sharma and Goyal (2017); Maity and Sahu (2018, 2019; Maity and Ganguly (2019); Maity (2019); and Agarwala et al. (2021) in the case of the Indian region also highlighted the importance of finance in economic development and role of financial institution in financial inclusion.

Research Gap
By reviewing the literature, it can be reasoned that "access to formal finance and availing formal financial services could play a significant role in the efforts of poverty reduction." Poor households belonging to the vulnerable sections can benefit from credit, savings, payment, and insurance services and money transfer facilities.

Literature reviews revealed that there is a gap in previous literature and there are limited studies found on the status of financial inclusion from the Indian perspective. Literature reviews presented in the earlier studies are very few at the macro level. The majority of the studies are only at the micro level but not at the macro level of empirical studies.

If we see the past literature, only a few of them are undertaken in the context of the Indian economic framework. Few have studied on selected banks (Dangi, 2012; Dhar, 2012; Gautam & Garg, 2014; Jain, 2015; Pathania et al., 2016), few have studied on selected regions (Ramji, 2009; Cnaan et al., 2012; Kumar, 2012b) or state (Burgess & Pande, 2005; Kodan et al., 2011; Kumar, 2013; Boro, 2015; Das & Guha, 2015), few have studied on household perspective (Kar & Dash, 2009), and even fewer have paid attention to rural population or marginalized section of the society (Bhanot et al., 2012; Bruntha & Indirapriyadharshini, 2015; Ranjani & Bapat, 2015).

The very few studies on rural population have tended to focus on only one district or in one state (Kodan & Chhikara, 2011; Shafi & Medabesh, 2012; Chakraborty & Barman, 2013; Jalaludeen, 2014; Sharma & Goyal, 2017) or a city or small region in a state (Joshi, 2014; Kulkarni & Warke, 2015), and they do not provide a comparative vantage point. In the same line, many other studies were also conducted based on national and international regions. As PSBs and Pvt. SBs have expanded their business all over the regions in India and a major percentage of banking business is held by them, i.e., in respect of no. of branches and volume of business, the present study has covered almost all the regions and the studies at macro level.

Having reviewed the status of financial inclusion in India and across the world, the present study has focused on the role of PSBs and Pvt. SBs in financial inclusion in India. Here the authors considered a large number of sophisticated econometric as well as statistical techniques to reveal the actual relationship among the variables.

The existing study involving India as observed from literature review shows that during earlier days even up to a third quadrant of the previous century was based mostly on observation or feedback of respondents and so on. In the absence of availability of computer-based software-related analysis, specific identifications of effectiveness of different measures applied or the then-existing performance rate or achievement rate could not be established. As obtained in this study of the last few decades different statistical measures like Pearson reliability testing, discriminatory analysis, Cronbach's alpha test, ANOVA analysis, and regression analysis measures are adopted to identify specifically the performance outcome of financial inclusion. The literature review as done in this work specifically identifies such research gap.

BIBLIOGRAPHY

BOOKS, JOURNALS, WORKING PAPERS ETC.

Agarwal, S., Amromin, G., Ben-David, I., Chomsisengphet, S., & Evanoff, D. D. (2015). Financial literacy and financial planning: Evidence from India. *Journal of Housing Economics, 27*, 4–21.

Agarwala, V., Sahu, T. N., & Maity, S. (2021). Efficiency of public sector banks in achieving the goal of PMJDY and PMMY. *International Journal of Economics and Business Research.* (Accepted for publication). https://doi.org/10.1504/IJEBR.2022.10038248

Ang, J. B. (2010). Finance and inequality: The case of India. *Southern Economic Journal, 76*(3), 738–761.

Banerjee, S., & Francis, G. (2014). Financial inclusion and social development. *International Journal of Scientific Research and Management*, 13–18.

Bansal, S. (2014). Perspective of technology in achieving financial inclusion in rural India. *Procedia Economics and Finance, 11*, 472–480.

Barot, P. (2017). Financial inclusion in India. *Imperial Journal of Interdisciplinary Research (IJIR)*, *3*(4), 1098–1104.

Basak, A. (2015). The role of urban cooperative banks and non-agricultural cooperative credit societies in financial inclusion: A study in Howrah District, West Bengal. *The IUP Journal of Management Research*, *XIV*(3), 81–98.

Bhanot, D., Bapat, V., & Bera, S. (2012). Studying financial inclusion in North-East India. *International Journal of Bank Marketing*, *30*(6), 465–484.

Bhat, A. L., & Bhat, B. J. (2013). Automated teller machines (ATMs): The changing face of banking in India. *The IUP Journal of Bank Management*, *XII*(4), 16–28.

Bhattacharyya, A., Lovell, C. A. K., & Sahay, P. (1997). The impact of liberalization on the productive efficiency of Indian commercial banks. *European Journal of Operational Research*, *98*, 332–345.

Boro, K. (2015). Prospects and challenges of technological innovation in banking industry of North East India. *Journal of Internet Banking & Commerce*, *20*(3), 1–6.

Bruntha, P., & Indirapriyadharshini, B. (2015). Enquiry into financial inclusion with special reference to street hawkers of Pollachi, Tamil Nadu. *The IUP Journal of Marketing Management*, *XIV*(4), 56–68.

Burgess, R., & Pande, R. (2005). Do rural banks matter? Evidence from the Indian social banking experiment. *American Economic Review*, *95*(3), 780–795.

Burgess, R., Wong, G., & Pande, R. (2005). Banking for the poor: Evidence from India. *Journal of the European Economic Association*, *3*(2–3), 268–278.

Chakraborty, A., & Barman, S. R. (2013). Financial inclusion in Tripura: Challenges and opportunities. *Journal of Commerce & Management Thought*, *IV*(4), 870–879.

Chakravarty, S. R., & Pal, R. (2013). Financial inclusion in India: An axiomatic approach. *Journal of Policy Modeling*, *35*, 813–837.

Chattopadhyay, S. K. (2011). *Financial inclusion in India: A case study of West Bengal* (RBI Working Paper Series: 8/2011). Retrieved from: http://www.rbi.org.in/scripts/PublicationsView.aspx?id=13517. Accessed 10 June 2016.

Chauhan, S. (2015). Acceptance of mobile money by poor citizens of India: Integrating trust into the technology acceptance model. *Info., Emerald Group Publishing Limited*, *17*(3), 58–68.

Chibango, C. (2014). Mobile money revolution: An opportunity for financial inclusion in Africa. *The International Journal of Humanities & Social Studies*, *2*(2), 59–67.

Cnaan, R. A., Moodithaya, M. S., & Handy, F. (2012). Financial inclusion: Lessons from rural South India. *Jnl Soc. Pol.*, *41*(1), 183–205.

Dangi, N., & Kumar, P. (2013). Current situation of financial inclusion in India and its future visions. *International Journal of Management and Social Sciences Research (IJMSSR)*, *2*(8), 155–166.

Dangi, V. (2012). Financial inclusion: A saga of Indian financial system. *Asia-Pacific Journal of Management Research and Innovation, 8*(2), 111–125.

Das, T., & Guha, P. (2015). A study on the differences in the banking parameters between pre- and post-financial inclusion periods: Some evidence for India. *The IUP Journal of Bank Management, XIV*(1), 39–56.

Dev, S. M. (2006). Financial inclusion: Issues and challenges. *Economic and Political Weekly, 41*(41), 4310–4313.

Dhar, S. (2012). Banking reforms for financial inclusion: Performance of selected Indian banks. *Amity Management Review, 2*(2), 34–39.

Gautam, T., & Garg, K. (2014). Union Bank of India: Initiatives towards IT-enabled financial inclusion. *South Asian Journal of Business and Management Cases, 3*(2), 149–156.

Ghosh, S. (2012). Determinants of banking outreach: An empirical assessment of Indian states. *The Journal of Developing Areas, 46*(2), 269–295.

Government of India. (2008, January). *Report of the committee on financial inclusion* (pp. 20). Economic Advisory Council to the Prime Minister, under the Chairmanship of C. Rangarajan.

Goyal, C. (2008). Financial inclusion in the northeastern region of India with special reference to Assam. *The ICFAI Journal of Applied Finance, 14*(12), 54–64.

Gupta, N. (2014). Financial inclusion in India: The way forward. *Pezzottaite Journals, 3*(3), 1255–1264.

Gupta, P., & Singh, B. (2013). Role of literacy level in financial inclusion in India: Empirical evidence. *Journal of Economics, Business and Management, 1*(3), 272–276.

Gupte, R., Venkataramani, B., & Gupta, D. (2012). Computation of financial inclusion index for India. *Procedia – Social and Behavioral Sciences, 37*, 133–149.

Gwalani, H., & Parkhi, S. (2014). Financial inclusion – Building a success model in the Indian context. *Procedia – Social and Behavioral Sciences, 133*, 372–378.

Iqbal, B. A., & Sami, S. (2017). Role of banks in financial inclusion in India. *Contaduría y Administración, 62*, 644–656.

Jain, S. (2015). A study of banking sector's initiatives towards financial inclusion in India. *Journal of Commerce & Management Thought, 6*(1), 55–77.

Jalaludeen, N. (2014). Is bank branch expansion driven by demand? – Some evidence from Kerala. *The IUP Journal of Bank Management, XIII*(1), 7–18.

Jones, J. H. M., Williams, M., Nilsson, E., & Thorat, Y. (2007). Training to address attitudes behaviour of rural bank managers in Madhya Pradesh, India: A programme to facilitate financial inclusion. *Journal of International Development, 19*, 841–851.

Joshi, N. C. (1998). Restructuring credit system for rural development. *Kurukshetra*, 36–38.

Joshi, V. (2014, October–December). Financial inclusion: Urban-poor in India. *SCMS Journal of Indian Management*, 29–37.

Kar, J., & Dash, P. K. (2009). Formal financial services for rural small savers: A case study of Orissa, India. *Annals of the University of Petroşani, Economics*, 9(2), 73–82.

Kaur, P., & Abrol, V. (2018). Measuring financial inclusion in Jammu & Kashmir state: An empirical study. *IOSR Journal of Business and Management*, 20(1), 37–44.

Khan, H. R. (2011). *Financial inclusion & financial stability – Are they two sides of the same coin?* Addressed at BANCON 2011, Chennai on November 4, Organized by Indian Bankers Association and Indian Overseas Bank.

Kodan, A. S., & Chhikara, K. S. (2011). Status of financial inclusion in Haryana: An evidence of commercial banks. *Management and Labour Studies*, 36(3), 247–267.

Kodan, A. S., Garg, N. K., & Kaidan, S. (2011). Financial inclusion: Status, issues, challenges and policy in northeastern region. *The IUP Journal of Financial Economics*, IX(2), 27–40.

Kozhikode, R. K., & Li, J. (2012). Political pluralism, public policies, and organizational choices: Banking branch expansion in India, 1948–2003. *Academy of Management Journal*, 55(2), 339–359.

Kulkarni, M. M., & Warke, P. (2015). The framework for assessment of ICT based financial inclusion management by nationalized banks with special reference to Marathwada region. *Journal of Commerce & Management Thought*, 6(4), 684–692.

Kumar, N. (2012a). An empirical analysis of financial inclusion across population groups in India. *The IUP Journal of Bank Management*, XI(1), 97–111.

Kumar, N. (2012b). *Financial inclusion and its determinants: Evidence from state level empirical analysis in India* (pp. 1–23). Retrieved from: https://www.researchgate.net/file.PostFileLoader.html?id…assetKey. Accessed 20 July 2016.

Kumar, N. (2013). Financial inclusion and its determinants: Evidence from India. *Journal of Financial Economic Policy*, 5(1), 4–19.

Kumar, S., & Gulati, R. (2008). An examination of technical, pure technical, and scale efficiencies in Indian public sector banks using data envelopment analysis. *Eurasian Journal of Business and Economics*, 1(2), 33–69.

Kunt, A. D., & Klapper, L. (2012, April). *Measuring financial inclusion* (Policy Research Working Paper, 6025). World Bank.

Kuri, P. K., & Laha, A. (2011). Determinants of financial inclusion: A study of some selected districts of West Bengal, India. *Indian Journal of Finance*, 5, 29–36.

Lokhande, M. A. (2011). Financial inclusion: Options for micro, small and medium enterprises. *Synergy*, IX(II), 39–50.

Mahadeva, M. (2008). Financial growth in India: Whither financial inclusion? *Margin—The Journal of Applied Economic Research, 2*(2), 177–197.

Mahadeva, M. (2009). Understanding financial abandoning from a micro perspective: Policy responses to promote inclusion in India. *Savings and Development, 33*(4), 405–430.

Mahajan, V., & Ramola, B. G. (1996). Financial services for the rural poor and women in India: Access and sustainability. *Journal of International Development, 8*(2), 211–224.

Maity, S. (2015). Financial inclusion in India: A study. In Kaushik Kundu (Ed.). Haldia Institute of Technology, School of Management and Social Science, published by *Partha Pratim Datta*, Purba Midnapore (pp. 292–304).

Maity, S. (2016a). Role of schedule commercial banks in financial inclusion: Progress and trends in India. In Nandi, J. K. & Sahu, T. N. (Eds.). Department of Commerce, Ghatal Rabindra Satabarsiki Mahavidyalaya, published by *Perfect Solution*, Kolkata (pp. 290–308).

Maity, S. (2016b). Payment bank license to India Post and its role in financial inclusion – An analysis. In Ghosh, S. & Sahu, T. N. (Eds.). Department of Commerce with Farm Management, Vidyasagar University, published by *Perfect Solution*, Kolkata (pp. 358–370).

Maity, S. (2019). Financial inclusion status in north eastern region: An evidence of commercial banks. *International Journal of Research in applied Management, Science and Technology, 4*(3), 1–11.

Maity, S., & Ganguly, D. (2019). Is demonetization really impact efficiency of banking sector – An empirical study of banks in India. *Asian Journal of Multidimensional Research, 8*(3), 315–327.

Maity, S., & Sahu, T. N. (2018). Role of public and private sector banks in financial inclusion in India – An empirical investigation using DEA. *SCMS Journal of Indian Management, 15*(4), 62–73.

Maity, S., & Sahu, T. N. (2019). A study on regional disparity of Bank performance towards financial inclusion. *Management Today (International Journal of Business Studies), 9*(1), 24–31.

Maity, S., & Sahu, T. N. (2020). Role of public sector banks towards financial inclusion during pre and post introduction of PMJDY: A study on efficiency review. *Rajagiri Management Journal, 14*(2), 95–105.

Maity, S., & Sahu, T. N. (2021). Mergers in banking industry: Some emerging issues. *International Journal of Services and Operations Management* (Accepted for publication). https://doi.org/10.1504/IJSOM.2021.10039421

Malik, R., & Yadav, S. (2014). Financial inclusion in India: An appraisal. *International Journal of Research, 1*(4), 593–602.

Padmanbhan, & Sumam. (2014). Financial inclusion: A study of Union Bank. *Indian Research Journal, 1*(March), 1–7.

Pathania, A., Ali, A., & Rasool, G. (2016). Quality dimension imperative for innovative financial inclusion: A case study of select banks in J&K. *Amity Business Review, 16*(2), 115–125.

Raina, N. (2014). An analytical study: Inclusive approach to banking by scheduled commercial banks as a key driver for inclusive growth. *Journal for Contemporary Research in Management*, 1–8.

Ramji, M. (2009). *Financial inclusion in Gulbarga: Finding usage in access* (Institute for Financial Management and Research Centre for Micro Finance Working Paper Series No. 26, pp. 1–37).

Ranjani, K. S., & Bapat, V. (2015). Deepening financial inclusion beyond account opening: Road ahead for banks. *Business Perspectives and Research, 3*(1), 52–65.

Rao, K. G. K. S. (2007). Financial inclusion: An introspection. *Economic and Political Weekly, 42*(5), 355–360.

Sachan, A., & Ali, A. (2006). Competing in the age of information technology in a developing economy: Experiences of an Indian bank. *Journal of Cases on Information Technology, 8*(2), 62–76.

Sakaria, S. (2013). Evaluation of financial inclusion strategy components: Reflections from India. *Journal of International Management Studies, 13*(1), 83–92.

Sarma, M., & Pais, J. (2008, September). *Financial inclusion and development: A cross country analysis* (pp. 1–28). Paper presented at the annual conference of the human development and capability association, New Delhi. Retrieved from: www.icrier.org/pdf/6nov08/Mandira%20Sarma-Paper.pdf. Accessed 20 July 2016.

Sehrawat, M., & Giri, A. K. (2016). Financial development and poverty reduction in India: An empirical investigation. *International Journal of Social Economics, 43*(2), 106–122.

Shafi, M., & Medabesh, A. H. (2012). Financial inclusion in developing countries: Evidences from an Indian state. *International Business Research, 5*(8), 116–122.

Sharma, D. (2016). Nexus between financial inclusion and economic growth. *Journal of Financial Economic Policy, 8*(1), 13–36.

Sharma, N., & Goyal, R. (2017). Pradhan Mantri Jan Dhan Yojana (PMJDY) – A conceptual study. *International Journal of Research-Granthaalayah, 5*(4), 143–152.

Sharma, R., & Sharma, S. (2014). Banking sector in India: An overview. *Global Journal of Commerce and Management Perspective, 3*(3), 37–39.

Singh, A. B. (2012). Mobile banking based money order for India Post: Feasible model and assessing demand potential. *Procedia – Social and Behavioral Sciences, 37*, 466–481.

Singh, C., Mittal, A., Garg, R., Goenka, A., Goud, R., Ram, K., ... & Kumar, U. (2014). *Financial inclusion in India: Select issues.* IIM Bangalore research paper (474).

Stephen, N., & Tom, T. R. (2015). The role of cooperative banks in financial inclusion. *The IUP Journal of Bank Management, XIV*(3), 55–64.

Stephens, M. C. (2012). *Promoting responsible financial inclusion: A risk-based approach to supporting mobile financial services expansion* (pp. 329–343). Retrieved from: https://www.ftc.gov/sites/default/files/documents/public_comments/ftc-host-workshop-mobile-payments-and-their-impact-consumers-project-no.124808-561018-00012%C2%A0/561018-00012-82712.pdf. Accessed 5 May 2017.

Swamy, V. (2011a). Financial inclusion in India: An evaluation of the coverage, progress and trends. *The IUP Journal of Financial Economics, IX*(2), 7–26.

Swamy, V. (2011b). Does government intervention in credit deployment cause inclusive growth? – An evidence from Indian banking. *International Journal of Business Insights & Transformation, 4*(1), 35–45.

Swamy, V. (2013). Institutional reforms in finance to the poor. *ASCI Journal of Management, 43*(1), 39–66.

Swamy, V. (2014). Financial inclusion, gender dimension, and economic impact on poor households. *World Development, 56*, 1–15.

Thyagarajan, S., & Venkatesan, J. (2008). *Cost-benefit and usage behaviour analysis of no frills accounts: A study report on Cuddalore district* (IFMR/CMF Working Paper). IFMR/CMF, Chennai.

CHAPTER 4

Determinants of Financial Inclusion

4.1 INTRODUCTION

The main driving force of an economy is the country's banking and non-banking institutions. The stronger and widespread banking systems help to strengthen the economy. Although the financial sector has made commendable progress in recent years, according to the recent World Bank report, financial inclusion status is not at the same level throughout the world and a large percentage of the population is still excluded from banking services. The differences are found country to county, region to region of a country, or even at local level within the region. In the Indian context, even after 50 years of bank nationalization large parts of population from across the regions are excluded from formal banking services, especially underprivileged sections. The issue of financial inclusion is influence by many factors. So measuring determinants is a significant issue to fulfill the target of financial inclusion. This chapter deals with the determinants of financial inclusion in the Indian context. Selected dependent variables, independent variables, control variables, input variables, and output variables are selected according to the different objectives set. The selected variables considered in this study are listed below according to different objectives.

In the first part, to analyze determinants, the study has set two dependent variables related to deposit and credit accounts (Reynolds, 2003; Leeladhar, 2005; Thorat, 2007; Sarma & Pais, 2008; Bihari, 2011; Kodan

© The Author(s), under exclusive license to Springer Nature
Singapore Pte Ltd. 2022
S. Maity, T. N. Sahu, *Financial Inclusion and the Role of Banking
System*, https://doi.org/10.1007/978-981-16-6085-6_4

& Chhikara, 2011; Ghosh, 2012; Shafi & Medabesh, 2012; Kumar, 2013; Fungacova & Weill, 2015; and Sharma, 2016) which measure financial inclusion. To study the factors that influence financial inclusion a total of 14 independent variables have been selected. These 14 independent variables are Average Population per Branch (APPB) with off-site ATMs, population per 1000 sq. km., literacy rate, number of factories, employment (person engaged), GDP (percent), per capita Net National Product (NNP), bank deposits to GDP, bank credit to GDP, per capita deposits, per capita credit, Credit-Deposit (C-D) ratio, total assets per branch, and gross Non-Performing Assets (NPAs) to gross advance.

Further, according to the third objective, to analyze disparity across regions, the study has selected five control variables of bank branches per 1000 sq. km., bank branches per 1000 population, deposits per capita, credit per capita, and C-D ratio. Again to analyze disparity across states and union territories, the study has selected two control variables of deposits and credit outstanding.

Statistical and Econometric Test Used
The study employed several statistical and econometric tests to study the determinants of financial inclusion and for obtaining concrete and reliable results.

Coefficient of Variation (CV)
To test consistency of growth performance, CV has been used [CV = Standard deviation / Mean]. CV is applied where the variability of two or more than two variables is compared. To be more variable for CV is greater or conversely less stable, less uniform, less consistent, or homogeneous and vice versa.

Pearson Correlation Coefficients
In statistics, correlation is a measure of linear correlation between two variables. Value of correlation will be within the range from +1 to −1. Value of correlation +1 is the positive correlation, "0" (zero) is no correlation, and −1 is total negative correlation.

Factor Analysis
"It is defined as a class of procedures that are primarily used for reduction of data and summarizing" (Malhotra & David, 2007). In this current study, the principal component analysis (PCA) has been used because it is

usually the preferred method of factor extraction, especially when the focus of an analysis searching for the underlying structure is truly exploratory, which is typically the case. Further, varimax rotations have been used to simplify component structure by maximizing the variance. This is one of the most popular methods used in several social sciences research papers. In addition, Eigen value is also used; it helps to find out the amount of variance in overall data. Finally, determination of factors based on factor score is estimated for each factor with a new name given about grouped variables. Below is the general form for the formula to compute scores on the first component extracted in a PCA.

$$F_i = w_{i1}x_1 + w_{i2}x_2 + w_{i3}x_3 + \ldots + w_{ik}x_k$$

Where,

F_i = Estimate of ith factor
w_{i1} = Factor (weight) score coefficient
x_i = The original variables
k = Number of variables

Bivariate Regression Analysis and Multiple Regression Analysis
Regression is a statistical technique for examining relationship between two or more explanatory variables with an endogenous variable, whose value is to be predicted, and independent or explanatory variables, about which knowledge is available. The objective of bivariate is to use an explanatory variable, whose values are known to predict a single endogenous variable. Both the models have been used for different objectives of the present study. When the problem involves two or more explanatory variables, it is termed multiple regression. Regression is a method for examining relationships between a dependent variable and explanatory variables and for hypotheses testing. The technique is used to find the equation that represents the relationship between variables. The equation is as follows:

$$Y = b_0 + b_1x_1 + b_2x_2 + b_3x_3 + \ldots$$

One-Way Analysis of Variance (ANOVA)
It is used to test the differences of means using F distribution among at least three groups. One-way ANOVA test has been used to find out whether there is any disparity across regions and states.

Tukey HSD Test
Tukey HSD Test is a post hoc test, also called Tukey's Honest Significant Difference test. Tukey's HSD test has been run to find out which specific groups' means are different. To find the significant difference between regions this test has been used.

Other than the above, other tests like mean, medium, quartile values, and standard deviation (SD) have been determined for the purpose of the study.

Scheme of Investigation
Different statistical and econometric tests have been applied according to objectives set for the study. These are enumerated below according to objectives.

Initially, the authors use descriptive statistics to understand the basic nature of factors and correlation coefficient of 14 independent variables to check multicollinearity if any. Due to the presence of multicollinearity, with the results of the correlation coefficient and VIF, the study uses PCA to eliminate the multicollinearity. Results of Kaiser-Meyer-Olkin (KMO) and Bartlett's Test are also found appropriate to run the PCA. Then with the three common PCA scores, two separate regressions have been employed with two dependent variables.

To analyze the disparity in financial inclusion across regions in India, first, authors have checked the significance difference between six regions with ANOVA test. However, differences between regions are not specifically identified from ANOVA test. Hence Tukey HSD Test has been conducted. Further, to measure the disparity across 35 states and union territories, the study first checks the significant difference between states and union territories with ANOVA test. Afterward, the authors have calculated mean, SD, and CV of deposits and credit outstanding separately. Whether there is a wide variation of deposit penetration and credit penetration across states, CV has been computed.

4.2   Determinants of Financial Inclusion

"As financial inclusion can contribute to alleviate poverty and boost economic growth, understanding determinants of financial inclusion is a major issue" (Raichoudhury, 2020). In the Indian context, the authors selected a total of 14 variables to measure factors which may impact on financial inclusion. To examine the factors, the study uses regression with 2 endogenous variables of financial indicators and 14 explanatory variables. In this study, PCA and multiple regression analyses have been combined to estimate penetration of deposit and penetration of credit which measures the financial inclusion. Three components with eigenvalues greater than 1 have been extracted in Varimax rotation which accounted for 97.748 percent of total variation.

According to previous literature, this study found an extensive list of factors which influence financial inclusion. These factors are income level, GDP, population, deposit, credit, education level, employment status, branch, gender, age group, GDP per capita, internet penetration, mobile subscribers, branches per 1000 sq. km., branches per 1 million/per capita, ATM per 1 million/per capita, religion, caste, bank's age, agriculture credit, National State Domestic Product, usage ratio, APPB, deposit or credit to State Domestic Product (SDP) ratio, deposit or credit per branch, deposits or credit to GDP, ATMs per 1000 sq. km., deposit to income ratio, assets, area (rural/urban) of residence, type of family (nuclear/joint) and distance from branch, and so on (Devlin, 2005; Bihari, 2011; Kodan et al., 2011; Kumar & Mohanty, 2011; Burgstaller, 2013; Chakravarty & Pal, 2013; Kumar, 2013; Kunt, 2014; Singh, 2014; Fungacova & Weill, 2015; Koku, 2015; Stephen & Tom, 2015; and Sharma, 2016).

4.2.1   Variables of the Study

Endogenous Variables
There are many dimensions to financial access. To analyze determinants of financial inclusion the study has set two endogenous variables. According to previous literature, the most widely accepted indicator is the populations that have any type of account (including all types of transactions, saving or loan accounts). According to Reynolds (2003), "one of the measurements of financial exclusion is not having a bank account." For

Leeladhar (2005) and Thorat (2007) "one common measure of financial inclusion is adults with bank accounts (deposit and credit)."

Hogarth et al. (2003), Sarma and Pais (2008), Bihari (2011), Shafi and Medabesh (2012), and Kumar (2013) have proposed a "number of bank accounts to population ratio as an indicator of penetration of banking system." On the basis of their study, "deposit and credit accounts per thousand of population have been constructed as a measure of financial inclusion" (Kodan & Chhikara, 2011; Ghosh, 2012; and Sharma, 2016), which constitutes our independent variables. Separate regressions have been carried out for each of them with a common set of explanatory variables.

Explanatory Variables
An essential variable to examine the segment of population to which branch caters is APPB. "Branch network has an unambiguous beneficial impact on financial inclusion" (Kumar, 2013). "Number of bank branches and ATMs express availability of banking services" (Dangi, 2012). In line with the same branch is an important variable. In earlier studies, the authors have found that due to the non-availability of data, ATMs have been eliminated from the analysis. Other than bank branch, ATMs also played a major role in expansion of banking services and also as per present data the number of ATMs exceeds the number of branches. The authors have collected the ATMs data from various sources and such data have been included in the present analysis. To make the variable stronger the authors have considered the off-site ATMs only as the on-site ATMs are located in the branch premises and in many cases customer can get their services from either one. Here the authors have clubbed the branch and off-site ATMs data to get better results. So, one of the independent variables is branch and off-site ATMs per thousand of population instead of only APPB. "Higher geographic and demographic penetration indicates easier geographic access and smaller distance between branch and customer" (Beck et al., 2007).

Among the other independent variables, the foremost is the population density. Population density is the number of people living in a square kilometer in a concerned location. It is determined by dividing total population living in the area by total area. Population is an important parameter which directly affects demand for banking. "Population density is an important aspect that could be considered while opening new branches" (Ansong et al., 2015; Kumar, 2013). Low-population density areas might be expected to be associated with few bank branches. "Higher population density or higher population per branch is expected to have more number of new branches" (Burgstaller, 2013). So, explanatory variable population per 1000 sq. km. is included as higher demand will naturally lead to more opening of accounts.

Population figures are available only for the census years 1991, 2001, and 2011. As per earlier studies, to overcome this limitation this study also considered the Average Annual Exponential Growth Rate (AAEGR) of population. To measure yearly population during 2002–2010 the authors have considered the AAEGR at 1.64 percent as per Census data 2011. This study also measures the same AAEGR of 1.64 percent for measuring population during 2012–2016.

Other than population, other socio-demographic factor is literacy ratio. From the literature review, it was found that literate people are more comfortable in using banking services than illiterate people. Devlin (2009), Arputhamani and Prasannakumari (2011), Bihari (2011), Singh et al. (2014), Fungacova and Weill (2015), and Koku (2015) in their study have found "a positive and statistically significant association between financial inclusion and literacy rate." People with low or having no formal education may feel frightened in accessing formal financial services given their incapability to write or read. "High illiteracy levels may prevent a large section of population from benefiting financial inclusion efforts" (Arora, 2012).

"Proportion of factories has been taken as a proxy for level of industrialization and sociological modernization. Usually, advanced economies with greater industrialization are expected to have a greater role for banking and financial activities" (Kumar, 2013). "Another factor is employment, which can also be associated with financial inclusion" (Goodwin et al., 1999). Employment status represents the employment status of individuals. "Insecure and Irregular employment or unemployment has high negative correlation and are less likely to participate in financial system" (Alama & Ausina, 2012). A cross-country study by King and Levine (1993) asserts that bank expansion and economic growth are positively correlated. Higher demand for banking services will naturally lead to profitable branch expansion. "GDP is a significant economic exhibitor to find out the growth of a country and due to this reason, authors used it widely as an indicator" (Chithra & Selvam, 2013; and Kamboj, 2014). "A higher economic growth or higher per capita income can be strong reasons for branch expansion as the banks can reasonably expect to generate more business from higher economic activities" (Burgstaller, 2013; Kunt, 2014). In those lines GDP and per capita income are considered as independent variables.

"Income is directly having a positive and significant role in determining level of financial inclusion" (Devlin, 2009; Kumar, 2013; Fungacova & Weill, 2015; Koku, 2015; and Stephen & Tom, 2015). "Both per capita income and population are expected to positively impact accessibility because they directly influence demand for bank services" (Evanoff, 1988). Income is measured by per capita NNP at current prices. Deposit income ratio is a primary indicator of level of deposit in the system. Information on the net national product is collected from Statistics on Indian Economy, RBI.

Further, "deposit to GDP ratio is a primary indicator of level of deposit in the system and credit to GDP portrays the level of credit utilization. Both deposits to GDP and credit to GDP denote usage of basic financial products in the financial system" (Kumar, 2013; and Sharma, 2016). "Higher ratios of deposit to GDP and credit to GDP are usually associated with higher banking and investment activities" (Swamy, 2011b). Iqbal and Sami (2017) "in their study found positive and significant impact of number of bank branch and C-D ratio on GDP."

"Per capita deposits and per capita credit have a significant impact on deposit accounts and credit accounts" (Kodan & Chhikara, 2011). Customers will come to buy a product or visit a shop on the basis of number of existing customers. If the existing customer is on higher side, the new customer will also come with believing that their product is good in comparison to others. So, deposit per capita and credit per capita are included as two independent variables in this analysis.

"C-D ratio is a fundamental indicator of how efficiently the deposits are mobilized and is utilized to carry out investment and capital formation activities" (Kodan & Chhikara, 2011). "A high C-D ratio is usually associated with higher investment and growth. Limited credit access may cause economic loss" (Chen & Jin, 2017). C-D ratio is considered separately as a measure of usage dimension to nullify the effect of higher deposit/ per capita in comparison of credit/ per capita.

"Bank size, as captured by assets, has a direct influence on number of operating branches" (Kumar, 2012a). Size of a branch depends on volume of assets. So, total asset per branch (₹) is another independent variable. "Increase in NPA ceases economic growth and measure soundness of financial status" (Harimaya & Kondo, 2012). "Increase NPA stops banks to take expansion decisions which ultimately impact in opening of deposit and credit accounts" (Maity & Sahu, 2019). So, gross NPA to gross advance is another independent variable.

4.2.2 Measures of Determinants

To test the significance of determinants separate regressions have been carried out with two endogenous variables with a common set of components score. When utilized as principal component scores as independent variables in multiple regression, they have significant effects on deposit accounts with two components and on credit accounts with single component for 97.3 percent and 97.7 percent variation respectively. Positive growth of deposit and credit accounts indicates improvement of financial inclusion. The use of deposit and credit accounts measurements might provide useful information on improvement of financial inclusion programs. The means with minimum and maximum values and SDs of 2 endogenous variables and all the selected 14 independent variables are presented in Table 4.1. After testing multicollinearity from correlation matrix as depicted in Table 4.2, the authors use PCA to reduce the variables into components and to make group between them.

The correlation matrix predicts that there is multicollinearity between the variables. In order to eliminate the problems of multicollinearity, PCA has been used in SPSS through data reduction process. As observed, results of correlation coefficient (Table 4.2) also show the intense correlation coefficient between the variables. The correlation coefficients are observed to be high and mostly above 0.5 and close to 1.000. Relationship between the variables has mostly been positive and highly significant ($p<0.01$). These correlations provide a measure of linear relations between the independent variables and also indicate existence of multicollinearity.

KMO and Bartlett's Test
KMO and Bartlett's test of sphericity have been used and the authors found that they are fit for application in factor analysis. KMO measures sampling adequacy value which is found to be 0.671 (Table 4.3), i.e., more than the 0.5 and we should confident that the application of PCA is appropriate for these data set. The result of Bartlett's test of sphericity was 658.999 and the test is highly significant ($p < 0.001$). According to these results, it could be said that available data sets were suitable for PCA.

Table 4.1 List of variables analyzed in the present study (descriptive statistics)

Sl. No.	Variables	Symbol	Units of measurement	Mean	Minimum	Maximum	Std. dev.
	Dependent Variables						
1	Number of deposit accounts per thousand of population	DA		652.6993	419.75	1201.72	264.86671
2	Number of credit accounts per thousand of population	CA		89.0407	53.92	118.12	20.94808
	Explanatory Variables						
1	Average population per branch and off-site ATMs	APPBA	in 000'	10.8540	5.71	14.88	3.44923
2	Population/1000 km^2	POPU	in 000'	357.2523	318.07	399.29	25.94095
3	Literacy rate	LITC		72.3080	66.10	78.87	4.08026
4	Number of factories	FAC	in 000'	174.3165	127.96	241.02	43.77542
5	Employment (total person engaged)	EMP	in million	11.0685	7.75	14.52	2.40405
6	GDP (%)	GDP		7.3800	3.80	10.30	1.86364
7	Per capita NNP	NNP	in 000'	47.3988	17.78	93.29	25.82619
8	Bank deposits as a percent of GDP	DGDP		61.9667	47.00	69.40	7.82456
9	Bank credit as a percent of GDP	CGDP		44.3067	25.10	53.40	10.05772
10	Per capita deposits of SCBs (₹)	DPC	in 000'	36.5617	10.99	73.59	21.19026
11	Per capita credit of SCBs (₹)	CPC	in 000'	26.9903	5.92	57.30	17.10816
12	Credit-deposit ratio	CDR		70.5680	53.40	78.00	8.59983
13	Total assets of SCBs per branch (₹)	ASSET	in billion	0.6217	0.23	0.98	0.27222
14	Gross NPA to gross advance	NPA		3.4993	2.26	7.49	1.34305

Source: Authors' calculation

Table 4.2 Correlation matrix

Variables	APPBA	POPU	LITC	FAC	EMP	GDP	NNP	DGDP	CGDP	DPC	CPC	CDR	ASSET	NPA
APPBA	1													
POPU	-0.989*	1												
LITC	-0.988*	1.000*	1											
FAC	-0.970*	0.954*	0.953*	1										
EMP	-0.980*	0.984*	0.985*	0.947*	1									
GDP	0.062	0.008	0.010	-0.134	-0.041	1								
NNP	-0.989*	0.984*	0.983*	0.970*	0.956*	-0.053	1							
DGDP	-0.864*	0.894*	0.896*	0.771*	0.921*	0.096	0.808*	1						
CGDP	-0.874*	0.911*	0.914*	0.807*	0.937*	0.059	0.830*	0.981*	1					
DPC	-0.994*	0.990*	0.989*	0.965*	0.966*	-0.040	0.998*	0.837*	0.851*	1				
CPC	-0.993*	0.992*	0.991*	0.969*	0.972*	-0.051	0.997*	0.844*	0.864*	0.998*	1			
CDR	-0.809*	0.864*	0.867*	0.771*	0.886*	0.068	0.779*	0.913*	0.973*	0.794*	0.814*	1		
ASSET	-0.987*	0.989*	0.990*	0.950*	0.993*	-0.039	0.962*	0.926*	0.937*	0.972*	0.977*	0.880*	1	
NPA	-0.317	0.334	0.329	0.363	0.224	0.126	0.433	-0.035	0.005	0.403	0.395	0.024	0.214	1

Source: Authors' calculation

*Significance level is 1 percent

Table 4.3   KMO and Bartlett's test

Kaiser-Meyer-Olkin measure of sampling adequacy		0.671
Bartlett's test of sphericity	Approx. Chi-Square	658.999
	Df	91
	Sig.	0.000

Source: Authors' calculation

Factor Extraction

Normally the number of factors to be retained is similar to the number of positive eigenvalues of the factors. An eigenvalue is defined as the amount of total variance explained by each factor, with the total amount of variability in the analysis equal to number of original variables in the analysis (i.e., each variable contributes one unit of variability to the total amount due to the fact that the variance has been standardized). PCA is the preferred method of factor extraction as it extracts maximum variance from a data set.

The middle part of Table 4.4 shows initial solution with eigenvalues greater than 1 and their percentage of variance explained. Further, in Table 4.4 the three rotated factors are displayed with percentage of variance explained and their eigenvalues. It is observed from the table that the first three factors contribute to 80.736 percent, 9.336 percent, and 7.676 percent, respectively, and the total contribution of these factors is 97.748 percent. As per initial solution, the first component is much more important than the second, the second component is more important than the third, and so on. We should note that component rotation does not affect total variance accounted by the model but does change how the variance is distributed among the retained components. The amount of total variance of three factors before rotation is just the same as after rotation. This makes it clear how important it is that we extract an appropriate number of factors.

Scree Test

A scree test is useful in determining the total amount of variance explained by each factor or component. It is a graph with principal components on the x-axis and eigenvalues on the y-axis. We should look for "knee," or bend, in the line to determine the component number. A typical scree plot

Table 4.4 Total variance explained

Component	Initial eigenvalues			Extraction sums of squared loadings			Rotation sums of squared loadings		
	Total	% of variance	Cumulative %	Total	% of variance	Cumulative %	Total	% of variance	Cumulative %
1	11.303	80.736	80.736	11.303	80.736	80.736	10.986	78.471	78.471
2	1.307	9.336	90.072	1.307	9.336	90.072	1.619	11.568	90.039
3	1.075	7.676	97.748	1.075	7.676	97.748	1.079	7.709	97.748
4	0.194	1.387	99.135						
5	0.083	0.596	99.731						
6	0.024	0.172	99.903						
7	0.008	0.059	99.962						
8	0.003	0.020	99.982						
9	0.002	0.014	99.996						
10	0.000	0.002	99.998						
11	0.000	0.001	100.000						
12	3.65E-005	0.000	100.000						
13	9.83E-006	7.02E-005	100.000						
14	3.57E-008	2.55E-007	100.000						

Source: Authors' calculation

Extraction method: PCA

will show the first one or two eigenvalues to be relatively large in magnitude, with magnitude of successive eigenvalues dropping off rather drastically. At some point, the line will appear to level off. This is indicative of the fact that these successive eigenvalues are relatively small and, for the most part, of equal size. In the present analysis, three components would be retained from the left-hand side from the knee of scree plot (Fig. 4.1).

Communalities

The communalities as presented in Table 4.5 represent the proportion of variance in the original variables, and solution was found to be high in all the 14 variables with ranges from 96.2 percent to 99.8 percent which are normally more than 70 percent. As the communality values of all the 14 explanatory variables were found quite high, only the first three principal components are appropriate for explaining variations in measures of financial inclusion.

Rotation

After extraction of factors, interpretation of the factors can be very difficult. To overcome this difficulty, factor rotation is the best choice by which solution of a factor is made more interpretable without altering underlying mathematical formation. Rotation is a complex mathematical procedure and it is sometimes helpful to consider it from a geometric perspective.

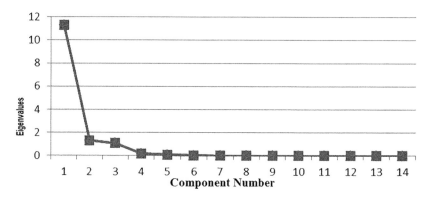

Fig. 4.1   Scree plot. (Source: Prepared by authors)

Table 4.5   Communalities

Statements/attributes	Initial	Extraction
APPBA	1.000	0.998
POPU	1.000	0.998
LITC	1.000	0.998
FAC	1.000	0.962
EMP	1.000	0.990
GDP	1.000	0.998
NNP	1.000	0.996
DGDP	1.000	0.968
CGDP	1.000	0.999
DPC	1.000	0.997
CPC	1.000	0.998
CDR	1.000	0.983
ASSET	1.000	0.998
NPA	1.000	0.996

Source: Authors' calculation

Extraction method: PCA

To carry out rotations there are several methods. In the present study the authors have considered varimax rotation. After varimax rotation of the factor, three components have been extracted which accounted for 97.748 percent of the original 14 variables (Table 4.4). Component pattern coefficients of the rotated components show the relative contribution of each explanatory variable to a particular component. The first component explained 78.471 percent of the 12 variables (APPBA, POPU, LITC, FAC, EMP, NNP, DGDP, CGDP, DPC, CPC, CDR, and ASSET), the second component explained 11.568 percent of another variable of Gross NPA to gross advance, and the third component explained 7.709 percent of another variable of GDP (percent).

Once rotated, it is ready to attempt an interpretation. Rotated component loading of 14 variables is presented in Table 4.6. The authors notice that each variable has a loading on each component, although in most cases each has a high loading on only one component. From the table the authors also notice that some of the variables have loaded relatively high on both components, but we will assign a given variable to the component with the higher loading as shown in bold form and attempt to interpret the same.

Table 4.6   Rotated component matrix (Rotation converged in nine iterations)

Attributes	Component		
	1	2	3
ASSET	0.990	0.112	-0.042
EMP	0.987	0.115	-0.041
LITC	0.974	0.221	0.004
CGDP	0.974	-0.154	0.096
POPU	0.973	0.227	0.002
APPBA	-0.959	-0.241	0.082
DGDP	0.958	-0.180	0.129
CPC	0.948	0.306	-0.067
DPC	0.941	0.321	-0.060
CDR	0.928	-0.154	0.115
NNP	0.926	0.358	-0.077
FAC	0.912	0.306	-0.165
NPA	0.119	0.965	0.083
GDP	-0.010	0.072	0.991

Source: Authors' calculation

Notes: Extraction method: PCA; rotation method: varimax with Kaiser normalization

Whether the loadings will be positive or negative depends upon the correlation between the variables in a component. If the variables (all) are positively correlated then the loadings will be positive. The loadings will be negative in case a few variables are negatively correlated.

The three rotated components are just as good as the initial components in explaining and reproducing the observed correlation matrix. In the rotated components, out of 14 variables, 11 are with high positive loadings and 1 with high negative loading under the first component, whereas gross NPA to gross advance has high positive loadings under the second component. Further, in the third component, GDP rate has high positive loading under the third component.

Component 1
In Table 4.6, the variables of high loadings are indicated. These variables are collected and organized based on their loadings. Thus, it is seen that the first component is loaded with 12 variables, namely, APPB (including off-site ATMs), population per 1000 sq. km., literacy rate, number of factories, employment, per capita NNP, bank deposits to GDP, credit to GDP, per capita deposits (₹), per capita credit (₹), C-D ratio, and total assets per branch (₹).

Component 2
The second component is observed to be loaded with a single variable of gross NPA to gross advance.

Component 3
The third component is observed to be loaded with also a single variable of GDP as percentage.

Observing the matrices and comparing the eigenvalues and percent of variance explained, component 1 which accounts for 78.471 percent is the most dominant factor to measure financial inclusion. The component 1 has 12 dominant determinants, with 11 variables having positive loadings and the remaining one having negative loading. The other two components having one variable each with 11.568 percent and 7.709 percent of variance explained respectively may also impact on financial inclusion. Now whether these components are significant or not the authors have run multiple regression.

Component scores derived from PCA have been used for regression analysis in order to eliminate multicollinearity problem. Separate regression has been run with the same set of three component scores. Results of multiple regression using principal component scores (PCSs) as independent variables and deposit and credit accounts as dependent variables are presented in Tables 4.7 and 4.8 respectively. When probabilities have been taken into consideration, the regressions of standardized deposit accounts on component 1 ($P<0.01$) and component 2 ($P<0.01$) both are statistically significant. Component 3 ($P>0.05$) is statistically non-significant. Value of constant is also significant at 1 percent level ($P<0.01$) of significance. The value R^2 is 0.973, that is, 97.30 percent of variation in the opening of deposit accounts which have been explained by all three components (Table 4.7). Positively significant effects components 1 and 2 on deposit accounts were found to measure the position of financial inclusion. The values of VIFs are 1 for all three components which also indicates that there is no multicollinearity between the components. Finally, the regression equation is fit because value of "F" statistics is significant at 0.01 level of significance. So, from the analysis, the study found that out of 14 selected variables, 13 variables have a significant impact on deposit accounts. Only the percentage of GDP rate is non-significant on deposit accounts.

Table 4.7   Regression results of deposit accounts with component scores

Indicators	Coefficients	Std. error	t-values	P-values	VIF
(Constant)	652.699	12.720	51.314	0.000*	
Principal Component Score 1	224.429	13.166	17.046	0.000*	1.000
Principal Component Score 2	131.903	13.166	10.018	0.000*	1.000
Principal Component Score 3	-21.932	13.166	-1.666	0.124	1.000
R^2	0.973				
Adjusted R^2	0.965				
F-statistics	131.236			0.000*	

Source: Authors' calculation
*Significance level is 1 percent

Table 4.8   Regression results of credit accounts with component scores

Indicators	Coefficients	Std. error	t-values	P-values	VIF
(Constant)	89.041	0.919	96.891	0.000*	
Principal Component Score 1	20.675	0.951	21.735	0.000*	1.000
Principal Component Score 2	0.903	0.951	0.949	0.363	1.000
Principal Component Score 3	0.776	0.951	0.816	0.432	1.000
R^2	0.977				
Adjusted R^2	0.971				
F-statistics	157.988			0.000*	

Source: Authors' calculation
*Significance level is 1 percent

Table 4.8 exhibits the regression results of credit account as dependent variable and component 1, component 2, and component 3 as explanatory variables. When probabilities have been taken into consideration, the regressions of standardized credit accounts on component 1 ($P<0.01$) which accounts for 12 independent variables and regression coefficient of constant ($P<0.01$) both are statistically significant. Component 2 ($P>0.05$), that is, gross NPA to gross advance and component 3 ($P>0.05$), that is, percentage of GDP, both are statistically non-significant. The value R^2 is 0.977, that is, 97.70 percent of variation in opening of credit accounts which is explained by all three components (Table 4.8). The values of VIFs are 1 for all three components which also indicates that there is no multicollinearity between the components. Finally, the regression equation is fit because value of "F" statistics is significant at 0.01 level of significance. So, from the analysis, this study found that out of 14 selected variables, 12 have a significant impact on credit accounts. Variables of Gross NPA to gross advance and percentage of GDP rate are non-significant on credit accounts.

In a nutshell, deposit account is expected to change with change in the first two components, that is, 13 independent variables and credit account are expected to change, with change in first component only, that is, 12 explanatory variables. So the authors conclude that in the Indian context according to deposit accounts, 13 factors (except GDP as a percentage) impact on financial inclusion and according to credit accounts there are 12 factors which impact on financial inclusion.

4.2.3   Disparity Across Regions and States in India

Financial Inclusion Status Across Regions in India
From the studies, the authors found that individual banks, RBI, and GOI have taken many initiatives to cover regions with bank branches and ATMs and by any other mode. More the supply, more will be the demand. People will open a saving or credit account if the access is easier within a short distance with minimum time period.

The present section analyzes the patterns and trends of economic discrimination across the regions and states. Based on literature, the authors identified five parameters to analyze disparity across regions and two parameters to analyze disparities across states, namely, branches (per 1000 sq. km. and per 1000 of population), deposits outstanding, credit outstanding, and C-D ratio. This chapter shows comparative study among these parameters during the period from 2001–2002 to 2015–2016. The regional discrimination in bank branches, deposits, credit outstanding, and C-D ratio shows a clear picture of regional discrimination on financial inclusion in India.

To study the status across regions and states the authors have set Hypothesis I. On the basis of review of literature, the authors identify five parameters, namely, branches per 1000 sq. km. (geographic outreach), branches per 1000 of population (demographic outreach), deposits, credit outstanding, and C-D ratio. To measure whether there is any disparity between states and regions the authors have analyzed the different indicators or parameters region-wise by applying ANOVA. For testing discrimination between different groups for homogeneity, ANOVA is essentially a procedure. For measuring the results p-value approach has been used. SPSS has been used for calculating the results of ANOVA.

The post hoc test also conducted to know significant difference between six regions penetration of branches, that is, Central Region (CR) with Chhattisgarh, Madhya Pradesh, Uttarakhand, and Uttar Pradesh; Eastern Region (ER) with Andaman and Nicobar Islands, Bihar, Jharkhand, Odisha, Sikkim, and West Bengal; North Eastern Region (NER) with Arunachal Pradesh, Assam, Manipur, Meghalaya, Mizoram, Nagaland, and Tripura; Northern Region (NR) with Chandigarh, Haryana, Himachal Pradesh, Jammu and Kashmir, Delhi, Punjab, and Rajasthan; Southern Region (SR) with Andhra Pradesh, Karnataka, Kerala, Lakshadweep, Puducherry, Tamil Nadu, and Telangana; and Western Region (WR) with Dadra and Nagar Haveli, Daman and Diu, Goa, Gujarat, and Maharashtra. An ANOVA test can tell us whether the present results are significant overall, but it won't tell us exactly where those differences lie. So to find the significant difference between the regions, a post hoc test has been conducted. Tukey HSD Test is a post hoc test and is also called Tukey's Honest Significant Difference test which has been run to find out which specific group's means (compared with each other) are different. The test compares all possible pairs of means

"Branch density denotes the spread of banks and level of comfort, convenience available for public to carry out banking pursuits" (Kumar, 2013). "Penetration of branches is an essential measure of financial inclusion which measured by number of branches per 1000 sq. km and number of branches per 1000 population" (Kodan & Chhikara, 2011).

To study regional imbalance of penetration of branches per 1000 sq. km. in CR, ER, NER, NR, SR, and WR, ANOVA statistics have been employed (Table 4.9). Since observed value F of 19.88 > critical value F of 3.24 (alternatively, since p-value < 0.01), the results explicitly explain that the test is significant at 1 percent level. So, null hypothesis will be rejected and alternative hypothesis will be accepted. Therefore, the authors conclude that there is a significant difference in penetration of branches per 1000 sq. km. in the six regions.

It has been found from the ANOVA test that there is a significant difference among the regions in terms of branches per 1000 sq. km. However, the differences between regions are not specifically identified from the

Table 4.9 ANOVA Results: Bank branches per 1000 sq. km. from April 2001 to March 2016

Source of variation	SS	df	MS	F	P-value	F crit
Between groups	2212.8892	5	442.5778	19.8831	0.000*	3.2433
Within groups	1869.7526	84	22.2590			
Total	4082.6417	89				

Source: Authors' calculation

*Significance level is 1 percent

ANOVA test. So, the authors have run Tukey HSD test to know difference between regions of CR, ER, NER, NR, SR, and WR. Based on results (Table 4.10), the study proves that expansions of branch in the regions with all combinations are significant at 1 percent level.

The test (post hoc) revealed that ER, SR, and WR do not have difference in mean scores while CR, NER, and NR have mean scores which are different from the scores of the other three regions. Since mean value of CR (12.83103), NER (4.26841), and NR (11.27829) is lower as compared to ER (17.31918), SR (19.29923), and WR (16.45586), the authors are led to believe that the branch expansion per 1000 sq. km. is little at a lower level in CR and NR than the other three regions of ER, SR, and WR. The results also revealed that branch expansion per 1000 sq. km. in NER is comparatively lower than the other five regions.

Based on the null hypothesis, an observation in this study establishes that the assumption that there is no disparity due to policies on financial inclusion across different regions of India is disproved. Accordingly, financial inclusion resulted in more penetration of branches per 1000 sq. km. in all three regions of ER, SR, and WR than CR, NER, and NR. Figure 4.2 also elucidates the average branches per 1000 sq. km. in the six regions of India.

"Branch network is used in financial inclusion studies to capture banking access and branch density" (Burgess & Pande, 2005). "The penetration of banks that measured by branches per 1,000 population is also an important measure of financial inclusion" (Kodan & Chhikara, 2011). To study the regional imbalance of penetration of branches per 1000 population in CR, ER, NER, NR, SR, and WR, ANOVA statistics have been

Table 4.10   Tukey HSD Test: Multiple Comparison of branch expansion per 1000 sq. km

Expansion of branches per 1000 sq. km.		Mean difference (A - B)	Std. error	Sig.
Region (A)	Region (B)			
Central Region	Eastern Region	-4.48816	0.27234*	0.000
	North Eastern Region	8.56261	0.71885*	0.000
	Northern Region	1.55273	0.04538*	0.000
	Southern Region	-6.46820	0.47343*	0.000
	Western Region	-3.62483	0.35048*	0.000
Eastern Region	Central Region	4.48816	0.27234*	0.000
	North Eastern Region	13.05077	0.98589*	0.000
	Northern Region	6.04089	0.26927*	0.000
	Southern Region	-1.98005	0.22722*	0.000
	Western Region	0.86332	0.18547*	0.000
North Eastern Region	Central Region	-8.56261	0.71885*	0.000
	Eastern Region	-13.05077	0.98589*	0.000
	Northern Region	-7.00988	0.72993*	0.000
	Southern Region	-15.03082	1.18840*	0.000
	Western Region	-12.18744	1.05228*	0.000
Northern Region	Central Region	-1.55273	0.04538*	0.000
	Eastern Region	-6.04089	0.26927*	0.000
	North Eastern Region	7.00988	0.72993*	0.000
	Southern Region	-8.02094	0.4598*	0.000
	Western Region	-5.17757	0.33214*	0.000
Southern Region	Central Region	6.46820	0.47343*	0.000
	Eastern Region	1.98005	0.22722*	0.000
	North Eastern Region	15.03082	1.18840*	0.000
	Northern Region	8.02094	0.45980*	0.000
	Western Region	2.84337	0.17184*	0.000
Western Region	Central Region	3.62483	0.35048*	0.000
	Eastern Region	-0.86332	0.18547*	0.000
	North Eastern Region	12.18744	1.05228*	0.000
	Northern Region	5.17757	0.33214*	0.000
	Southern Region	-2.84337	0.17184*	0.000

Source: Authors' calculation

*Significance level is 1 percent

Average Branch per 1000 sq. km.

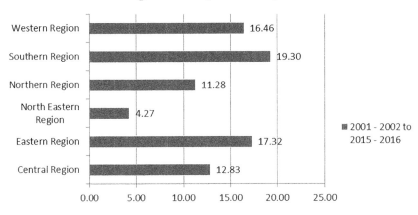

Fig. 4.2 Average branches per 1000 sq. km. in the six regions of India (for the period from 2001–2002 to 2015–2016). (Source: Prepared by authors)

Table 4.11 ANOVA Results: Bank branches per 1000 population from April 2001 to March 2016

Source of variation	SS	df	MS	F	P-value	F crit
Between groups	0.0110	5	0.0022	18.5942	0.000*	3.2433
Within groups	0.0099	84	0.0001			
Total	0.0209	89				

Source: Authors' calculation

*Significance level is 1 percent

employed (Table 4.11). Since observed value F of 18.59 > critical value F of 3.24 (alternatively, since p-value < 0.01), the results explicitly explain that test is significant at 1 percent level. So, null hypothesis will be rejected and alternative hypothesis will be accepted. Therefore, there is a significant difference in penetration of branches per 1000 population in the six regions.

To find where the differences lie among the six regions of CR, ER, NER, NR, SR, and WR in terms of branch penetration per 1000 population the authors have run Tukey HSD test. This study has found that all the combinations of regions are significant at 1 percent, except SR and WR or vice versa that are significant at 5 percent.

Based on Table 4.12, the test revealed that NR, SR, and WR do not have difference in mean scores while mean scores of CR, ER, and NER which are different from the scores of other three regions and significant at 1 percent level of significance ($p < 0.01$). Since mean values of CR (0.03125), ER (0.02818), and NER (0.02452) are lower as compared to NR (0.05143), SR (0.04910), and WR (0.04843), the authors are led to believe that the branch expansion per 1000 of population is little at a lower level in CR, ER, and NER than the other three regions of NR, SR, and WR.

Based on the null hypothesis, the assumption that there is no disparity due to banking policies on financial inclusion across regions is disproved. Accordingly, financial inclusion resulted in more branch penetration per 1000 population in NR, SR, and WR than CR, ER, and NER. Figure 4.3 also elucidates that average branches per 1000 population in the six regions of India.

To study regional imbalance of deposit penetration in CR, ER, NER, NR, SR, and WR, ANOVA statistics have been employed (Table 4.13). Since observed value F of 14.09 > critical value F of 3.24 (alternatively, since p-value < 0.01), the results explicitly explain that test is significant at 1 percent level. So, alternative hypothesis will be accepted and null hypothesis will be rejected. Therefore, there is a significant difference in deposit penetration per capita in the six regions.

To find where the differences lie among the six regions of CR, ER, NER, NR, SR, and WR in terms of deposit penetration per capita the authors have run Tukey HSD test. Based on the results of Table 4.14, Tukey HSD test proves that deposit penetration per capita in all the regions with all combinations is significant at 1 percent level.

The test (post hoc) revealed that CR, ER, and NER do not have a difference in the mean scores while NR, SR, and WR have mean scores which are different from the scores of the other three regions. Since the mean value of CR (0.01755), ER (0.01964), and NER (0.01666) is lower as compared to NR (0.05972), SR (0.03930), and WR (0.07700), the

Table 4.12 Tukey HSD Test: Multiple comparisons of branch expansion per 1000 population

Expansion of branches per 1000 population		Mean difference (A - B)	Std. error	Sig.
Region (A)	Region (B)			
Central Region	Eastern Region	0.00307	0.00037*	0.000
	North Eastern Region	0.00674	0.00032*	0.000
	Northern Region	-0.02018	0.00772*	0.000
	Southern Region	-0.01785	0.00511*	0.000
	Western Region	-0.01718	0.00528*	0.000
Eastern Region	Central Region	-0.00307	0.00037*	0.000
	North Eastern Region	0.00366	0.00012*	0.000
	Northern Region	-0.02325	0.00235*	0.000
	Southern Region	-0.02092	0.00168*	0.000
	Western Region	-0.02025	0.00172*	0.000
North Eastern Region	Central Region	-0.00674	0.00032*	0.000
	Eastern Region	-0.00366	0.00012*	0.000
	Northern Region	-0.02692	0.00228*	0.000
	Southern Region	-0.02459	0.00161*	0.000
	Western Region	-0.02392	0.00166*	0.000
Northern Region	Central Region	0.02018	0.00199*	0.000
	Eastern Region	0.02325	0.00235*	0.000
	North Eastern Region	0.02692	0.00228*	0.000
	Southern Region	0.00233	0.00069*	0.004
	Western Region	0.00300	0.00073*	0.001
Southern Region	Central Region	0.01785	0.00132*	0.000
	Eastern Region	0.02092	0.00168*	0.000
	North Eastern Region	0.02459	0.00161*	0.000
	Northern Region	-0.00233	0.00069*	0.004
	Western Region	0.00067	0.00029**	0.044
Western Region	Central Region	0.01718	0.00136*	0.000
	Eastern Region	0.02025	0.00172*	0.000
	North Eastern Region	0.02392	0.00166*	0.000
	Northern Region	-0.00300	0.00073*	0.001
	Southern Region	-0.00067	0.00029**	0.044

Source: Authors' calculation

*Significance level is 1 percent
**Significance level is 5 percent

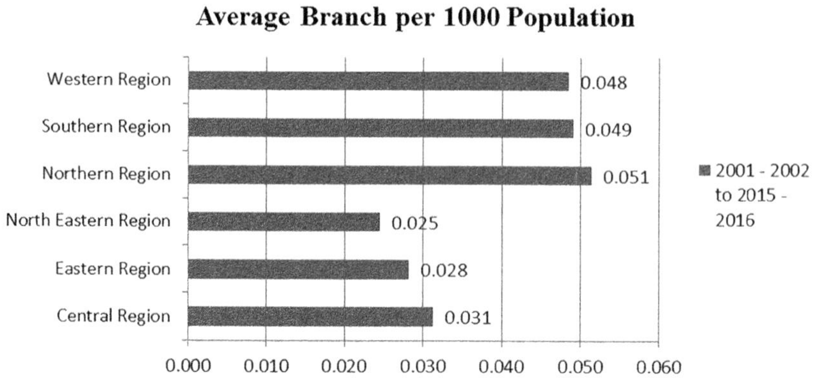

Average Branch per 1000 Population

Fig. 4.3   Average branches per 1000 population in the six regions of India (for the period from 2001–2002 to 2015–2016). (Source: Prepared by authors)

Table 4.13   ANOVA Results: Deposit penetration per capita from April 2001 to March 2016

Source of variation	SS	df	MS	F	P-value	F crit
Between groups	0.0481	5	0.0096	14.092	0.000*	3.2433
Within groups	0.0573	84	0.0007			
Total	0.1054	89				

Source: Authors' calculation

*Significance level is 1 percent

authors are led to believe that deposit penetration is lower level in CR, ER, and NER than the other three regions of NR, SR, and WR. The results also revealed that deposit penetration in WR is comparatively higher than the other regions followed by NR and SR.

Based on null hypothesis, the study finds that the assumption that there is no disparity due to banking policies on financial inclusion across regions is disproved. Accordingly, financial inclusion resulted in more deposit penetration in all the three regions of WR, NR, and SR than CR, ER, and NER. Figure 4.4 also elucidates the average deposit per capita (₹ in million) in the six regions of India.

Table 4.14 Tukey HSD Test: Multiple comparisons of deposit per capita

Deposit per capita		Mean difference (A – B)	Std. error	Sig.
Region (A)	Region (B)			
Central Region	Eastern Region	-0.00210	0.00041*	0.000
	North Eastern Region	0.00089	0.00022*	0.001
	Northern Region	-0.04217	0.00554*	0.000
	Southern Region	-0.02175	0.00356*	0.000
	Western Region	-0.05945	0.00924*	0.000
Eastern Region	Central Region	0.00210	0.00041*	0.000
	North Eastern Region	0.00299	0.00045*	0.000
	Northern Region	-0.04007	0.00513*	0.000
	Southern Region	-0.01966	0.00316*	0.000
	Western Region	-0.05735	0.00884*	0.000
North Eastern Region	Central Region	-0.00089	0.00022*	0.001
	Eastern Region	-0.00299	0.00045*	0.000
	Northern Region	-0.04306	0.00553*	0.000
	Southern Region	-0.02264	0.00358*	0.000
	Western Region	-0.06034	0.00922*	0.000
Northern Region	Central Region	0.04217	0.00554*	0.000
	Eastern Region	0.04007	0.00513*	0.000
	North Eastern Region	0.04306	0.00553*	0.000
	Southern Region	0.02042	0.00208*	0.000
	Western Region	-0.01728	0.00378*	0.000
Southern Region	Central Region	0.02175	0.00356*	0.000
	Eastern Region	0.01966	0.00316*	0.000
	North Eastern Region	0.02264	0.00358*	0.000
	Northern Region	-0.02042	0.00208*	0.000
	Western Region	-0.03770	0.00577*	0.000
Western Region	Central Region	0.05945	0.00924*	0.000
	Eastern Region	0.05735	0.00884*	0.000
	North Eastern Region	0.06034	0.00922*	0.000
	Northern Region	0.01728	0.00378*	0.000
	Southern Region	0.03770	0.00577*	0.000

Source: Authors' calculation

*Significance level is 1 percent

Average Deposit per Capita (₹ in million)

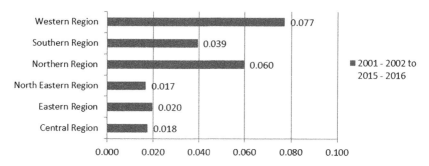

Fig. 4.4 Average deposit per capita (₹ in million) in the six regions of India (for the period from 2001–2002 to 2015–2016). (Source: Prepared by authors)

To study the regional imbalance of credit penetration per capita in CR, ER, NER, NR, SR, and WR, ANOVA statistics have been employed (Table 4.15). Since observed value F of 14.82 > critical value F of 3.24 (alternatively, since p-value < 0.01), the results explicitly explain that test is significant at 1 percent level. So, alternative hypothesis will be accepted and null hypothesis will be rejected. Therefore, there is a significant difference in credit penetration per capita in the six regions.

To find the differences lie among the six regions of CR, ER, NER, NR, SR, and WR in terms of credit penetration per capita the authors have also run Tukey HSD test. Based on Table 4.16, Tukey HSD test proves that deposit penetration per capita in all regions with all combinations between them is significant at 1 percent level of significance.

The test (post hoc) revealed that CR, ER, and NER do not have difference in mean scores while NR, SR, and WR have mean scores which are different from the scores of the other three regions. Since the mean value of CR (0.00795), ER (0.00923), and NER (0.00574) is lower as compared to NR (0.04611), SR (0.03449), and WR (0.06442), the authors are led to believe that credit penetration is lower level in CR, ER, and NER than the other three regions of NR, SR, and WR. The results also revealed that credit per capita in NER is comparatively lower than the other five regions and WR is comparatively higher than the other five regions.

Table 4.15 ANOVA Results: Credit penetration per capita from April 2001 to March 2016

Source of variation	SS	Df	MS	F	P-value	F crit
Between groups	0.0442	5	0.0088	14.8233	0.000*	3.2433
Within groups	0.0501	84	0.0006			
Total	0.0943	89				

Source: Authors' calculation

*Significance level is 1 percent

Based on null hypothesis, the assumption that there is no disparity due to banking policies on financial inclusion across regions is disproved. Accordingly, financial inclusion resulted in excessive credit penetration in WR compared to SR, NR, ER, CR, and NER. Moreover, NR and SR have asserted excessive credit penetration compared to CR, ER, and NER. Figure 4.5 also elucidates average credit per capita (₹ in million) in the six regions of India.

The region-wise C-D ratio is one of the indicators used to evaluate the performance of banks at the regional level in the context of its role to enable development of the region (Kodan et al., 2011).

To study regional imbalance of C-D ratio in CR, ER, NER, NR, SR, and WR, ANOVA statistics have been employed (Table 4.17). Since observed value of F of 111.40 is much > critical value of F of 3.24 (alternatively, since p-value < 0.01), the results explicitly explain that test is significant at 1 percent level. So, null hypothesis will be rejected and alternative hypothesis will be accepted. Therefore, there is a significant difference in C-D ratio between the six regions.

To find the differences lie among the six regions in terms of C-D ratio the authors have also run Tukey HSD test. Based on Table 4.18, Tukey HSD test proves that deposit penetration per capita in all the regions with all combinations are significant at 1 percent level except combination of WR and SR or vice versa are non-significant.

The test (post hoc) revealed that CR and ER do not have difference in mean scores while NER, NR, SR, and WR have mean scores which are different from the scores of other two regions. Since mean value of CR (0.46592), ER (0.48082), and NER (0.35308) is lower as compared to

Table 4.16   Tukey HSD Test: Multiple comparisons of credit per capita (₹ billion)

Credit per capita		Mean difference (A − B)	Std. error	Sig.
Region (A)	Region (B)			
Central Region	Eastern Region	−0.00128	0.00020*	0.000
	North Eastern Region	0.00221	0.00044*	0.000
	Northern Region	−0.03816	0.00686*	0.000
	Southern Region	−0.02654	0.00481*	0.000
	Western Region	−0.05647	0.00980*	0.000
Eastern Region	Central Region	0.00128	0.00020*	0.000
	North Eastern Region	0.00350	0.00055*	0.000
	Northern Region	−0.03688	0.00674*	0.000
	Southern Region	−0.02525	0.00470*	0.000
	Western Region	−0.05519	0.00968*	0.000
North Eastern Region	Central Region	−0.00221	0.00044*	0.000
	Eastern Region	−0.00350	0.00055*	0.000
	Northern Region	−0.04037	0.00729*	0.000
	Southern Region	−0.02875	0.00524*	0.000
	Western Region	−0.05868	0.01022*	0.000
Northern Region	Central Region	0.03816	0.00686*	0.000
	Eastern Region	0.03688	0.00674*	0.000
	North Eastern Region	0.04037	0.00729*	0.000
	Southern Region	0.01162	0.00207*	0.000
	Western Region	−0.01831	0.00307*	0.000
Southern Region	Central Region	0.02654	0.00481*	0.000
	Eastern Region	0.02525	0.00470*	0.000
	North Eastern Region	0.02875	0.00524*	0.000
	Northern Region	−0.01162	0.00207*	0.000
	Western Region	−0.02993	0.00501*	0.000
Western Region	Central Region	0.05647	0.00980*	0.000
	Eastern Region	0.05519	0.00968*	0.000
	North Eastern Region	0.05868	0.01022*	0.000
	Northern Region	0.01831	0.00307*	0.000
	Southern Region	0.02993	0.00501*	0.000

Source: Authors' calculation

*Significance level is 1 percent

Average Credit per Capita (₹ in million)

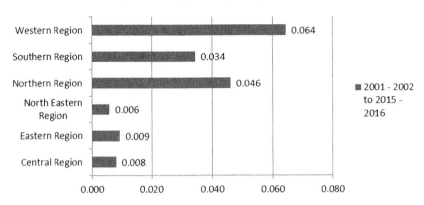

Fig. 4.5   Average credit per capita (₹ in million) in the six regions of India (for the period from 2001–2002 to 2015–2016). (Source: Prepared by authors)

Table 4.17   ANOVA Results: C-D ratio from April 2001 to March 2016

Source of variation	SS	df	MS	F	P-value	F crit
Between groups	3.6897	5	0.7379	111.3976	0.000*	3.2433
Within groups	0.5565	84	0.0066			
Total	4.2462	89				

Source: Authors' calculation

*Significance level is 1 percent

NR (0.80177), SR (0.90252), and WR (0.86422), the authors are led to believe that C-D ratio is lower level in CR, ER, and NER than the other three regions of NR, SR, and WR. The results also revealed that C-D ratio in NER is comparatively lower than the other five regions and SR is comparatively higher than the other five regions.

Based on null hypothesis, the assumption that there is no disparity due to banking policies on financial inclusion across regions is disproved. Accordingly, financial inclusion resulted in an excessive C-D ratio in SR compared to WR, NR, ER, CR, and NER. Moreover, WR and NR have asserted excessive C-D ratio compared to CR, ER, and NER. Figure 4.6 also elucidates the average C-D ratio in the six regions of India.

Table 4.18   Tukey HSD Test: Multiple comparisons of C-D ratio

Credit deposit ratio		Mean difference (A – B)	Std. error	Sig.
Region (A)	Region (B)			
Central Region	Eastern Region	-0.01491	0.00810*	0.001
	North Eastern Region	0.11284	0.00971*	0.000
	Northern Region	-0.33585	0.02326*	0.000
	Southern Region	-0.43660	0.01512*	0.000
	Western Region	-0.39831	0.01317*	0.000
Eastern Region	Central Region	0.01491	0.00810*	0.001
	North Eastern Region	0.12775	0.00773*	0.000
	Northern Region	-0.32094	0.02942*	0.000
	Southern Region	-0.42170	0.01896*	0.000
	Western Region	-0.38340	0.01550*	0.000
North Eastern Region	Central Region	-0.11284	0.00970*	0.000
	Eastern Region	-0.12775	0.00773*	0.000
	Northern Region	-0.44869	0.03258*	0.000
	Southern Region	-0.54945	0.02306*	0.000
	Western Region	-0.51115	0.01054*	0.000
Northern Region	Central Region	0.33585	0.02326*	0.000
	Eastern Region	0.32094	0.02942*	0.000
	North Eastern Region	0.44869	0.03258*	0.000
	Southern Region	-0.10075	0.01658*	0.000
	Western Region	-0.06246	0.03095*	0.002
Southern Region	Central Region	0.43660	0.01512*	0.000
	Eastern Region	0.42170	0.01896*	0.000
	North Eastern Region	0.54945	0.02306*	0.000
	Northern Region	0.10075	0.01658*	0.000
	Western Region	0.03830	0.02498	0.861
Western Region	Central Region	0.39831	0.01317*	0.000
	Eastern Region	0.38340	0.01550*	0.000
	North Eastern Region	0.51115	0.01054*	0.000
	Northern Region	0.06246	0.03095*	0.002
	Southern Region	-0.03830	0.02498	0.861

Source: Authors' calculation

*Significance level is 1 percent

Average Credit - Deposit Ratio

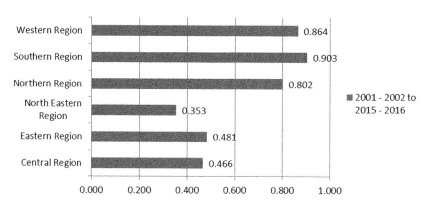

Fig. 4.6 Average C-D ratio in the six regions of India (for the period from 2001–2002 to 2015–2016). (Source: Prepared by authors)

From Tables 4.11, 4.13, 4.15, 4.17, and 4.19 it is quite evident that F values are greater than F critical value; hence, null hypothesis is rejected and alternative hypothesis is accepted. It has been found from the ANOVA test that there is a significant difference among the regions in terms of branches per 1000 sq. km., bank branches per 1000 populations, deposits per capita, credit per capita, and C-D ratio. However, differences between regions are not specifically identified from the ANOVA test. Hence Tukey HSD Test has been conducted. From Tables 4.12, 4.14, 4.16, 4.18, and 4.20, the test revealed that in respect of branches per 1000 sq. km. SR, ER, and WR are comparatively in a better position than CR, NER, and NR. In respect of other parameters of branches per 1000 populations, deposits per capita, credit per capita, and C-D Ratio, SR, WR, and NR are comparatively in a better position than CR, NER, and ER. In respect of all the parameters considered, SR and WR are in an advantageous position than the other four regions of ER, CR, NER, and NR.

Financial Inclusion Status Across States in India
To check the significant difference between states, ANOVA statistics have been employed. The ANOVA results have been presented in Tables 4.19 and 4.20. Since observed values F of 23.52 and 23.27 are greater than

Table 4.19   ANOVA Results: Deposits (state-wise) from April 2001 to March 2016

Source of variation	SS	df	MS	F	P-value	F crit
Between groups	2,076,566,687	34	61,075,491	23.517	0.000*	1.6894
Within groups	1,272,544,913	490	2,597,030			
Total	3,349,111,600	524				

Source: Authors' calculation

*Significance level is 1 percent

Table 4.20   ANOVA Results: Credit outstanding (state-wise) from April 2001 to March 2016

Source of variation	SS	df	MS	F	P-value	F crit
Between groups	1,706,040,500	34	50,177,662	23.273	0.000*	1.6894
Within groups	1,056,474,539	490	2,156,070			
Total	2,762,515,039	524				

Source: Authors' calculation

*Significance level is 1 percent

critical value F of 1.69 (alternatively, since p-value < 0.01), the results explicitly explain that both the tests are significant at 1 percent level. So, null hypothesis will be rejected and the alternative hypothesis will be accepted. Therefore, there is a significant difference in deposit and credit penetration in the 35 states and union territories.

After analyzing the ANOVA test, the authors have calculated the mean, SD, and CV of deposits and credit outstanding separately. Whether there is a wide variation of deposit penetration and credit penetration across states the CV has been computed. With CV the authors found which state or union territories have highest stability or highest volatility in deposits and credit penetration.

Table 4.21 displays state-wise mean, SD, and CV of deposit and credit outstanding for the period from 2001–2002 to 2015–2016. As per the table, Maharashtra (₹10,674.93 billion) has the maximum mean value of deposits, followed by Delhi (₹4868.31 billion), Uttar Pradesh (₹3215.78 billion), Karnataka (₹2919.25 billion), Tamil Nadu (₹2749.89 billion),

Table 4.21   Deposit and credit penetration in states and union territories

States/union territories	Deposits			Credit outstanding		
	Mean	SD	CV	Mean	SD	CV
Haryana	1048.20	777.70	74.19	733.58	613.01	83.56
Himachal Pradesh	285.00	197.28	69.22	104.74	69.73	66.57
Jammu and Kashmir	363.08	242.48	66.78	153.83	97.87	63.63
Punjab	1344.46	814.77	60.60	951.87	677.69	71.20
Rajasthan	1098.62	787.04	71.64	908.25	684.67	75.38
Chandigarh	288.15	175.23	60.81	321.00	206.99	64.48
Delhi	4868.31	2990.93	61.44	4279.76	3252.38	75.99
Arunachal Pradesh	39.05	29.61	75.83	9.86	7.82	79.30
Assam	462.00	329.83	71.39	175.89	128.09	72.83
Manipur	27.37	20.34	74.31	9.97	7.03	70.54
Meghalaya	78.07	58.03	74.33	21.31	13.73	64.43
Mizoram	23.57	18.88	80.08	9.93	7.09	71.39
Nagaland	37.53	24.63	65.62	10.93	8.31	76.00
Tripura	73.21	53.38	72.92	23.74	18.37	77.38
Bihar	1027.95	733.12	71.32	315.01	249.80	79.30
Jharkhand	662.18	477.25	72.07	207.78	145.24	69.90
Odisha	852.44	673.61	79.02	404.94	275.23	67.97
Sikkim	28.85	19.28	66.83	9.12	5.25	57.49
West Bengal	2688.83	1851.99	68.88	1594.16	1100.54	69.04
Andaman and Nicobar Islands	15.15	9.44	62.34	5.49	4.24	77.11
Chhattisgarh	465.44	345.84	74.30	256.55	217.96	84.96
Madhya Pradesh	1228.08	896.03	72.96	707.53	529.01	74.77
Uttar Pradesh	3215.78	2240.09	69.66	1386.41	1031.71	74.42
Uttarakhand	436.28	284.56	65.22	140.07	107.13	76.49
Goa	263.11	166.21	63.17	71.57	46.88	65.49
Gujarat	2245.87	1578.33	70.28	1533.47	1243.48	81.09
Maharashtra	10674.93	7471.26	69.99	9791.99	6997.81	71.46
Dadra and Nagar Haveli	11.46	9.65	84.22	5.18	7.12	137.37
Daman and Diu	15.95	11.06	69.38	3.12	2.78	89.08
Andhra Pradesh	2011.04	1239.12	61.62	2042.91	1501.91	73.52
Karnataka	2919.25	2163.51	74.11	2090.00	1502.59	71.89
Kerala	1567.87	1047.22	66.79	1014.68	728.12	71.76
Tamil Nadu	2749.89	1868.99	67.97	3157.60	2273.78	72.01
Lakshadweep	3.92	2.84	72.45	0.35	0.29	83.50
Puducherry	57.46	35.31	61.46	36.35	28.85	79.38

Source: Authors' calculation

and West Bengal (₹2688.83 billion). Contrarily Lakshadweep (₹3.92 billion) has the lowest mean value of deposits, followed by Dadra and Nagar Haveli (₹11.46 billion), Andaman and Nicobar Islands (₹15.15 billion), and Daman and Diu (₹15.95 billion). In respect of credit outstanding Maharashtra (₹9791.99 billion) has the maximum mean value, followed by Delhi (₹4279.76 billion), Tamil Nadu (₹3157.60 billion), Karnataka (₹2090.00 billion), and Andhra Pradesh (₹2042.91 billion). Contrarily Lakshadweep (₹0.35 billion) has lowest the mean value of credit outstanding, followed by Daman and Diu (₹3.12 billion). In both deposits and credit outstanding the state of Maharashtra has the maximum mean value and Lakshadweep has the lowest mean value. Though Maharashtra has the highest mean value and Lakshadweep has the lowest mean value, as per the Census Data 2011 in Maharashtra 68.9 percent of HHs were availing banking services and in Lakshadweep 85.3 percent of HHs were availing banking services. This reflects that deposits and credits in Lakshadweep were shared by maximum population, whereas in Maharashtra less percentage of population shared the deposits and credits; that is, a small group of people shared the maximum portion of deposits and credits.

As per the CV value as tabulated the study found that state-wise deposits displayed the highest stability than credit outstanding. According to state-wise deposits, Punjab displayed the highest stability of deposits with least CV of 60.60 percent and Dadra and Nagar Haveli displayed the highest volatility with maximum CV of 84.22 percent. Again Sikkim has displayed the highest stability of credit amount with least CV of 57.49. On the other side, Dadra and Nagar Haveli has displayed the highest volatility of credit amount with maximum CV of 137.37.

Based on the above analysis the null hypothesis that there is no disparity due to banking policies on financial inclusion across states is disproved. Accordingly the status of financial inclusion between states and union territories is not similar.

On the basis of analysis between regions and states, the authors finally concluded that there is a significant disparity in financial inclusion across regions and states. This analysis signifies that although growths of deposits and credits have taken place, they have been uneven in the states and regions over time.

4.3   Key Findings and Their Interpretations

It is evident from the empirical results and previous literature that "banking penetration, availability of banking services and usage of banking services in terms of deposits and credit lead to financial inclusion" (Reynolds, 2003; Thorat, 2007; Sarma & Pais, 2008; Bihari, 2011; Kodan & Chhikara, 2011; Ghosh, 2012; Shafi & Medabesh, 2012; and Kumar, 2013) and higher economic growth (Kelkar, 2009; Chakravarty & Pal, 2013; Anzoategui et al., 2014; Kunt, 2014; Jain, 2015; Unnikrishnan & Jagannathan, 2015; and Sharma, 2016). However, it must be kept in mind that the mere opening of bank accounts (including the no-frills accounts) may lead to very limited usage of banking services as observed by Kempson et al. (2004). Although one cannot ignore this, "the opening of bank accounts initiates the flow of money and assists in improving the economy" (Sharma, 2016).

Findings on the relationship between different independent variables and dependent variables are consistent with a large body of empirical studies including Carbo et al. (2005), Devlin (2005), Devlin (2009), Bihari (2011), Kodan et al. (2011), Kumar and Mohanty (2011), Diniz et al. (2012), Kumar (2012a), Kumar (2012b), Kumar (2013), Wentzel et al. (2013), Jalaludeen (2014), Belas et al. (2015), Koku (2015), Stephen and Tom (2015), Zins and Weill (2016), Abor et al. (2017), Ajide (2017), Barot (2017), Chauvet and Jacolin (2017), Chen and Jin (2017), Iqbal and Sami (2017), Ouma et al. (2017), and Musau et al. (2018).

Determinants of Financial Inclusion
"Financial inclusion in terms of number of deposit and loan accounts leads to better economic development and growth" (Sharma, 2016). The study focuses on measuring the factors influencing financial inclusion status in the Indian context. From the analysis, the authors found 13 significant factors for measuring financial inclusion in terms of deposit accounts and 12 significant factors in terms of credit accounts. According to Shafi and Medabesh (2012), "for financial inclusion requires that households/ adults should have a bank account." The study found a significant effect of APPB (including off-site ATMs), population per 1000 sq. km., literacy rate, number of factories, employment, per capita NNP, deposits to GDP, credit to GDP, per capita deposits, per capita credit, credit-deposit ratio,

and total assets per branch on deposit and credit accounts which influence the financial inclusion status.

The PCA study found that the first component is loaded with high loadings of 12 variables out of 14 variables selected in this analysis. So, the study concludes that these 12 variables are the essential factors which impact on financial inclusion. Their positive (with positive rotated component matrix scores) growth enhances financial inclusion or vice versa. And negative (with negative rotated component matrix scores) growth enhances financial inclusion or vice versa.

Gross NPA (Component 2) which accounts for 11.568 percent of variance has a significant impact only on deposit accounts but no impact on credit accounts. GDP (Component 3) which accounts for 7.709 percent of variance has no significant impact on both deposit and credit accounts. These findings are consistent with the results of Evanoff (1988), Hogarth et al. (2003), and Rhine and Greene (2006) in the US context; Devlin (2005), Devlin (2009), and Nice and Irvine (2010) in the UK context; Burgstaller (2013) in the Austria context; Bihari (2011), Kumar (2012b), Bhanot et al. (2012), Ghosh (2012), Kumar (2013), and Stephen and Tom (2015) in the Indian context; and Lanzillotti and Saving (1969), Honohan (2008), Arora (2012), Bhat and Bhat (2013), Bansal (2014), Kostov et al. (2014), Fungacova and Weill (2015), and Kundu (2015) in the context of different countries with respect to different variables considered in this study.

So as per the results, GDP does not impact on financial inclusion. This result contradicts Kunt (2014) and Iqbal and Sami (2017) that having an account in a formal institution increases with GDP per capita. The study also contradicts Ranjani and Bapat (2015) where their analysis suggests that to achieve financial inclusion, it is not enough if bank accounts are opened. Banks must also look at flexibility and timeliness in services. Moreover, it is clear that the other significant variables strongly influence the financial inclusion status in India.

Financial Inclusion Status Across Regions and States in India
Significant differences have been found between the six regions in geographic penetration of branches per 1000 sq. km. According to the result of ANOVA, the study has found that there is a disparity in financial inclusion across regions. Further, applying Tukey HSD test study also found

more penetration of branches per 1,000 sq. km. in ER, SR, and WR compared to CR, NER, and NR.

According to the ANOVA results, the study has found that there is a significant difference in demographic penetration of branches per 1000 population in the six regions. Tukey HSD test proves that expansion of branches in NR, SR, and WR is more powerful compared to CR, ER, and NER.

Further, there is a significant difference in deposits per capita in the six regions. According to Tukey HSD test, the authors have also found that financial inclusion resulted in more deposit penetration per capita in NR, SR, and WR than CR, ER, and NER.

According to the ANOVA results, the authors found that there is a significant difference in credit per capita in the six regions. Further, according to Tukey HSD test the study proves that credit per capita in NR, SR, and WR are more powerful compared to CR, ER, and NER.

An ANOVA result indicates that there is a significant difference in C-D ratio between the six regions. According to Tukey HSD test, the study also proves that C-D ratio in SR is comparatively better than WR, NR, CR, ER, and NER. The C-D ratio of NER is comparatively low than that of the other five regions and all-India level. Again, WR and NR have asserted excessive C-D ratio compared to CR, ER, and NER.

From the results of ANOVA and post hoc test, the authors finally conclude that region-wise banks have a strong role toward financial inclusion in the three regions of NR, SR, and WR than the other three regions of CR, ER, and NER. In this regard, the regulators should take initiative and instruct banks to expand their branches to the excluded regions and provide banking service to the excluded people for availing formal banking services.

According to the calculated value of CV, this study found that state-wise or region-wise deposits displayed the highest stability than credits outstanding. State-wise Punjab has displayed the highest stability of deposits and Sikkim has displayed the highest stability of credits outstanding with least coefficient of variation. Contrarily Dadra and Nagar Haveli displayed the highest volatility of both deposit and credit penetration. Therefore this study extensively evidences the disparity in financial inclusion across regions and states.

The results are in line with the previous empirical studies by Goyal (2008), Mahadeva (2008), Swamy (2011a), Chakravarty and Pal (2013),

Das and Guha (2015), and Ghosh and Sahu (2021) in the Indian context who have found that there is regional disparity. The disparity is
found even at the district level. Ghosh and Sahu (2021) suggest
Chandigarh be placed at the top in terms of mean financial inclusion
scores. A study by Ramji (2009) found that 70 percent of her sample
remains without a bank account in Gulbarga district in northern
Karnataka which is considered to be one of the most developmentally
backward districts in the state, and in 2007, the RBI formally declared
Gulbarga to be 100 percent financially included. Goyal (2008), Mahadeva
(2008), Kodan et al. (2011), Bhanot et al. (2012), Boro (2015), and
Das and Guha (2015) in their study found that in the NE states of India,
the position of financial inclusion was found to be poor in comparison to
the all-India level. An investigation by Kodan and Chhikara (2011)
found that the aggregate financial inclusion status of India is somewhat
lower as compared to Haryana. Ghosh (2012) "indicates significant differences across states in case of deposit and loan accounts." In a study,
Ansong et al. (2015) have found "evidence of inequality in access to
financial services, and bank branches which are disproportionately more
accessible in urban south compared to rural north."

This present result is also not surprising, since existing theoretical and
empirical studies have not found any lesser differences in financial inclusion across regions or states. Lower inclusion in most states or regions is
found due to geographical location, economic factors, social factors,
and so on.

BIBLIOGRAPHY

BOOKS, JOURNALS, WORKING PAPERS ETC.

Abor, J. Y., Amidu, M., & Issahaku, H. (2017). Mobile telephony, financial inclu-
sion and inclusive growth. *Journal of African Business*, 1–24.
Ajide, K. B. (2017). Determinants of financial inclusion in sub-Saharan Africa
countries: Does institutional infrastructure matter? *CBN Journal of Applied
Statistics*, 8(2), 69–89.
Alama, L., & Ausina, E. T. (2012). Bank branch geographic location patterns in
Spain: Some implications for financial exclusion. *Growth and Change, 43*(3),
505–543.

Ansong, D., Chowa, G., & Adjabeng, B. K. (2015). Spatial analysis of the distribution and determinants of bank branch presence in Ghana. *International Journal of Bank Marketing, 33*(3), 201–222.

Anzoategui, D., Kunt, A. D., & Peria, M. S. M. (2014). Remittances and financial inclusion: Evidence from El Salvador. *World Development, 54,* 338–349.

Arora, R. U. (2012). Financial inclusion and human capital in developing Asia: The Australian connection. *Third World Quarterly, 33*(1), 179–199.

Arputhamani, J. A., & Prasannakumari, K. (2011). Financial inclusion through micro finance: The way to rural development, a case study of Rajapalayan block in Virudhunagar district. *KKIMRC International Journal of Research in Finance and Accounting, 1*(1), 94–115.

Bansal, S. (2014). Perspective of technology in achieving financial inclusion in rural India. *Procedia Economics and Finance, 11,* 472–480.

Barot, P. (2017). Financial inclusion in India. *Imperial Journal of Interdisciplinary Research (IJIR), 3*(4), 1098–1104.

Beck, T., Kunt, A. D., & Peria, M. S. M. (2007). Reaching out: Access to and use of banking services across countries. *Journal of Financial Economics, 85,* 234–266.

Belas, J., Koraus, M., & Gabcova, L. (2015). Electronic banking, its use and safety. Are three differences in the access of Bank customers by gender, education and age? *International Journal of Entrepreneurial Knowledge, 3*(2), 16–28.

Bhanot, D., Bapat, V., & Bera, S. (2012). Studying financial inclusion in North-East India. *International Journal of Bank Marketing, 30*(6), 465–484.

Bhat, A. L., & Bhat, B. J. (2013). Automated teller machines (ATMs): The changing face of banking in India. *The IUP Journal of Bank Management, XII*(4), 16–28.

Bihari, S. C. (2011). Growth through financial inclusion in India. *Journal of International Business Ethics, 4*(1), 28–41.

Boro, K. (2015). Prospects and challenges of technological innovation in banking industry of North East India. *Journal of Internet Banking & Commerce, 20*(3), 1–6.

Burgess, R., & Pande, R. (2005). Do rural banks matter? Evidence from the Indian social banking experiment. *American Economic Review, 95*(3), 780–795.

Burgstaller, J. (2013). Bank office outreach, structure and performance in regional banking markets. *Regional Studies, 47*(7), 1131–1155.

Carbo, S., Edward, P. M. G., & Molyneux, P. (2005). *Financial exclusion.* Palgrave Macmillan.

Chakravarty, S. R., & Pal, R. (2013). Financial inclusion in India: An axiomatic approach. *Journal of Policy Modeling, 35,* 813–837.

Chauvet, L., & Jacolin, L. (2017). Financial inclusion, bank concentration and firm performance. *World Development, 97*(September), 1–13.

Chen, Z., & Jin, M. (2017). Financial inclusion in China: Use of credit. *Journal of Family and Economic Issues, 38*(4), 528–540.
Chithra, N., & Selvam, M. (2013). *Determinants of financial inclusion: An empirical study on the inter-state variations in India*. Retrieved from: http://www.ssrn.com/abstract=2296096. Accessed 28 Apr 2018.
Dangi, V. (2012). Financial inclusion: A saga of Indian financial system. *Asia-Pacific Journal of Management Research and Innovation, 8*(2), 111–125.
Das, T., & Guha, P. (2015). A study on the differences in the banking parameters between pre- and post-financial inclusion periods: Some evidence for India. *The IUP Journal of Bank Management, XIV*(1), 39–56.
Devlin, J. F. (2005). A detailed study of financial exclusion in the UK. *Journal of Consumer Policy, 28*, 75–108.
Devlin, J. F. (2009). An analysis of influences on total financial exclusion. *The Service Industries Journal, 29*(8), 1021–1036.
Diniz, E., Birochi, R., & Pozzebon, M. (2012). Triggers and barriers to financial inclusion: The use of ICT-based branchless banking in an Amazon county. *Electronic Commerce Research and Applications, 11*, 484–494.
Evanoff, D. D. (1988). Branch banking and service accessibility. *Journal of Money, Credit, and Banking, 20*(2), 191–202.
Fungacova, Z., & Weill, L. (2015). Understanding financial inclusion in China. *China Economic Review, 34*, 196–206.
Ghosh, S. (2012). Determinants of banking outreach: An empirical assessment of Indian states. *The Journal of Developing Areas, 46*(2), 269–295.
Ghosh, S., & Sahu, T. N. (2021). Financial inclusion and economic status of the states of India: An empirical evidence. *Economic Notes*. https://doi.org/10.1111/ecno.12182
Goodwin, D., Adelman, L., Middleton, S., & Ashworth, K. (1999). *Debt, money management and access to financial services: Evidence from the 1999 PSE survey of Britain* (1999 PSE Survey Working Paper 8). Centre for Research in Social Policy, Loughborough University.
Goyal, C. (2008). Financial inclusion in the northeastern region of India with special reference to Assam. *The ICFAI Journal of Applied Finance, 14*(12), 54–64.
Harimaya, K., & Kondo, K. (2012). Determinants of branch expansion by Japanese regional banks. *The IUP Journal of Bank Management, XI*(2), 7–25.
Hogarth, J. M., Anguelov, C. E., & Lee, J. (2003). Why households don't have checking accounts. *Economic Development Quarterly, 17*(1), 75–94.
Honohan, P. (2008). Cross-country variation in household access to financial services. *Journal of Banking & Finance, 32*, 2493–2500.
Iqbal, B. A., & Sami, S. (2017). Role of banks in financial inclusion in India. *Contaduríay Administración, 62*, 644–656.
Jain, S. (2015). A study of banking sector's initiatives towards financial inclusion in India. *Journal of Commerce & Management Thought, 6*(1), 55–77.

Jalaludeen, N. (2014). Is bank branch expansion driven by demand? – Some evidence from Kerala. *The IUP Journal of Bank Management, XIII*(1), 7–18.

Kamboj, S. (2014). Financial inclusion and growth of Indian economy: An empirical analysis. *The International Journal of Business & Management, 2*(9), 175–179.

Kelkar, V. (2009). Financial inclusion for inclusive growth. *ASCI Journal of Management, 39*(1), 55–68.

Kempson, E., Atkinson, A., & Pilley, O. (2004). *Policy level response to financial exclusion in developed economies: Lessons for developing countries.* Report of Personal Finance Research Centre, University of Bristol.

King, R., & Levine, R. (1993). Finance and growth: Schumpeter might be right. *Quarterly Journal of Economics, 108*(3), 717–738.

Kodan, A. S., & Chhikara, K. S. (2011). Status of financial inclusion in Haryana: An evidence of commercial banks. *Management and Labour Studies, 36*(3), 247–267.

Kodan, A. S., Garg, N. K., & Kaidan, S. (2011). Financial inclusion: Status, issues, challenges and policy in northeastern region. *The IUP Journal of Financial Economics, IX*(2), 27–40.

Koku, P. S. (2015). Financial exclusion of the poor: A literature review. *International Journal of Bank Marketing, 33*(5), 654–668.

Kostov, P., Arun, T., & Annim, S. (2014). Banking the unbanked: The Mzansi intervention in South Africa. *Indian Growth and Development Review, 7*(2), 118–141.

Kumar, B., & Mohanty, B. (2011). Financial inclusion and inclusive development in SAARC countries with special reference to India. *Vilakshan, XIMB Journal of Management,* (September), 13–22.

Kumar, N. (2012a). An empirical analysis of financial inclusion across population groups in India. *The IUP Journal of Bank Management, XI*(1), 97–111.

Kumar, N. (2012b). *Financial inclusion and its determinants: Evidence from state level empirical analysis in India* (pp. 1–23). Retrieved from: https://www.researchgate.net/file.PostFileLoader.html?id...assetKey. Accessed 20 July 2016.

Kumar, N. (2013). Financial inclusion and its determinants: Evidence from India. *Journal of Financial Economic Policy, 5*(1), 4–19.

Kundu, D. (2015). Addressing the demand side factors of financial inclusion. *Journal of Commerce & Management Thought, 6*(3), 397–417.

Kunt, A. D. (2014). Presidential address: Financial inclusion. *Atlantic Economic Journal, 42,* 349–356.

Lanzillotti, R. F., & Saving, T. R. (1969). State branching restrictions and the availability of branching services: Comment. *Journal of Money, Credit and Banking, 1*(4), 778–788.

Leeladhar V. (2005). *Taking banking services to the common man – Financial inclusion.* Commemorative Lecture at the Fedbank Hormis Memorial Foundation at Ernakulam on December 2.

Mahadeva, M. (2008). Financial growth in India: Whither financial inclusion? *Margin—The Journal of Applied Economic Research, 2*(2), 177–197.

Maity, S., & Sahu, T. N. (2019). Is the efficiency of banks degenerating due to the mounting of non-performing assets? An empirical investigation using DEA. *Malaysian Management Journal, 23*, 65–86.

Malhotra, K. N., & David, F. B. (2007). *Marketing research – An applied approach* (3rd European ed.). Prentice Hall – Financial Times Publishing.

Musau, S., Muathe, S., & Mwangi, L. (2018). Financial inclusion, GDP and credit risk of commercial banks in Kenya. *International Journal of Economics and Finance, 10*(3), 181–195.

Nice, K., & Irvine, A. (2010). Living on a low income and using banks to pay bills. *Journal of Poverty and Social Justice, 18*(1), 53–67.

Ouma, S. A., Odongo, T. M., & Were, M. (2017). Mobile financial services and financial inclusion: Is it a boon for savings mobilization? *Review of Development Finance, 7*, 29–35.

Raichoudhury, A. (2020). Major determinants of financial inclusion: State-level evidences from India. *Vision, 24*(2), 151–159.

Ramji, M. (2009). *Financial inclusion in Gulbarga: Finding usage in access* (Institute for Financial Management and Research Centre for Micro Finance Working Paper Series No. 26, pp. 1–37).

Ranjani, K. S., & Bapat, V. (2015). Deepening financial inclusion beyond account opening: Road ahead for banks. *Business Perspectives and Research, 3*(1), 52–65.

Reynolds, F. (2003). Promoting financial inclusion. *Poverty, 114*, 1–7.

Rhine, S. L. W., & Greene, W. H. (2006). The determinants of being unbanked for U.S. immigrants. *The Journal of Consumer Affairs, 40*(1), 21–40.

Sarma, M., & Pais, J. (2008, September). *Financial inclusion and development: A cross country analysis* (pp. 1–28). Paper presented at the annual conference of the human development and capability association, New Delhi. Retrieved from: www.icrier.org/pdf/6nov08/Mandira%20Sarma-Paper.pdf. Accessed 20 July 2016.

Shafi, M., & Medabesh, A. H. (2012). Financial inclusion in developing countries: Evidences from an Indian state. *International Business Research, 5*(8), 116–122.

Sharma, D. (2016). Nexus between financial inclusion and economic growth. *Journal of Financial Economic Policy, 8*(1), 13–36.

Singh, C., Mittal, A., Garg, R., Goenka, A., Goud, R., Ram, K., ... & Kumar, U. (2014). *Financial inclusion in India: Select issues.* IIM Bangalore research paper (474).

Singh, U. (2014). Financial literacy and financial stability are two aspects of efficient economy. *Journal of Finance, Accounting and Management, 5*(2), 59–76.

Stephen, N., & Tom, T. R. (2015). The role of cooperative banks in financial inclusion. *The IUP Journal of Bank Management, XIV*(3), 55–64.

Swamy, V. (2011a). Financial inclusion in India: An evaluation of the coverage, progress and trends. *The IUP Journal of Financial Economics, IX*(2), 7–26.

Swamy, V. (2011b). Does government intervention in credit deployment cause inclusive growth? – An evidence from Indian banking. *International Journal of Business Insights & Transformation, 4*(1), 35–45.

Thorat, U. (2007). *Financial inclusion – The Indian experience*. Speech at the HMT-DFID financial inclusion conference 2007, Whitehall Place, London, UK on June 19.

Unnikrishnan, R., & Jagannathan, L. (2015). Unearthing global financial inclusion levels and analysis of financial inclusion as a mediating factor in global human development. *Serbian Journal of Management, 10*(1), 19–32.

Wentzel, J. P., Diatha, K. S., & Yadavalli, V. S. S. (2013). An application of the extended technology acceptance model in understanding technology-enabled financial service adoption in South Africa. *Development Southern Africa, 30*(4–5), 659–673.

Zins, A., & Weill, L. (2016). The determinants of financial inclusion in Africa. *Review of Development Finance, 6*, 46–57.

CHAPTER 5

Role of Banking System on Finanscial Inclusion

5.1 Introduction

"The study on financial inclusion is extremely momentous for the society, since, outcomes of exclusion are quite harmful" (Maity & Sahu, 2021b). Without available sources of affordable credit, poor or low-income people may have to borrow from unorganized sectors or sources including money lenders at high costs. A large percentage of population are not only excluded financially because of low branch penetration or not having bank branches but also rejected by the service providers due to low-income group. Inclusion of disadvantaged sections of the community in the formal financial sector is the major objective for most of the countries. "In recent times financial inclusion is the primary object of the Government" (Maity & Sahu, 2021b). Banks are the major financial service providers to fill the challenges of financial inclusion. In developing economies (like India), banks have a very crucial role, as they mobilize savings and allocate credit for investment and production. "Bank network has an unambiguous beneficial impact on financial inclusion" (Maity & Sahu, 2021b). The selected dependent and independent variables considered are listed below according to different objectives.

According to the fourth objective set, to examine the impact of branch network expansion on financial inclusion, the authors considered two dependent variables of deposit and credit accounts and an independent variable of the number of branches (including off-site

S. Maity, T. N. Sahu, *Financial Inclusion and the Role of Banking System*, https://doi.org/10.1007/978-981-16-6085-6_5

ATMs). Afterward, to test factors of various branch expansion policies the study has selected dependent variable of opening of a new bank branch and to find factors which influence opening of a new branch this study has considered six independent variables of deposit to GDP, deposit per branch, credit to GDP, credit per branch, branch per 1000 sq. km., and APPB.

To evaluate the technology-based mobile banking solutions for greater financial inclusion, the authors have considered two dependent variables of deposit and credit accounts and a common independent variable of number of mobile banking transactions. Then to measure factors of technology-based banking transactions, the study has considered a dependent variable as the number of banking transactions through mobile and five independent variables as fixed telephone lines per capita, mobile connection per capita, internet user per capita, literacy rate, and logarithm value of GDP (NNP). Afterward, in the last part of this objective for comparative analysis between the PSBs and Pvt. SBs in implementing mobile banking, the authors have considered banking transaction through mobile in volume and value as control variables.

At last, to analyze the sixth objective the authors have considered eight variables as control variables to compare between PSBs and Pvt. SBs. These control variables are APPB, population per ATM, deposits to GDP, credit to GDP, deposits per capita, credit per capita, C-D ratio, and assets per office. To measure the performance of selected banks through Data Envelopment Analysis (DEA), this study has selected two outputs of deposits and credits with two input variables of branch and value of assets.

Statistical and Econometric Test Used
To study the role of banking system on financial inclusion the study has employed several statistical and econometric tests for obtaining concrete and reliable results.

Stepwise Regression Analysis
Stepwise regression has been made to determine which independent variables contributed to the variation in the dependent variables set. If at least one variable is significant then null hypothesis is rejected and the alternative hypothesis is accepted.

One-Way Analysis of Variance (ANOVA) and T-Test
The term "t-test" was introduced by William Sealy Gosset in 1908. The t-test which is a special case of ANOVA is used to measure the significant difference in mean values between the two sample groups.

Data Envelopment Analysis (DEA)
The present study measures performance of the Indian banking sector with respect to technical efficiency. It is very easy to calculate the efficiency of an organization when it has only one input and one output that is measured by dividing one by another and can be compared with different years or with other organizations. In the current market situation, any organization or sector has many inputs and outputs. In these circumstances, it becomes complicated to measure efficiency by just dividing one by another. At this juncture as proposed by Charnes, Cooper, and Rhodes (1978), DEA is appropriate in measure of efficiency in a decision making unit (DMU) within the homogeneous organization.

Further, the study employed bivariate regression analysis, multiple regression analysis, and factor analysis which were already discussed in the previous chapter. Other than the above, other tests like mean, median, quartile values, and standard deviation (SD) have been determined.

Scheme of Investigation
Different statistical and econometric tests have been applied according to objectives set for the study. These are enumerated below according to objectives.

To measure the impact of branch expansion on financial inclusion, bivariate regression has been run to test the significant effect of branch (including off-site ATMs) on deposit and credit accounts. To measure factors that influence branch expansion the study uses descriptive statistics to understand the basic nature of factors and correlation coefficient to check the existence of multicollinearity between the variables. Due to the existence of multicollinearity, the study uses multiple regressions with two component scores as an explanatory variable. The results of KMO and Bartlett's Test were also found appropriate.

To examine the impact of technology-based mobile banking, the study has run two bivariate regression analyses with two dependent variables and a common independent variable. To check the factors which influence mobile banking, multiple regressions, Variance inflation factor (VIF), and stepwise regression have been tested. Lastly, t-test with a coefficient of variance has been tested to check the significant difference between PSBs and Pvt. SBs in adoption of mobile banking.

To investigate the significant difference between PSBs and Pvt. SBs, t-test with CVs has been checked. Then to measure the performance of 20 selected banks, the study has run DEA, both under Charnes, Cooper, and Rhodes' (CCR) and Banker, Charnes, and Cooper's (BCC) input-oriented models. With the quartile value the authors further classified inefficient banks into four groups as most inefficient, below average, above average, and marginally inefficient.

5.2   BRANCH-BASED BANKING ON FINANCIAL INCLUSION

5.2.1   Impact of Bank Branch Network Expansion on Financial Inclusion

Branches of banks are the principal interface between public and banks and as such play an important role in financial intermediation. Without the presence of branches everywhere, there can be no banking access for people. The easiest way to ensure better financial inclusion is expansion on banking service network and removing various obstacles in accessing financial services from banks by very poor people. Since independence, GOI and RBI have taken numerous initiatives to improve banking access by people of both urban and rural areas. From time to time regulators have issued various guidelines for expansion policy of branches in India. All the SCBs and non-SCBs should adhere to these guidelines to continue their business in India and abroad. In the previous part of this chapter, the authors found 14 factors that may influence financial inclusion of which 13 variables found significant on deposit accounts and 12 variables found significant on credit accounts. According to PCA in measuring factors of financial inclusion, though the authors have found that the first component which combines 12 variables together has a significant impact on deposit and credit accounts, it is difficult to say how the 12 independent variables impact individually on deposit and credit accounts.

To check whether bank branch network expansion significantly impacts on financial inclusion and to measure how branches significantly impact, the authors have run two separate regression with two dependent variables of deposit and credit accounts with a common independent variable of number of branches (including off-site ATMs). The same independent variable is considered in measuring determinants in this study. Now banks are very much interested to open off-site ATMs instead of a new branch due to cost-effectiveness. And as a result during the last few years, numbers of ATMs are increasing at a higher growth rate than the number of bank branches. So this study has combined here off-site ATMs with branches and ignores the on-site ATMs as they are located in same premises of the branch. To reduce the overload of banking service in the branch in rural and semi-urban areas it is easier to install ATM either in the same building or in different places.

"A bank account is a primary requirement which enables access to any banking service or product" (Mahadeva, 2008). "Financial inclusion, as measured by the proportion of individuals having a formal account and formal savings" (Fungacova & Weill, 2015). According to Chakravarty and Pal (2013), "deposit and credit accounts per thousand people with other geographic and demographic penetration are the indicators of outreach of banking services." Further, Kodan and Chhikara (2011) have analyzed the financial inclusion status of an Indian state based on deposit and credit accounts, population per branch, and uses ratio. According to Shafi and Medabesh (2012), full financial inclusion requires that all households/adults should have an account for making and receiving payments and parking savings through deposits and insurance. "Around the globe, opening a bank account or account in a formal financial institution is the entry point for participate in financial transactions" (Kunt & Klapper, 2013).

It is evident from Table 5.1 that the deposit accounts which measure financial inclusion is positively and statistically significant related to the

Table 5.1 Regression results of deposit accounts with a number of branches and off-site ATMs

Indicators	Coefficients	Std. Err.	t-values	p-values
(Constant)	58.301	13.168	4.427	0.001*
Number of branches and off-site ATMs	0.005	0.000	49.123	0.000*
R^2	0.995			
Adjusted R^2	0.994			
VIF	1.000			
F-statistics	2413.033			0.000*

Source: Authors' calculation

*Significance level is 1 percent

Table 5.2   Regression results of credit accounts with a number of branches and off-site ATMs

Indicators	Coefficients	Std. Err.	t-values	p-values
(Constant)	47.964	6.979	6.873	0.000*
Number of branches and off-site ATMs	0.001	0.000	6.405	0.000*
R²	0.759			
Adjusted R²	0.741			
VIF	1.000			
F-statistics	41.028			0.000*

Source: Authors' calculation
*Significance level is 1 percent

expansion of branch network. The regression coefficient of both constant and deposit accounts is significant. Therefore, the null hypothesis "financial inclusion is positively and significantly not related to expansion of branch network" has not been accepted. Value of R^2 is 0.995 or 99.5 percent. It means 99.5 percent variation in deposit accounts is occurring due to expansion of branch network, that is, physical branch including off-site ATMs. Finally, the regression equation is fit ($p < 0.001$). Thus, financial inclusion and expansion of branch are interlinked.

Table 5.2 exhibits that the credit account which also measures financial inclusion is significantly influenced by the expansion of branch network. The regression coefficient of both constant and credit accounts is significant. Therefore, the null hypothesis "expansion of branch network is significantly not affected financial inclusion in the form of credit accounts" is not accepted. Value of R^2 is 0.759 or 75.9 percent. It means 75.9 percent variation in credit accounts is occurring due to expansion of branch network, that is, physical branch including off-site ATMs. Finally, the regression equation is fit ($p < 0.001$).

Therefore, the hypothesis that bank branch network expansion does not have any significant impact on financial inclusion is rejected and alternative hypothesis that bank branch network expansions have a significant impact on financial inclusion is accepted.

5.2.2   Determinants of Branch Expansion

The opening of a new branch depends upon many factors (Kumar, 2012). Based on previous literature, to test determinants of various branch expansion policies, the authors considered opening of a new branch in a year (Alama & Ausina, 2012) is the endogenous variable. A cross-country study by King and Levine (1993) shows that branch expansion and economic growth are positively correlated. Calcagnini et al. (1999), in their study of determinants of branch expansion in Italy, assumed each bank as having a two-stage decision-making process: (1) how many branches to open; and (2) in which provinces to site them. Before opening a bank branch in a province, it should have fulfilled minimum criteria. So, opening of new branches in a financial year is a dependent variable in this present analysis. "As the decision of new branches in a year is based on different factors of the previous year, all independent variables in present research are considered with a lag of one year" (Jalaludeen, 2014).

Among the explanatory variables, the foremost is deposit to GDP and credit to GDP. "An economy has reached full access, if deposit to GDP ratio is 100 percent and development of the financial system measures by this indicator" (Peachey & Roe, 2004). To capture whether more new branches are opening in a region, state, or district with a higher deposit to GDP ratio, this study includes the variable deposit to GDP (Burgess & Pande, 2005; Kunt et al., 2011; Jalaludeen, 2014) as an independent variable. As one of the important functions of a branch is to ensure adequate flow of credit to support economic growth, it is expected that more new branches are to be open in a region, state, or district where existing branches have higher credit to GDP ratio to enhance more credit distribution. "Limited credit access may cause economic loss for a country" (Chen & Jin, 2017). So, in line with the first independent variable the authors also included credit to GDP as another variable.

High deposits and credits influence bank decisions to open more new branches. Apart from the above aspects, banks may consider the business (credit and deposit) of the existing branches while making their choices of opening new branches in a district or region. So, the authors incorporated two more independent variables deposit per branch and credit per branch to capture the impact of business of existing branches to open a new branch (Jalaludeen, 2014).

The geographical coverage of existing branches (Beck et al., 2007; Burgess & Pande, 2005; Kunt et al., 2011; Inoue & Hamori, 2016) is also an important aspect that could be considered while opening new branches. The region, state, or districts having higher branches per 1000 sq. km. are expected to have more number of new branches, since additional branches will have the opportunity of being involved with higher volume of activities because present branches do not appear to be capable to satisfy the total need of the community. So, branches per 1000 sq. km. are included as one of the independent variables.

Though banks have the freedom to choose the location of the new branches, they are still required to submit their branch expansion plan to RBI with a number of supporting documents and statistics on business potential, level of financial inclusion, and so on, of the location where the new branches are proposed to be open. So, one can expect that while deciding on a new branch, banks would consider the level of financial inclusion in the particular region or district also. Accordingly, a variable APPB is included to represent the number of population served by a branch (Beck et al., 2007).

So, the authors consider opening of new branches (dependent variable) in a year and six independent variables of deposit to GDP, deposit per branch, credit to GDP, credit per branch, branch per 1000 sq. km., and APPB. To determine whether the six variables have any significant impact on opening of new branches in next year, first only multiple regressions have been applied to the data with one dependent variable of opening of branch in a year and six independent variables of the lag period is considered. To check the multicollinearity, if any, the authors have tested the correlation coefficient. On the presence of multicollinearity interpretation of results may be inaccurate.

To remove the multicollinearity, factor analysis has been conducted to determine the components of six variables of deposit to GDP (dgdp), deposit per branch (dpbr), credit to GDP (cgdp), credit per branch (cpbr), branch per 1000 sq. km. (bptsk), and population per branch (appb). PCA has been conducted by utilizing varimax rotation. To determine the number of components under PCA the study has considered four criteria (eigenvalue, variance, scree plot, and residuals) and on the basis of the four criteria, the study considered two components to run the PCA. List of variables considered in the present analysis and their descriptive statistics with mean value, minimum value, maximum value, and SD are presented in Table 5.3.

The correlation coefficient ranged from 0.895 to 0.999 as presented in Table 5.4. From the correlation matrix, the variables are observed to have substantial correlations between the variables and also indicate the existence of multicollinearity.

Before using factor analysis KMO and Bartlett's test of sphericity have been tested whether the data are suitable for factor analysis (Table 5.5).

Table 5.3   List of variables analyzed (descriptive statistics)

Sl. No.	Variables	Symbol	Mean	Minimum	Maximum	Std. dev.
	Dependent variable:					
1	Branch open	bropen	2942.600	116.00	7071.00	2253.3791
	Explanatory variables:					
1	Deposit to GDP	dgdp	0.474	0.34	0.61	0.0839
2	Deposit per branch	dpbr	56.654	21.04	89.51	25.0743
3	Credit to GDP	cgdp	0.341	0.17	0.50	0.1088
4	Credit per branch	cpbr	42.197	10.34	73.53	22.94056
5	Branch per 1000 sq. km.	bptsk	13.337	9.66	21.85	4.1589
6	Average population per branch	appb	26.533	17.00	33.00	5.8781

Source: Authors' calculation

Table 5.4   Correlation matrix

Variables	dgdp	dpbr	cgdp	cpbr	bptsk	appb
dgdp	1					
dpbr	0.978*	1				
cgdp	0.986*	0.988*	1			
cpbr	0.976*	0.999*	0.990*	1		
bptsk	0.922*	0.911*	0.895*	0.916*	1	
appb	-0.952*	-0.964*	-0.936*	-0.965*	-0.973*	1

Source: Authors' calculation

a Significance level is 1 percent

Table 5.5   KMO and Bartlett's Test

Kaiser-Meyer-Olkin Measure of Sampling Adequacy		0.725
Bartlett's test of sphericity	Approx. chi-square	245.963
	Df	15
	Sig.	0.000

Source: Authors' calculation

The KMO value with greater than 0.5 and the significant value of Bartlett's Test suggest that variables chosen for conducting factor analysis have a high relationship. According to the results of the above two tests, the data were found to be most appropriate for applying factor analysis.

The PCA has been conducted using data reduction, which utilized the eigenvalue criteria and varimax rotation. Applying the four methods of interpretation, the authors first examine the eigenvalues in Table 5.6 of total variance. Since one component has eigenvalue >1, we may retain one component. Based on eigenvalue, it would appear that one component should be interpreted; however, this may be an oversimplification of reduction of original data. Furthermore, addition of a second component certainly improved the fit of the model to these empirical data.

After rotation of two components, the first component accounts for 56.113 percent of total variance against 96.410 percent before the rotation of two components. While the second component accounts for 42.980 percent of the total variances against 2.684 percent prior to rotation of two components. Then scree plot is assessed and it indicates that eigenvalues after two components levels have insignificant values (Fig. 5.1).

Based on initial eigenvalue and variance explained, it would appear that one component should be interpreted; however, this may be an oversimplification of reduction of original data. The scree plot, rotated eigenvalue, residuals, and variance after rotation suggest that inclusion of second component may improve the model. The communality values of variables (Table 5.7) were also found high in all the independent variables of dgdp (98.00 percent), dpbr (99.40 percent), cgdp (99.40 percent), cpbr (99.40 percent), bptsk (99.40 percent), and appb (98.90 percent).

The residuals (Table 5.8) also reveal that the model is consistent with the empirical data with two components. Furthermore, addition of a

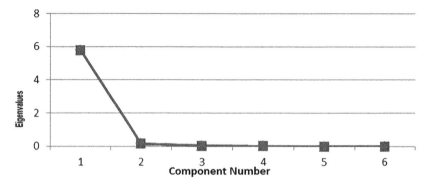

Fig. 5.1   Scree plot. (Source: Prepared by authors)

Table 5.6 Total variance explained

Component	Initial eigenvalues			Extraction sums of squared loadings			Rotation sums of squared loadings		
	Total	% of variance	Cumulative %	Total	% of variance	Cumulative %	Total	% of Variance	Cumulative %
1	5.785	96.410	96.410	5.785	96.410	96.410	3.367	56.113	56.113
2	0.161	2.684	99.093	0.161	2.684	99.093	2.579	42.980	99.093
3	0.038	0.628	99.722						
4	0.014	0.240	99.961						
5	0.002	0.034	99.996						
6	0.000	0.004	100.000						

Source: Authors' calculation

Extraction Method: PCA

Table 5.7 Communalities

Statements/ attributes	Initial	Extraction
dgdp	1.000	0.980
dpbr	1.000	0.994
cgdp	1.000	0.994
cpbr	1.000	0.994
bptsk	1.000	0.994
appb	1.000	0.989

Source: Authors' calculation

Extraction Method: PCA

Table 5.8   Reproduced correlations

		dgdp	dpbr	cgdp	cpbr	bptsk	appb
Reproduced correlation	dgdp	0.980[b]					
	dpbr	0.987	0.994[b]				
	cgdp	0.983	0.992	0.994[b]			
	cpbr	0.987	0.994	0.992	0.994[b]		
	bptsk	0.919	0.915	0.890	0.918	0.994[b]	
	appb	-0.959	-0.959	-0.942	-0.961	-0.981	0.989[b]
Residual[a]	dgdp						
	dpbr	-0.009					
	cgdp	0.002	-0.004				
	cpbr	-0.011	0.005	-0.002			
	bptsk	0.003	-0.004	0.005	-0.002		
	appb	0.006	-0.006	0.006	-0.004	0.008	

Source: Authors' calculation

Extraction Method: PCA

[a]Computed between observed and reproduced correlations
[b] Reproduced communalities

second component certainly improved the fit of the model to these empirical data. For this later reason, the authors have proceeded with the interpretation of two-component solution.

Rotated component loadings from varimax rotation are presented in Table 5.9. From the table, the authors notice that each variable has a loading on each component, although each has a high loading on only one component. "The two rotated components are just as good as initial components in explaining and reproducing the observed correlation matrix"

Table 5.9   Rotated component matrix[a]

Attributes	Component	
	1	2
gdp	0.849	0.523
dpbr	0.816	0.572
cpbr	0.812	0.579
dgdp	0.794	0.591
bptsk	0.527	0.847
appb	-0.642	-0.759

Source: Authors' calculation

Extraction method: PCA; rotation method: varimax with Kaiser normalization

[a]Rotation converged in three iterations

(Noorshella et al., 2015). Whether the loading of each component will be positive or negative depends on correlation of variables of the components. If correlations between the variables are positive, loadings result will be positive or vis-à-vis if correlations between the variables are negative, loadings result between the variables is negative. In the rotated components, credit to GDP, deposit per branch, credit per branch, and deposit to GDP all have high positive loadings on first component and low loadings on the second component. Whereas branch per 1000 sq. km. has high positive loading on second component and low loading on first component. Again, APPB has high negative loading on the second component and low negative loading on the first component. The principal objective of PCA is to find a strong correlation between variables considered in the study and components considered in PCA. Items with the highest loadings are credit to GDP and branch per 1000 sq. km.

So, the results of rotated component matrix conclude that deposit to GDP, deposit per branch, credit to GDP, and credit per branch fall under first group. These variables have positive loadings and addressed economic development. The second component included the remaining two variables of branch per 1000 sq. km. and APPB. Among these two variables, branch per 1000 sq. km. has positive loading and the other variable of APPB has negative loading. Component number 2 has been named as geographic and demographic penetration.

After principal component score values were obtained from two components, the scores values have been used as independent variables and

Table 5.10   Results of multiple regression analysis of branch open

Indicators	Coefficients	Std. Err.	t-values	p-values	VIF
(Constant)	2942.600	229.857	12.802	0.000*	
Principal component score 1	1840.523	237.924	7.736	0.000*	1.000
Principal component score 2	1005.432	237.924	4.226	0.001*	1.000
R^2	0.866				
Adjusted R^2	0.844				
Durbin-Watson test	1.514				
F-statistics	38.850			0.000*	

Source: Authors' calculation

a Significance level is 1 percent

opening of branches considered as an endogenous variable. Results of multiple regression analysis using principal component scores as explanatory variables and branch open as dependent variable are presented in Table 5.10. The results revealed that multicollinearity has been removed as the VIF is 1 in both the component scores. The results also revealed that the Durban-Watson test is 1.514 which indicates that there is no autocorrelation.

In the regression analysis opening of branch on component 1 and component 2 ($p < 0.01$) both are positively significant and 86.60 percent of the variation in opening branch is explained by the two components. So, this study concludes that opening of branch in a year is expected to change, with change in lag year values of deposit to GDP, deposit per branch, credit to GDP, credit per branch, and branch per 1000 sq. km. with positive effects and one independent variable of APPB with negative effects. The final model can be written as:

$$\text{Branch open} = 2942.600 + 1840.523^* \left(\text{PCS}_1\right) + 1005.432^* \left(\text{PCS}_2\right)$$

5.3   TECHNOLOGY-BASED BANKING
ON FINANCIAL INCLUSION

5.3.1   Technology-Based Banking Through Mobile

The rationale for using mobile banking as a product to promote financial inclusion is that even 71 years after independence, a large percentage of

Indians do not have access to banking services. Prior to mobile banking expansion, internet banking through PC was the main source for using internet banking. Due to expansion of using mobile devices and keeping in mind the cost of a PC, the importance of using mobile banking has been growing rapidly and reduces the importance of using internet banking through PC. Mobile banking or internet banking gives customers anytime access to their banks. A combination of improvements in technology and customer profile change is helping banks reduce their cost of real estate by as much as 30–40 percent depending on the location in cities and even more in smaller towns laying the foundation for improved profitability.

While there is a gradual shift to enable customer to be able to do all basic banking activities through ATMs, mobile phone banking, net banking, and branches are meant to become points for selling of financial products, financial counseling, and assistance. Due to technology up-gradation and involvement of the technology in banking sectors worldwide, we can see major changes in products and services. The up-gradation of technology changes people's habits from branch-based banking systems with limited time access to any time banking and now ATMs, POS, online banking, and mobile banking have become part of the payment system. This technology allows banks to increase the range of their products and market them more effectively. Implementation of technology not only improves the banking services with flexibility but also reduces cost for providing services through the introduction of ATMs, internet, mobile, and so on. In a study, Nyagilo (2017) finds that an increase in mobile banking in Kenya leads to increase in financial inclusion.

Mobile banking means using a mobile device to offer various banking services. As per RBI guidelines, mobile banking involves banking transactions (both debit and credit facility to the accounts) through mobile. In today's world, mobile banking is a popular term.

5.3.2 Information Technology (IT)–Enabled Financial Inclusion

"Technology is the key driver of revolutionary changes in the Indian financial sector with the growing demand for various financial services" (Das & Guha, 2015). "The growth of telecommunication infrastructure especially mobile penetration has created an opportunity in achieving the objective of financial inclusion" (Mishra & Bisht, 2013). "The higher mobile penetration and low rate of banking accessibility have given an opportunity to expand the banking services through mobile" (Sanz & Lima, 2013). To study information technology–enabled financial inclusion the authors have set Hypothesis III. To study the same hypothesis the authors have run regression in SPSS. As per previous analysis and studies deposit and credit accounts per capita which measure financial inclusion are dependent variables. Technology-based mobile banking, that is, the number of mobile banking transactions, is an independent variable. The authors have run two regressions: one with deposit accounts and another with credit accounts as dependent variable with common explanatory variable as banking transaction through mobile.

Table 5.11 depicts the regression results of deposit accounts per capita as dependent variable and the number of banking transactions through mobile per capita as an independent variable. The value of R^2 is 0.815 or 81.5 percent. It means 81.5 percent variation in deposit accounts is occurring due to number of banking transactions through mobile. Finally, the regression equation is fit as $p < 0.05$. Thus, the authors can conclude that financial inclusion and technology-based banking transaction are interlinked.

Table 5.12 exhibits that the credit account which also measures financial inclusion is significantly influenced by banking transactions through mobile. The regression coefficient of constant and credit accounts both are significant. The value of R^2 is 0.850 or 85.0 percent. It means 85.0 percent variation in credit accounts is occurring due to technology-based mobile banking solutions. Finally, the regression equation is fit as $p < 0.01$.

Table 5.11 Regression results of deposit accounts with the number of banking transactions through mobile

Indicators	Coefficients	Std. Err.	t-values	p-values
(Constant)	0.753	0.058	13.087	0.000*
Number of mobile banking transaction	1.861	0.443	4.204	0.014**
R^2	0.815			
Adjusted R^2	0.769			
VIF	1.000			
F-statistics	17.676			0.014**

Source: Authors' calculation

* Significance level is 1 percent and ** Significance level is 5 percent

Table 5.12 Regression results of credit accounts with the number of banking transactions through mobile

Indicators	Coefficients	Std. Err.	t-values	p-values
(Constant)	0.103	0.002	63.530	0.000*
Number of mobile banking transaction	0.059	0.012	4.758	0.009*
R^2	0.850			
Adjusted R^2	0.812			
VIF	1.000			
F-statistics	22.642			0.009*

Source: Authors' calculation

*Significance level is 1 percent

From the above analyses this study found that credit accounts significant at 1 percent level and deposit accounts significant at 5 percent level. Therefore, the null hypothesis that "technology-based mobile banking solutions do not significantly affect financial inclusion" is not accepted.

5.3.3 Determinants of Technology-Based Banking Transactions Through Mobile

In order to focus more sharply on the determinant of technology-based banking transactions, multiple regressions have been used. The full model regression was fitted with five independent variables of fixed telephone lines per capita (Tel Line), mobile connection per capita (Mob Conn), internet user per capita (Internet User), literacy rate (Lt Rate), and GDP (NNP) log value (Log NNP). As mobile service is the alternative to telephone and before capturing the whole market by mobile handset, these services have been provided by telephone only. Due to easy handling of mobile handset and its low cost with several types of services, mobile connections have reached a peak level. As such reason telephone lines per capita is one of our predictor variables.

Description of Variables

Mobile phones usage all over the world has witnessed a significant increase in recent times. Due to technology trends and high mobile penetration the banking industry has found that mobile can occupy a significant place in banking services. Through mobile, banking services can be expanded in a short time including in unbanked areas.

One of the biggest innovations to reach remote areas of rural households anywhere in the world is the access of mobile. Through mobile, we can reach the entire world. So reach to un-reach through mobile devices is an excellent concept of expansion banking service or formal financial service. With wide network of mobile access, banks are now giving importance to mobile banking as an important technology tool to deliver banking services.

Usage of mobile has multiple benefits like voice call, information gathering, exchange of information, and camera which motivate users to buy the devices. Mobile devices are user-friendly and to be able to use this device the owner does not need any form of training. Also, due to reduction in price of mobiles and due to their multiple uses the owner of a mobile device finds it comfortable to use compared to other devices, namely, PC or laptop, installation of internet connection, and so on. For the said reasons mobile phones are more accessible to the poor than other kinds of ICT.

In developing countries we find more accessible mobile devices compared to other kinds of ICT devices. In the present regression analysis mobile banking transactions per capita (Mob Tran) is a dependent variable. There are five independent variables in the model. The selected independent variables are being taken based upon the previous literatures on financial inclusion and their availability. On the other hand level of economic development, financial literacy, mobile phone penetration, fixed telephone line penetration, internet user penetration, and log value of NNP hold are taken as explanatory variables.

Mobile penetration is expected to have a positive effect on banking transactions. The fixed telephone subscriber per capita is another ICT variable. Though telephone lines have decreased significantly during the last few years due to expansion of mobile devices, they are expected to have a positive effect on banking transactions, as well as on financial inclusion. Banks provide a range of financial transactions over telephone, without a need to visit a bank branch or ATM.

PC per household is a significant ICT variable. Without visiting the bank branch, we use PC with internet connectivity for different banking services. Due to non-availability of data, the same has been ignored from the present research.

Literacy is important for internet banking (e-banking) or mobile banking (Boro, 2015). Arputhamani and Prasannakumari (2011) find that in the Indian context there is a positive association between literacy rate and financial inclusion and the same is statistically significant. Per capita income and literacy rate are proxy variables of level of development and financial literacy.

Regression Analysis of ICT Indicators on Financial Inclusion
First, this study has run multiple regressions with all the five independent variables of telephone lines per capita, mobile connection per capita, internet user per capita, literacy rate, and GDP (NNP) log value as selected on the basis of previous literature, with the one dependent variable of banking transaction through mobile. The logarithm of GDP is used as one of the independent variables in this quantitative analysis as level of development. After running multiple regressions in SPSS this study found multicollinearity (VIF > 7) of variable "fixed telephone lines per capita." And as such out of five independent variables, the variable of fixed telephone line per capita is excluded because of multicollinearity.

The result of multiple regressions is depicted in Table 5.13. After removing the variable of telephone line per capita, the value of R^2 and adjusted R^2 with all the four explanatory variables has been 0.996 and 0.982 respectively which is slightly higher than value of R^2 and adjusted R^2 with the independent variable of internet user with 0.906 and 0.883 respectively. Table 5.13 also allows us to check multicollinearity in this regression models. From the table, the authors found that VIF of all the independent variables has been less than 6. So, there is no multicollinearity between the variables. This study finds that all four independent variables

Table 5.13 Regression results of ICT indicators on financial inclusion

Indicators	Coefficients	Std. Err.	Standardized coefficients	t-values	p-values	VIF
(Constant)	0.033	0.144		0.230	0.856	
Mob conn	0.429	0.143	0.216	3.008	0.204	1.467
Internet user	1.012	0.086	1.153	11.767	0.054	2.733
Lt rate	0.599	0.258	0.238	2.322	0.259	3.000
Log NNP	-0.449	0.105	-0.582	-4.263	0.147	5.300
R^2	0.996					
Adjusted R^2	0.982					
F-statistics	70.953				0.089	

Source: Authors' calculation

are non-significant predictors of the endogenous variable. Though all the independent variables are insignificant, we can see that internet user has a higher impact on banking transaction through mobile than mobile connection, literacy rate, and log value GDP (NNP) by comparing the standardized coefficients (beta 1.153 vs. betas' 0.216, 0.238, and −0.582 respectively). In order to test which explanatory variable is more powerful and whether the same is significant or not, the authors have run stepwise regression in SPSS.

As the data on ICT infrastructure variables are available from April 2010, the authors have analyzed the same through stepwise regression for a short data period as available. By applying stepwise regression the authors have tried to find which explanatory variables contribute the most to technology-based banking transactions through mobile. Software SPSS has been used to test the hypothesis with stepwise regression methods. The stepwise regression revealed that only internet users contributed the most and also significant. Table 5.14 shows variables entered/removed in the present analysis. There have been two steps in the stepwise multiple regressions with a 0.05 significance level for entry and a 0.10 significance level for removal. The output results turn out that only internet user is useful to predict financial inclusion (Banking transaction through mobile).

Table 5.15 shows the results of regression model summary and overall fit statistics. The authors find that the R^2 of the analysis is 0.906, while the adjusted R^2 is 0.883. This means that the variable internet user explains 90.6 percent of the variance in mobile banking.

Table 5.15 also shows the F-test internet users and dependent variable of banking transaction through mobile which measure the level of using technology to get banking service. The linear regression's F-test measures the null hypothesis that technology-based mobile banking solutions do not have any significant impact on mobile banking. The stepwise regression shows that there is a significant amount of variance in mobile

Table 5.14   Variable entered/removed

Model	Variables		Method
	Entered	Removed	
I	Internet user		Stepwise (criteria probability of 'F' to enter <= 0.050, remove <= 0.100)

Source: Authors' calculation

Table 5.15   Regression (stepwise) results of ICT indicators on financial inclusion

Indicators	Coefficients	Std. Err.	t-values	p-values
(Constant)	-0.091	0.032	-2.802	0.049
Internet user	0.836	0.135	6.210	0.003
R^2	0.906			
Adjusted R^2	0.883			
VIF	1.000			
F-statistics	38.566			0.003

Source: Authors' calculation

Table 5.16   Excluded variables

Variables	Beta In	t	Sig.	Partial correlation	Collinearity statistics	
					Tolerance	VIF
Tel line	0.285	0.698	0.535	0.374	0.161	6.202
Mob conn	0.172	0.919	0.426	0.469	0.695	1.439
Lt rate	-0.078	-0.396	0.719	-0.223	0.761	1.314
Log NNP	-0.311	-1.561	0.217	-0.669	0.436	2.292

Source: Authors' calculation

banking. In the stepwise regression, the authors find both intercept and internet users are highly significant which indicates internet users and, mobile banking has a significant relationship. Finally, the regression equation is fit because the value of "F" statistics is significant ($p < 0.01$). Now the authors can interpret as: for every 1 unit increase in internet user per capita, we will see an additional 0.836 unit of mobile banking transaction per capita. The results of excluded variables in the stepwise regression model are presented in Table 5.16 and from the results the authors find that all the excluded variables are insignificant.

5.3.4   Comparative Analysis Between the PSBs and Pvt. SBs in Implementing Mobile Banking

This part analyzes the difference between PSBs and Pvt. SBs in implementing mobile banking. A comparison between PSBs and Pvt. SBs has been presented regarding adoption of mobile banking based on the data available from 2010 to 2011.

The average banking transactions through mobile of PSBs and Pvt. SBs have been 61.469 million and 54.904 million respectively as depicted in Table 5.17. Further, the average mobile banking in value of PSBs and Pvt. SBs has been ₹226.2 billion and ₹621.2 billion respectively. The CAGR of volume of mobile banking of PSBs and Pvt. SBs has been 101 percent and 176 percent respectively. To check the significant difference between PSBs and Pvt. SBs, Fisher's t-test has been applied for the study period from April 2010 to March 2016.

In respect of volume, calculated value of t-test is 0.166, while the tabulated value of t-test at 5 percent level of significance is 2.228. Since calculated value of t-test is < tabulated value, the results explicitly explain that the test is not significant ($p > 0.05$) and in volume there is no significant difference between the two groups.

In respect of values, the calculated value of t-test is 0.825, while the tabulated value of t-test at 5 percent level of significance is 2.228. Since the calculated value of t-test is lower than the tabulated value, the results explicitly explain that the test is not significant ($p > 0.05$) and in value there is no significant difference between the two groups. On the basis of the above analysis, the authors concluded that there is no significant difference between PSBs and Pvt. SBs in adoption of mobile banking.

Table 5.17   Banking transaction through mobile of PSBs and Pvt. SBs

Year	Volume		Value (₹ '000)	
	Public sector banks	Private sector banks	Public sector banks	Private sector banks
2010–2011	5,107,756	1,267,414	3,257,215	2,422,724
2011–2012	21,040,596	3,364,948	9,479,741	6,793,061
2012–2013	37,714,653	12,300,659	21,449,975	31,241,346
2013–2014	54,933,783	33,756,946	43,586,854	157,789,481
2014–2015	82,321,554	77,321,220	213,663,297	751,393,033
2015–2016	167,356,179	201,410,975	1,065,911,305	2,776,495,760
Average	61,468,587	54,903,694	226,224,731	621,022,568
CAGR	100.95	175.57	218.40	309.11
CV	95.08	140.52	185.15	176.18
T	0.166		0.825	
Sig.	0.436		0.220	

Source: Authors' calculation

Though there is no significant difference between the two groups, the mean score in value shows that Pvt. SBs are comparatively in a better position than PSBs in adoption of mobile banking.

5.4   COMPARATIVE ROLE OF PUBLIC AND PRIVATE SECTOR BANKS AND MEASURES IT PERFORMANCE

5.4.1   Comparative Role of PSBs and Pvt. SBs in Financial Inclusion

The regulators started the financial inclusion initiatives in 1969 through nationalization of banks. With the nationalization of banks, PSBs came into existence as social banking. Among the various institutions, PSBs hold a predominant position in the banking industry. Moreover, their participation in social banking activities is quite significant than the other participating banks (Martínez-Campillo et al., 2020). PSBs have been highly involved in these socio-economic development programs. To expand more banking coverage including in rural regions, the second phase of bank nationalization started in 1980 and in 1993 regulators started giving licenses to Pvt. SBs. Due to the significant growth the Pvt. SBs are also placed in a significant position compared to PSBs. Due to vast geographical expansion, both the PSBs and Pvt. SBs have played a significant role in financial inclusion. In respect of the Indian context, the authors have studied in detail whether there is any disparity between PSBs and Pvt. SBs toward financial inclusion and which bank group is in an advanced position than the other group and also which banks are comparatively in a better position among the sample banks.

Without a sound banking system, the economy cannot function smoothly and efficiently. The efficient banks can keep safe deposit and provide financial assistance and only then the regulator can achieve the target of financial inclusion. From the point of view of customers, efficient banks can offer better services due to their reasonable operational cost. In the present analysis first this study has comparatively analyzed the significant differences between the PSBs and Pvt. SBs with various financial parameters as selected from the previous literature by applying t-test. After analyzing the same the authors have applied the DEA model to compare between the selected banks and between two groups.

To study and analyze the comparative role of PSBs and Pvt. SBs on financial inclusion the authors have used the key indicators of availability and usage of banking service. The indicators are APPB (branch expansions), population per ATM (expansion of ATMs), deposits to GDP ratio, credit to GDP ratio, deposits per capita (deposit mobilization), credit per capita (credit penetration), C-D ratio, and assets per branch. All of these indicators are important parameters for measuring financial inclusion (Beck et al., 2007; Kunt et al., 2011; Kumar, 2013; and Jalaludeen, 2014). So, the authors have considered all these indicators to compare role toward financial inclusion by the two groups of PSBs and Pvt. SBs. Fisher's t-test has been applied to test any significant difference between PSBs and Pvt. SBs. Table 5.18 presents a comparison of financial inclusion parameters between the two bank groups.

Regarding branch expansion, APPB in respect of PSBs has been significantly declined from 35,307 in March 2002 to 22,941 in March 2016. In respect of Pvt. SBs the same has also been significantly declined from 493,433 in March 2002 to 70,338 in March 2016. Regarding ATM

Table 5.18 Comparison of financial inclusion parameters between PSBs and Pvt. SBs in India

Parameters	Bank group	N	Average	CAGR	CV	t-value	Sig.
Average population per branch	PSBs	15	30,777.33	(3.03)	16.96	5.30	0.000*
	Pvt. SBs.	15	235,318.61	(12.99)	63.50		
Average population per ATM	PSBs	6	20,471.16	(17.63)	40.38	2.58	0.015**
	Pvt. SBs.	6	34,740.85	(13.63)	30.92		
Deposits as % of GDP	PSBs	15	0.38	2.48	14.78	16.22	0.000*
	Pvt. SBs.	15	0.11	9.11	29.32		
Credit as % of GDP	PSBs	15	0.27	5.94	27.21	8.70	0.000*
	Pvt. SBs.	15	0.09	10.14	36.31		
Deposits per capita	PSBs	15	20142.99	13.95	60.14	4.26	0.000*
	Pvt. SBs.	15	6076.94	21.33	67.89		
Credit per capita	PSBs	15	15,099.34	17.79	67.36	3.53	0.001*
	Pvt. SBs.	15	5160.32	22.47	75.46		
Credit-deposits ratio	PSBs	15	0.70	3.38	15.61	3.06	0.002*
	Pvt. SBs.	15	0.81	0.94	9.75		
Assets per office	PSBs	15	693.06	11.03	44.05	6.72	0.000*
	Pvt. SBs.	15	1333.51	3.54	15.53		

Source: Authors' calculation

* Significance level is 1 percent and ** Significance level is 5 percent

expansion, population per ATM in respect of PSBs and Pvt. SBs has declined from 31,716 in March 2011 to 12,023 in March 2016 and 55,280 in March 2011 to 26,563 in March 2016 respectively.

Deposits to GDP of PSBs have increased from 0.3258 in March 2002 to 0.4589 in March 2016 and of Pvt. SBs have increased from 0.0499 in March 2002 to 0.1694 in March 2016. Further, credit to GDP of PSBs has increased from 0.1626 to 0.3645 and in respect of Pvt. SBs it has increased from 0.0401 in March 2002 to 0.1550 in March 2016.

Regarding deposit penetration, deposits per capita of Pvt. SBs were ₹978 in March 2002 which further increased to ₹14,655 in March 2016 and deposits per capita of PSBs were ₹6383 in March 2002 and, further, they increased to ₹39,704 in March 2016.

Regarding credit penetration, credit per capita of PSBs has been increased from ₹3185 in March 2002 to ₹31,537 in March 2016 and of Pvt. SBs it has increased from ₹785 in March 2002 to ₹13,410 in March 2016.

Table 5.18 shows that there is a significant difference in APPB, deposits to GDP, credit to GDP, deposit per capita, credit per capita, C-D ratio, asset per office by PSBs, and Pvt. SBs at 1 percent level of significance. It means the APPB, deposits to GDP, credit to GDP, deposit per capita, credit per capita, C-D ratio, assets per office in PSBs, and Pvt. SBs were having significant differences at 1 percent level. Table 5.18 also shows that there is a significant difference in population per ATM by PSBs and Pvt. SBs at 5 percent level of significance. It means the average population per ATM of PSBs and Pvt. SBs were having significant differences at 5 percent level.

It is found from t-test that mean differences with an unequal variance of financial inclusion parameters between the two bank groups are significant. Accordingly, there is a significant difference between Pvt. SBs and PSBs on financial inclusion in India, and positive growth of branch and ATM expansion, deposit mobilization, and credit penetration do bring financial inclusion.

5.4.2   Performance Measures of PSBs and Pvt. SBs

According to t-test, the authors find out if there exists a significant difference between groups or not. However, it is not clear which individual bank is more efficient and which one is less efficient or which group is comparatively better than others. To measure the individual efficiency of banks the DEA efficiency measurement has been applied. "The application of DEA can be found in several services and industries since its inception in 1978" (by Charnes, Cooper, and Rhodes). In the public sector and private sector, this technique has been used widely to measure efficiency. In a recent study by Maity and Sahu (2017) used the DEA model to measure the performance of SBI and Associates banks of two different periods. The primary objective of the bank is to mobilize deposits and disbursement of credit from the deposits mobilized. The target is to have a bank account for all so that all can be a part of the development process. Due to their prime role, many previous studies also considered these two parameters as financial inclusion dimensions (Mahadeva, 2008; Kodan & Chhikara, 2011; Shafi & Medabesh, 2012; Chakravarty & Pal, 2013; Kunt & Klapper, 2013; Fungacova & Weill, 2015; Kumar, 2013; Maity & Sahu, 2018b). Considering the prime role of the banks and previous literature, in the present study also these dimensions are considered as indicators of financial inclusion. In this regard from the Indian perspective, the study considers that the number of branches (Kodan et al., 2011; Das & Guha, 2015) and total assets (Kumar, 2012) are two input variables.

Bhattacharyya et al. (1997) in their analysis to measure the performance of different bank groups under the DEA model include advances, investment, and deposits as output variables and two types of expenses, that is, operating expenses and interest expenses, as input variables. "Performance of any institution is often evaluated in terms of its efficiency in the use of its resources" (Saha & Ravisankar, 2000). Sathye (2003) in his analysis used interest expenses, non-interest expenses, deposits, and staff members as input variables and interest income, non-interest income, and net loans as output variables to measure the performance of banks.

In practice, the banks use various resources to serve the customers in the form of deposits and credits. Accordingly, the authors have set branch and total assets size as input variables. Based on the objective of the study and prime role of the banks, the present study considered volume of deposits and credits as output parameters. To measure efficient banks, we need to measure maximum output with minimum input. As the study is going to measure the performance of banks with regard to financial inclusion, these two variables are found to be appropriate as output.

In the present study, the different selected banks from PSBs and Pvt. SBs represent DMUs. Here, DMUs' number is 20 (selected 20 banks), that is, "more than twice the number (i.e., eight) of input and output factors in this analysis. Therefore, in the present analysis, the proposed DEA model has high construct validity" (Golany & Roll, 1989, Drake & Howcroft, 1994).

To increase the validity in the present analysis, the authors examine the "assumptions of isotonicity relationship by the correlation among the selected input and output factors" (Golany & Roll, 1989). "The isotonicity relationship expresses a rise in any input should not result in a loss in any output" (Maity & Sahu, 2020). The result of correlation matrix (Table 5.19) does not violet the isotonicity assumptions.

In the present study, two input variables and two output variables have been used to evaluate the efficiency levels of banks. Branch is one input variable, "as the additional branches attract more total customer for the bank as a whole" (Berger et al., 1997). Another input variable is assets (total assets), as the value of assets signifies the branch size (Kumar, 2012). The two output variables are deposit and advance which are the financial inclusion parameters. The efficiency score will be 1 for technically efficient DMU. An efficiency score < 1 considered as inefficient DMU and the DMU is operating either at Decreasing Returns to Scale (DRS) or at Increasing Returns to Scale (IRS).

Table 5.20 summarizes the DEA results. The efficiency scores of 20 banks obtained from CCR and BCC models have been presented in the table along with the magnitude of overall technical inefficiency (OTIE). The score measures "By how much can input quantities be proportionally decreased without changing the output quantities produced?" (Kumar & Gulati, 2008). The results indicate that the selected Indian banking industry has been characterized with lower asymmetry of efficiency scores of 79.02 percent to 100 percent and average scores of 0.949 for PSBs and Pvt. SBs as presented in descriptive statistics in Table 5.21. This suggests that average PSBs and Pvt. SBs, if producing their outputs on the efficient

Table 5.19 Correlation among the input and output factors

Factors	Assets	Branch	Deposits	Credit
Assets	1			
Branch	0.9304	1		
Deposits	0.9917	0.9588	1	
Credit	0.9985	0.9354	0.9943	1

Source: Authors' calculation

Table 5.20   DEA results of PSBs and Pvt. SBs under CCR and BCC models

Sr. No.	Banks (DMUs)	OTE score (CRS)	OTIE score (%)	PTE score (VRS)	PTIE score (%)	SE score	SIE score (%)	RTS
1	State Bank of India	0.9325	6.75	1.0000	0.00	0.9325	6.75	DRS
2	Bank of Baroda	0.9678	3.22	1.0000	0.00	0.9678	3.22	DRS
3	Bank of India	0.9729	2.71	0.9984	0.16	0.9744	2.56	DRS
4	Punjab National Bank	0.9627	3.73	0.9915	0.85	0.9709	2.91	DRS
5	Canara Bank	0.9880	1.20	1.0000	0.00	0.9880	1.20	DRS
6	Union Bank of India	0.9840	1.60	0.9949	0.51	0.9891	1.09	DRS
7	IDBI Ltd.	1.0000	0.00	1.0000	0.00	1.0000	0.00	CRS
8	Central Bank of India	0.9816	1.84	0.9950	0.50	0.9866	1.34	DRS
9	Syndicate Bank	0.9978	0.22	1.0000	0.00	0.9978	0.22	DRS
10	Indian Overseas Bank	0.9602	3.98	0.9665	3.35	0.9935	0.65	DRS
11	ICICI Bank Ltd.	0.7902	20.98	1.0000	0.00	0.7902	20.98	DRS
12	HDFC Bank Ltd.	0.8530	14.70	0.8868	11.32	0.9619	3.81	DRS
13	Axis Bank Ltd.	0.8441	15.59	0.8719	12.81	0.9681	3.19	DRS
14	YES Bank	1.0000	0.00	1.0000	0.00	1.0000	0.00	CRS
15	IndusInd Bank Ltd.	0.8645	13.55	0.9066	9.34	0.9536	4.64	IRS
16	Kotak Mahindra Bank Ltd.	0.9416	5.84	0.9943	0.57	0.9470	5.30	IRS
17	The Federal Bank Ltd.	0.9470	5.30	0.9476	5.24	0.9993	0.07	DRS
18	The Jammu & Kashmir Bank Ltd.	1.0000	0.00	1.0000	0.00	1.0000	0.00	CRS
19	The South Indian Bank Ltd.	1.0000	0.00	1.0000	0.00	1.0000	0.00	CRS
20	The Karur Vysya Bank Ltd.	0.9856	1.44	1.0000	0.00	0.9856	1.44	IRS
	Average	0.9487	5.1320	0.9777	2.2328	0.9703	2.9677	

Source: Authors' calculation

Table 5.21 Descriptive statistics of OTE scores for PSBs and Pvt. SBs

Statistics	All banks	Efficient banks	Inefficient banks
N (PSBs)	10	1	9
AOTE (PSBs)	0.9748	1.0000	0.9720
N (Pvt. SBs)	10	3	7
AOTE (Pvt. SBs)	0.9226	1.0000	0.8894
N (PSBs and Pvt. SBs)	20	4	16
AOTE (PSBs and Pvt. SBs)	0.9487	1.0000	0.9359
SD	0.0616	0	0.0627
Minimum	0.7902	1.0000	0.7902
First quartile	0.9371	1.0000	0.8985
Median	0.9703	1.0000	0.9615
Third quartile	0.9929	1.0000	0.9828
Maximum	1.0000	1.0000	0.9978
AOTIE (%)	5.1320	0	6.4150

Notes: AOTE = Average overall technical efficiency; and AOTIE = Average overall technical inefficiency

Source: Authors' calculation

frontier instead of their current (virtual) location, would need only 94.87 percent (PSBs with 97.48 percent and Pvt. SBs with 92.26 percent) of the inputs. This study opines that the OTIE score is to the tune of 5.13 percent for the Indian banking sector. This concludes that the banking sector can reduce branch and assets (inputs) by at least 5.13 percent (PSBs with 2.52 percent and Pvt. SBs with 7.74 percent). From the output maximization point of view, PSBs have 1.03 times (i.e., 1/0.975) and Pvt. SBs have the scope of producing 1.08 times (i.e., 1/0.923) and all of the twenty banks have the scope of producing 1.05 times (i.e., 1/0.949) as much as outputs from the same level of inputs. Among the selected banks considered in the study, four are technically efficient and the rest banks are marginally inefficient or inefficient due to efficiency scores <1. The efficient 4 banks in the selected 20 Indian banks are IDBI Bank Ltd., the Jammu & Kashmir Bank Ltd., the South Indian Bank Ltd., and YES Bank. The remaining 16 banks have OTE score less than 1 which means that they are technically less efficient or inefficient. The four overall efficient banks have equal PTE and TE with scores 1 and thus present constant returns to scale (CRS).

In particular, six DMUs (i.e., Bank of Baroda, Canara Bank, ICICI Bank Ltd., State Bank of India, Syndicate Bank, and the Karur Vysya Bank Ltd.) have the PTE scores equal to 1 while their SE scores are less than 1.

A DMU may be scale-inefficient if it exceeds the most productive scale size (thus experiencing DRS), or if it is smaller than the most productive scale size (thus having not taken the full advantage of IRS). Indeed, most of the inefficient banks present the DRS that can decrease their scales to possible improve their efficiencies. Only three inefficient banks (i.e., IndusInd Bank Ltd., Kotak Mahindra Bank Ltd., and the Karur Vysya Bank Ltd.) present IRS that can increase the scales to effectively improve their efficiencies. In particular, 11 scale inefficient banks (i.e., State Bank of India, Bank of Baroda, Bank of India, Punjab National Bank, Canara Bank, Union Bank of India, Central Bank of India, Syndicate Bank, ICICI Bank Ltd., Kotak Mahindra Bank Ltd., and the Karur Vysya Bank Ltd.) have their PTE scores higher than SE scores, respectively. This implies that overall inefficiency is primarily due to the SE.

These inefficient banks can improve their efficiency by reducing inputs or increasing the proportionate output. The efficiency scores among the inefficient groups range from 0.7902 (ICICI Bank Ltd.) to 0.9978 (Syndicate Bank). This implies that ICICI Bank Ltd. and Syndicate Bank can potentially reduce their present input requirement by 20.98 percent and 0.22 percent respectively (without changing the output quantity) or increase their output level by 1.266 times (i.e., $1/0.7902$) and 1.002 times (i.e., $1/0.9978$) respectively while leaving their input levels unchanged. Alternatively, the same interpretation of rest inefficient banks can be extended with OTE scores for the sample banks. On the whole, this study observes that OTIE levels ranged from 0.22 percent to 20.98 percent among inefficient PSBs.

Classification of Inefficient Banks
According to the analysis, 16 banks are less efficient or inefficient among the 20 selected banks. But all these less efficient or inefficient banks are not in the same position. There may be a little bit inefficient (nearer to efficient) or most inefficient. To classify them this study uses quartile values of OTE scores obtained from the CCR model. By applying the quartile values the authors classified them into four categories, namely, most inefficient (Category I), below average (Category II), above average (Category III), and marginally inefficient (Category IV). The banks of category I are the worst performer in collection of deposits and disbursement of credit. Again the banks of category IV are operating at a high level of operating efficiency in collection of deposits and disbursement of credit

even though they are not fully efficient. Table 5.22 shows the results of classification of inefficient banks.

The OTE scores below the first quartile (Table 5.21) have been included in the most inefficient category and the OTE score above the third quartile but less than 1 included in the marginally inefficient category. The OTE scores above the first quartile but less than median are included in the below-average category and the OTE scores above the median value but less than third quartile are included in the average category. Accordingly, there are significant differences among the inefficient banks.

"The banks attaining OTE and PTE scores equal to 1 are known as globally efficient and locally efficient banks, respectively" (Kumar & Gulati, 2008). Table 5.20 also depicts that ten banks have PTE scores equal to 1 and they are locally efficient banks. Among them, four banks have acquired the status of globally efficient banks and lie on the efficient frontier under CRS assumption. The rest six banks—namely, State Bank of India, Bank of Baroda, Canara Bank, Syndicate Bank, ICICI Bank Ltd., and the Karur Vysya Bank Ltd.—attained PTE score equal to 1 and lie on the efficient frontier. The PTE scores equal to 1 and OTE <1 of these six banks confirm that they are efficient under VRS assumption but have not been found to be efficient under CRS assumption. This concludes that the OTIE in these banks is not caused by poor input utilization or managerial inefficiency, rather caused by inappropriate scale size.

It has been further noticed that out of the remaining ten banks (having PTE<1) five banks have PTE score less than SE score (i.e., Indian Overseas

Table 5.22 Classification of inefficient PSBs and Pvt. SBs

Category I	Category II	Category III	Category IV
IndusInd Bank Ltd. (17)	Indian Overseas Bank (13)	Central Bank of India (9)	Syndicate Bank (5)
HDFC Bank Ltd. (18)	The Federal Bank Ltd. (14)	Bank of India (10)	Canara Bank (6)
Axis Bank Ltd. (19)	Kotak Mahindra Bank Ltd. (15)	Bank of Baroda (11)	The Karur Vysya Bank Ltd. (7)
ICICI Bank Ltd. (20)	State Bank of India (16)	Punjab National Bank (12)	Union Bank of India (8)

Note: Figures in the brackets are rank

Source: Authors' calculation

Table 5.23   Descriptive statistics of OTE, PTE, and SE scores for PSBs and Pvt. SBs

Statistics	OTE	PTE	SE
N (PSBs)	10	10	10
Average efficiency (PSBs)	0.9748	0.9946	0.9801
N (Pvt. SBs)	10	10	10
Average efficiency (Pvt. SBs)	0.9226	0.9607	0.9606
N (PSBs and Pvt. SBs)	20	20	20
Average efficiency (PSBs and Pvt. SBs)	0.9487	0.9777	0.9703
SD	0.0616	0.0411	0.0468
Minimum	0.7902	0.8719	0.7902
First quartile	0.9371	0.9790	0.9649
Median	0.9703	0.9992	0.9861
Third quartile	0.9929	1.0000	0.9986
Maximum	1.0000	1.0000	1.0000
Average inefficiency (%)	5.1320	2.2328	2.9677

Source: Authors' calculation

Bank, HDFC Bank Ltd., Axis Bank Ltd., IndusInd Bank Ltd., and the Federal Bank Ltd.). This concludes that the inefficiency in these five banks is primarily attributed due to managerial inefficiency rather than to the SE.

From the analysis, the authors observed that OTIE in the PSBs and Pvt. SBs is due to both PTIE (i.e., poor input utilization) and SIE (i.e., failure to operate at most productive scale size). Table 5.23 shows that APTE for the 20 banks has been observed to be 0.9777 which implies that 2.2 percent points of 5.1 percent of OTIE is due to managerial inefficiency and the rest, that is, 2.9 percent is due to scale size. Also, "higher mean and lower SD of the PTE scores compared to SE scores indicate that a lower portion of OTIE is due to PTIE" (Kumar & Gulati, 2008).

5.5   KEY FINDINGS AND THEIR INTERPRETATIONS

Branch-Based Banking on Financial Inclusion

Bivariate regression of deposit accounts as dependent variable and the number of branches (including off-site ATMs) as independent variable indicate that expansion of branch has a significant impact ($p < 0.01$) on the number of deposit accounts. And 99.5 percent ($R^2 = 0.995$) of the variation in opening of deposit accounts has been explained by expansion of branch.

Bivariate regression of credit accounts as dependent variable and the number of branches (including off-site ATMs) as independent variable indicate that expansion of branch has a significant impact ($p < 0.01$) on the number of credit accounts. And 75.9 percent ($R^2 = 0.759$) of the variation in opening of credit accounts has been explained by expansion of branch and off-site ATMs.

This finding of a significant relationship is consistent with the previous study of Ansong et al. (2015) in the Ghana context; Burgess et al. (2005), Mahadeva (2008), Kumar (2013), Kundu (2015), and Pathania et al. (2016) in the Indian context; Collard (2007) in the UK context; Evanoff (1988) in the US context; Alama and Ausina (2012) in the Spain context; and Beck et al. (2007) and Ergungor (2010) in the context of different countries, that opening of a new branch and or new ATMs provides access to banks.

Results indicate a significant influence of component 1, namely, credit to GDP, deposit per branch, credit per branch, and deposit to GDP, which accounts for 56.113 percent of total variance for expansion of branch. All the high loadings of component 1 are positive of the four variables of deposit to GDP, deposit per branch, credit to GDP, and credit per branch. The positive loadings indicate that there is a positive relationship between the independent and dependent variable. So, in the lag year if it was found that in a particular region or state, there is higher deposit to GDP, deposit per branch, credit to GDP, and credit per branch, then there are more chances for opening of a new branch in the ensuing year of the particular region or states. Due to these reasons, this study found that there is a disparity among opening branches region-wise or state-wise. Bank will be comfortable with opening of branches in a particular place if they found that the existing branch of the particular place or region has a higher deposit to GDP, higher deposit per branch, higher credit to GDP, or higher credit per branch.

Results also indicate a significant influence of component 2, namely, the branch per 1000 sq. km. and APPB, which accounts for 42.980 percent of total variance for expansion of branch. On this basis, the factors behind opening of new branches were identified as branch per 1000 sq. km. and APPB of the lag period. Among the two high loadings of component 2, branch per 1000 sq. km. is positive and APPB is negative. The positive loadings indicate that there is a positive relationship between the independent and dependent variables; on the other side negative loading indicates there is a negative relationship between independent and dependent variables. So, in the lag year if it was found that in a particular region or state, there is a higher number of branches per 1000 sq. km., there are more chances for opening of a new branch in the ensuing year of the particular region or states. Alternatively, lower population per branch in the lag year also have higher chances for the opening of a new branch in the ensuing year of that particular region to capture the banking business. Bank will be comfortable with the opening of branches in a particular place if they found a higher rate of branch per 1000 sq. km. or a lower rate of APPB.

In multiple regressions the authors have found that the value of R^2 is 0.8660 which indicates that 86.60 percent of the variations in opening of new branches have been explained by the two components and both the components are significant at 1 percent level of significance. So, the authors conclude that the entire selected six independent variables of deposit to GDP, deposit per branch, credit to GDP, credit per branch, branch per 1000 sq. km., and APPB have a significant impact on expansion of new branch. Inoue and Hamori (2016), in their investigation in the context of sub-Saharan Africa, find that there is a positive relationship between the number of bank branches and real GDP per capita. A number of studies show "a high correlation between the rate of financial deepening measured as the percentage of credit with respect to GDP or number of loans per capita and increases in GDP per capita" (Beck et al., 2007; Sanz & Lima, 2013). The present study also is partially consistent with Iqbal and Sami (2017) that branch and C-D ratio have a significant and positive impact on GDP and furthermore ATMs growth have no significant impact.

The result of the present study is also consistent with the previous study of Boufounou (1995) that volume of bank deposit is attracted by each branch in Greece. Result of the present analysis is consistent with the earlier study of Kumar (2012) and Jalaludeen (2014) in the Indian context.

The results of multiple regressions contradict the findings of Hirtle (2007) in the US bank branch context that size of a branch is not dependent upon the deposits per branch or branch performance. This is due to the fact that opening of a new branch or expansion of branch size is an overall strategy of banks. "Branch based banking still has a role in promoting financial inclusion" (Ansong et al., 2015). "In developed and developing countries, the government has used branch expansion policies to ensure that banks open branches where poor people reside" (Panagariya, 2006). Moreover, on the basis of present analysis and presentation of data, this study has found a strong positive impact of one-year lag value of the selected six variables on opening of a new branch. Therefore, "banks will open a new branch where the business from the existing branch is at higher side or already have more number of branches" (Maity & Sahu, 2018a).

Technology-Based Banking on Financial Inclusion
No country in the world would progress without science and technology. Due to rapid technological innovation, we have found rapid changes in providing and accessing banking services. There may be a variety of reasons for the lack of provision of appropriate products and services. Banks may have problems offering financial services in all the regions with a physical branch. In the banking sector, several banks have introduced several technological measures that enhance the services provided to the consumers. "The introduction of technology based services will reduce cost and enhance outreach and may prove to be an effective tool for greater financial inclusion in rural areas as it has happened in other countries like Kenya" (Nyagilo, 2017).

"The high mobile penetration and low banking access have the scope of utilising mobile technologies as origin of accessibility in all countries of the region" (Sanz & Lima, 2013). "Increasing internet penetration with the increase in mobile subscribers in rural and urban areas have created a huge opportunity for banking institutions" (Boro, 2015). So in this scenario, mobile banking is a better choice for expanding banking services. Turan and Sharma (2010) examined the quality of e-banking provided by various bank groups in the Indian urban areas. Alexandre et al. (2011), Hinson (2011), Singh (2012), Mishra and Bisht (2013), Chauhan (2015), and Kundu (2015) in the Indian context; Sanz and Lima (2013) in the Africa context; and Berger and Deyoung (2006) in their study in US context find that progress in technology has facilitated the geographic expansion of banking industry. Singh (2012) and Sahu and Maity (2021) in the Indian context; Nyagilo (2017) in the rural Kenya context; Honohan (2008); and Mishra and Bisht (2013) in the context of different countries find that mobile banking has a positive and significant influence on financial inclusion. "Mobile banking is the way to bridge the gap in access to financial services" (Ansong et al., 2015).

In bivariate regression, the study finds that there is significant effect of mobile banking transactions on deposit and credit accounts. The stepwise regression states that internet user per capita has a significant effect on mobile banking transaction. The other factors of mobile connection per capita, literacy rate, and GDP (NNP) log value have no significant effect on mobile banking transactions. This result is consistent with earlier study of Nyagilo (2017) in rural Kenya context that mobile banking has a positive and significant influence; that is, increase in mobile banking leads to more financial inclusion. This study is consistent with the previous study of Amore et al. (2013), Chava et al. (2013), and Laeven et al. (2015) in the case of the US and Bansal (2014) in the Indian context. This is due to the fact that technological innovation and finance have a strong connection.

According to the results of stepwise regression, the authors have found that the use of the internet plays an important role in expansion of mobile banking. This indicates the fact that internet connectivity as well as using of the internet either through mobile or through PC plays an important role in financial inclusion. The value of R^2 (0.906) explains that 90.6 percent of ICT-based mobile banking transactions have a highly significant relationship with internet users. Results of the present analysis are consistent with the previous study of Kostov et al. (2014) in the case of South Africa of literacy variable. Kulkarni and Warke (2015) in their analysis find that non-availability of network connection is a major hurdle in ICT-based FI. The insignificant results of literacy rate on mobile banking are contradicting the findings of Belas et al. (2015) in the Slovak Republic that higher education intensively uses electronic banking.

It appears that internet users mainly chase trend of financial inclusion. Bansal (2014) in his investigation finds modern ICT would directly or indirectly reflect support in achieving financial inclusion. "There is a general consensus that technological innovations are altering the traditional brick-and-mortar banking model" (King, 2014; and Ansong et al., 2015). "If it is not possible to offer financial services to all with the financial setup, then mobile technologies can be used to reach the unbanked areas" (Hinson, 2011). "Providing banking services through mobile helps banks' access with lower investment" (Kulkarni & Warke, 2015).

Comparative Role of PSBs and Pvt. SBs and Measures It Performance
Fisher's t-test clearly indicates that the position of availability of banking service of PSBs and Pvt. SBs is significantly different from each other. A significant difference has been found between PSBs and Pvt. SBs in respect of population per branch and population per ATM. However, the status of availability of banking services in terms of population per office and population per ATMs of PSBs has been superior to Pvt. SBs. Average

population per office and average population per ATM of PSBs have been 30,777 and 20,471, respectively. APPB and average population per ATM of Pvt. SBs have been 235,319 and 34,741 respectively. Also, the growth rate of population per ATM of PSBs is much more satisfactory than Pvt. SBs with -17.63 percent and -13.63 percent respectively. However, in respect of growth of population per branch Pvt. SBs are much ahead of PSBs. As because growth (CAGR) rate of population per branch of Pvt. SBs has been -12.99 percent compared to -3.03 percent in the case of PSBs. Negative CAGR population per branch and population per ATM indicate an improvement of financial inclusion status. With an increase in branches and ATMs, population per branch or population per ATM will reduce (negative relation).

A significant difference is found between PSBs and Pvt. SBs in respect of deposit as a percentage of GDP and credit as a percentage of GDP. This study has found that the p-value ($p < 0.01$) in both the analyses is significant at 1 percent level of significance. Though PSBs are in a better position (with highest average value) than Pvt. SBs in respect of deposit as a percentage of GDP and credit as a percentage of GDP, the growth rate of Pvt. SBs is comparatively better than PSBs.

A significant difference has been found between the PSBs and Pvt. SBs in respect of deposits per capita and credit per capita. Values of p ($p < 0.01$) in both the analyses are found to be significant at 1 percent level of significance. During the study period, deposit per capita and credit per capita of PSBs have been ₹20,143 and ₹15,099 respectively. Whereas, in the case of Pvt. SBs, deposit per capita and credit per capita have been only ₹6077 and ₹5160 respectively. The authors have also found a significant p-value ($p < 0.01$) at 1 percent level of significance. Though PSBs are in a better position in respect of deposits per capita and credit per capita, the growth rate of Pvt. SBs is comparatively better than the PSBs during the period under study. CAGR of deposit per capita and credit per capita of Pvt. SBs have been 21.33 percent and 22.47 percent respectively. Whereas in respect of PSBs, CAGR of deposit per capita and credit per capita have been 13.95 percent and 17.79 percent respectively.

A significant difference is found in respect of C-D ratio between the PSBs and Pvt. SBs. The C-D ratio of PSBs (0.70) is low as compared to Pvt. SBs (0.81). In the analysis p-value ($p < 0.01$) is also found to be significant at 1 percent level of significance.

The study also found that there is a significant difference between the assets per branch of PSBs and Pvt. SBs. In the analysis p-value (p < 0.01) is also found to be significant at 1 percent level of significance and value of t-test is also higher than the tabulated value. Both indicate that there is a significant difference in assets per branch of PSBs and Pvt. SBs. During the period, average assets of PSBs have been ₹30,334 billion, whereas in the case of Pvt. SBs it has been ₹10,989 billion. Assets per branch of PSBs (₹693 million) are much lower as compared to Pvt. SBs (₹1334 million).

While comparing their performance this study finds that among the selected 20 banks, 4 banks (i.e., IDBI Bank Ltd., the Jammu & Kashmir Bank Ltd., the South Indian Bank Ltd., and YES Bank) have been globally efficient and six banks have been locally efficient (i.e., State Bank of India, Bank of Baroda, Canara Bank, Syndicate Bank, ICICI Bank Ltd., and the Karur Vysya Bank Ltd.). The assumptions of isotonicity were also found appropriate to run the DEA. According to the analysis for globally efficient banks score value is 1 both under CCR model (CRS assumption) and BCC model (VRS assumption). Contrarily locally efficient banks' score value is 1 only under the BCC model (VRS assumption) and OTIE in these banks is not caused by poor input utilization, but rather caused by the operations of banks with inappropriate scale size. Also, this study concludes that on the basis of AOTE score or AOTIE (percent), PSB group is comparatively is in a little better position than Pvt. SB group toward playing their role in financial inclusion. This result is consistent with Bhattacharyya et al.'s (1997) findings that only 2 of 28 PSBs are found to be efficient in the final year of the sample period (1986–1991) and that PSBs are most efficient and privately owned banks are least efficient (Dhar, 2012). Sathye (2003) shows that the mean efficiency score of Indian banks compares well with the world and the score of private bank is lower than that of public and foreign banks. Maity and Sahu (2021a) in their analysis also found that foreign banks on average are working efficiently far better than the public and private banks and further that the Pvt. SB group is more efficient than the PSB group. The result is in line with the study by Maity (2020).

Kumar and Gulati (2008) in their analysis found that of the 27 PSBs, 13 PSBs are under DRS, all 7 efficient banks and SBI are under CRS, and the rest 6 PSBs are under IRS. The results of Bhattacharyya et al. (1997) also show that of the 43 frontier banks, 33 displayed DRS and only foreign-owned banks showed IRS. In the present study of the 20 banks, 13 banks (9 PSBs and 4 Pvt. SBs) are under DRS, 3 Pvt. SBs are under IRS, and 4 banks are under CRS. Though PSBs are under DRS, in line with the earlier findings of Dangi (2012), PSBs have dominated in removing financial exclusion followed by Pvt. SBs. According to the results, this study found that most big banks are less efficient than small banks. This is due to their bigger size and high cost. Berger and Humphrey (1992) in their study during the 1980s found that high-cost banks experienced a higher rate of failure than more efficient banks. Further, Maity et al. (2020) show that the dominant big private banks are efficient and with higher technical efficiency scores.

Pastor et al. (1997) in a broader context applied DEA of 427 banks from eight developed countries. They found a mean efficiency value of 0.86, with the highest efficiency value of 0.95 for France and lowest efficiency value of 0.55 for the UK. In another paper, Lozano-Vivas et al. (2002) computed efficiency scores for commercial banks across ten EU countries and found Spain to be highly efficient (with average score of 0.82) and Italy to be least efficient (with average score of 0.33).

The mean efficiency score was found to be 0.885 as estimated by Kumar and Gulati (2008) for the study period of 2004–2005 of Indian PSBs with efficiency scores of inefficient banks ranging from 0.632 to 0.974. The efficiency estimated by Sathye (2003) has been found to be 0.83 and 0.62 (mean efficiency) under two models for the study period of 1997–1998, which compares well with the score estimated by Bhattacharya et al. (1997) for the study period of 1986–1991, with scores from 0.79 to 0.80. Further, Saha and Ravishankar (2000) have found efficiency scores from 0.58 to 0.74 of 25 PSBs in 1995 and the mean score was 0.69. In the present study mean efficiency score of PSBs is 0.97 and that of Pvt. SBs is 0.92 which compares well with the previous studies. These indicate that banks are improving their efficiency level.

Though in volume and numbers PSBs hold a major percentage due to their long presence in the market, the growth rate of Pvt. SBs compared to PSBs is much superior throughout the period under study. The results of higher growth in both the groups may be due to various initiatives considered in the recent past. The lower scores for Pvt. SBs could be because these banks are in the expansion phase and could have higher number of branches and higher amount of fixed assets employed which have yet to start generating returns.

BIBLIOGRAPHY

BOOKS, JOURNALS, WORKING PAPERS ETC.

Alama, L., & Ausina, E. T. (2012). Bank branch geographic location patterns in Spain: Some implications for financial exclusion. *Growth and Change, 43*(3), 505–543.

Alexandre, C., Mas, I., & Radcliffe, D. (2011). Regulating new banking models to bring financial services to all. *Challenge, 54*(3), 116–134.

Amore, M., Schneider, C., & Zaldokas, A. (2013). Credit supply and corporate innovation. *Journal of Financial Economics, 109*(3), 835–855.

Ansong, D., Chowa, G., & Adjabeng, B. K. (2015). Spatial analysis of the distribution and determinants of bank branch presence in Ghana. *International Journal of Bank Marketing, 33*(3), 201–222.

Arputhamani, J. A., & Prasannakumari, K. (2011). Financial inclusion through micro finance: The way to rural development, a case study of Rajapalayan block in Virudhunagar district. *KKIMRC International Journal of Research in Finance and Accounting, 1*(1), 94–115.

Bansal, S. (2014). Perspective of technology in achieving financial inclusion in rural India. *Procedia Economics and Finance, 11*, 472–480.

Beck, T., Kunt, A. D., & Peria, M. S. M. (2007). Reaching out: Access to and use of banking services across countries. *Journal of Financial Economics, 85*, 234–266.

Belas, J., Koraus, M., & Gabcova, L. (2015). Electronic banking, its use and safety. Are three differences in the access of Bank customers by gender, education and age? *International Journal of Entrepreneurial Knowledge, 3*(2), 16–28.

Berger, A. N., & Deyoung, R. (2006). Technological progress and the geographic expansion of the banking industry. *Journal of Money, Credit, and Banking, 38*(6), 1485–1513.

Berger, A. N., & Humphrey, D. B. (1992). Measurement and efficiency issues in commercial banking. In Z. Griliches (Ed.), *Output measurement in services sector* (pp. 245–279). University of Chicago Press.

Berger, A. N., Leusner, J. H., & Mingo, J. J. (1997). The efficiency of bank branches. *Journal of Monetary Economics, 40*, 141–162.

Bhattacharyya, A., Lovell, C. A. K., & Sahay, P. (1997). The impact of liberalization on the productive efficiency of Indian commercial banks. *European Journal of Operational Research, 98*, 332–345.

Boro, K. (2015). Prospects and challenges of technological innovation in banking industry of North East India. *Journal of Internet Banking & Commerce, 20*(3), 1–6.

Boufounou, P. V. (1995). Evaluating bank branch location and performance: A case study. *European Journal of Operational Research, 87*, 389–402.

Burgess, R., & Pande, R. (2005). Do rural banks matter? Evidence from the Indian social banking experiment. *American Economic Review, 95*(3), 780–795.

Burgess, R., Wong, G., & Pande, R. (2005). Banking for the poor: Evidence from India. *Journal of the European Economic Association, 3*(2–3), 268–278.

Calcagnini, G., De, B. R., & Hester, D. D. (1999, October 29–30). *Determinants of bank branch expansion in Italy.* SIDE (Italian Economic Association), 40th Meeting.

Chakravarty, S. R., & Pal, R. (2013). Financial inclusion in India: An axiomatic approach. *Journal of Policy Modeling, 35*, 813–837.

Charnes, A., Cooper, W. W., & Rhodes, E. (1978). Measuring the efficiency of decision making units. *European Journal of Operational Research, 2*(6), 429–444.

Chauhan, S. (2015). Acceptance of mobile money by poor citizens of India: Integrating trust into the technology acceptance model. *Info., Emerald Group Publishing Limited, 17*(3), 58–68.

Chava, S., Oetti, A., Subramanian, A., & Subramanian, K. (2013). Banking deregulation and innovation. *Journal of Financial Economics, 109*(3), 759–774.

Chen, Z., & Jin, M. (2017). Financial inclusion in China: Use of credit. *Journal of Family and Economic Issues, 38*(4), 528–540.

Collard, S. (2007). Toward financial inclusion in the UK: Progress and challenges. *Public Money & Management, 27*(1), 13–20.

Dangi, V. (2012). Financial inclusion: A saga of Indian financial system. *Asia-Pacific Journal of Management Research and Innovation, 8*(2), 111–125.

Das, T., & Guha, P. (2015). A study on the differences in the banking parameters between pre- and post-financial inclusion periods: Some evidence for India. *The IUP Journal of Bank Management, XIV*(1), 39–56.

Dhar, S. (2012). Banking reforms for financial inclusion: Performance of selected Indian banks. *Amity Management Review, 2*(2), 34–39.

Drake, L., & Howcroft, B. (1994). Relative efficiency in the branch network of a UK bank: An empirical study. *Omega, 22*(1), 83–90.

Ergungor, O. E. (2010). Bank branch presence and access to credit in low- to moderate-income neighborhoods. *Journal of Money, Credit and Banking, 42*(7), 1321–1349.

Evanoff, D. D. (1988). Branch banking and service accessibility. *Journal of Money, Credit, and Banking, 20*(2), 191–202.

Fungacova, Z., & Weill, L. (2015). Understanding financial inclusion in China. *China Economic Review, 34*, 196–206.

Golany, B., & Roll, Y. (1989). An application procedure for DEA. *Omega, 17*(3), 237–250.

Hinson, R. E. (2011). Banking the poor: The role of mobiles. *Journal of Financial Services Marketing, 15*(4), 320–333.

Hirtle, B. (2007). The impact of network size on bank branch performance. *Journal of Banking & Finance, 31*, 3782–3805.

Honohan, P. (2008). Cross-country variation in household access to financial services. *Journal of Banking & Finance, 32*, 2493–2500.

Inoue, T., & Hamori, S. (2016). Financial access and economic growth: Evidence from sub-Saharan Africa. *Emerging Markets Finance & Trade, 52*, 743–753.

Iqbal, B. A., & Sami, S. (2017). Role of banks in financial inclusion in India. *Contaduría y Administración, 62*, 644–656.

Jalaludeen, N. (2014). Is bank branch expansion driven by demand? – Some evidence from Kerala. *The IUP Journal of Bank Management, XIII*(1), 7–18.

King, B. (2014). *Breaking banks: The innovators, rogues, and strategists rebooting banking*. John Wiley & Sons.

King, R., & Levine, R. (1993). Finance and growth: Schumpeter might be right. *Quarterly Journal of Economics, 108*(3), 717–738.

Kodan, A. S., & Chhikara, K. S. (2011). Status of financial inclusion in Haryana: An evidence of commercial banks. *Management and Labour Studies, 36*(3), 247–267.

Kodan, A. S., Garg, N. K., & Kaidan, S. (2011). Financial inclusion: Status, issues, challenges and policy in northeastern region. *The IUP Journal of Financial Economics, IX*(2), 27–40.

Kostov, P., Arun, T., & Annim, S. (2014). Banking the unbanked: The Mzansi intervention in South Africa. *Indian Growth and Development Review, 7*(2), 118–141.

Kulkarni, M. M., & Warke, P. (2015). The framework for assessment of ICT based financial inclusion management by nationalized banks with special reference to Marathwada region. *Journal of Commerce & Management Thought, 6*(4), 684–692.

Kumar, N. (2012). An empirical analysis of financial inclusion across population groups in India. *The IUP Journal of Bank Management, XI*(1), 97–111.

Kumar, N. (2013). Financial inclusion and its determinants: Evidence from India. *Journal of Financial Economic Policy, 5*(1), 4–19.

Kumar, S., & Gulati, R. (2008). An examination of technical, pure technical, and scale efficiencies in Indian public sector banks using data envelopment analysis. *Eurasian Journal of Business and Economics, 1*(2), 33–69.

Kundu, D. (2015). Addressing the demand side factors of financial inclusion. *Journal of Commerce & Management Thought, 6*(3), 397–417.

Kunt, A. D., Cordova, E. L., Pería, M. S. M., & Woodruff, C. (2011). Remittances and banking sector breadth and depth: Evidence from Mexico. *Journal of Development Economics, 95*, 229–241.

Kunt, A. D., & Klapper, L. (2013). Measuring financial inclusion: Explaining variation in use of financial services across and within countries. In *Brookings papers on economic activity* (pp. 279–321). Spring.

Laeven, L., Levine, R., & Michalopoulos, S. (2015). Financial innovation and endogenous growth. *Journal of Financial Intermediation, 24*, 1–24.

Lozano-Vivas, A., Pastor, J. T., & Pastor, J. M. (2002). An efficiency comparison of European banking systems operating under different environmental conditions. *Journal of Productivity Analysis, 18*, 59–77.

Mahadeva, M. (2008). Financial growth in India: Whither financial inclusion? *Margin—The Journal of Applied Economic Research, 2*(2), 177–197.

Maity, S., & Sahu, T. N. (2017). Pre-merger performance measures of state bank of India and its associate banks using data envelopment analysis. *Business Spectrum, VII*(2), 16–26.

Maity, S., & Sahu, T. N. (2018a). Bank branch expansion and financial inclusion: Evidence from selected commercial banks in India. *Al-Barkaat Journal of Finance & Management, 10*(1), 48–65.

Maity, S., & Sahu, T. N. (2018b). Role of public and private sector banks in financial inclusion in India – An empirical investigation using DEA. *SCMS Journal of Indian Management, 15*(4), 62–73.

Maity, S., & Sahu, T. N. (2020). Role of public sector banks towards financial inclusion during pre and post introduction of PMJDY: A study on efficiency review. *Rajagiri Management Journal, 14*(2), 95–105.

Maity, S., & Sahu, T. N. (2021a). How far the Indian banking sectors are efficient?: An empirical investigation. *Asian Journal of Economics and Banking.* https://doi.org/10.1108/AJEB-02-2021-0016

Maity, S., & Sahu, T. N. (2021b). Financial inclusion in north-eastern region: An investigation in the state of Assam. *VILAKSHAN – XIMB Journal of Management.* https://doi.org/10.1108/XJM-09-2020-0118

Maity, S., Sahu, T. N., & Biswas, D. (2020). Assessing efficiency of private sectors banks in India: An empirical investigation using DEA. *International Journal of Financial Services Management, 10*(2), 138–155.

Martínez-Campillo, A., Wijesiri, M., & Wanke, P. (2020). Evaluating the double bottom-line of social banking in an emerging country: How efficient are public banks in supporting priority and non-priority sectors in India? *Journal of Business Ethics, 162*(2), 399–420.

Mishra, V., & Bisht, S. S. (2013). Mobile banking in a developing economy: A customer-centric model for policy formulation. *Telecommunications Policy, 37*, 503–514.

Noorshella, C. N., Abdullah, A. M., & Nursalihah, A. R. (2015). Examining the key factors affecting e-service quality of small online apparel businesses in Malaysia. *SAGE Open, 5*(2). https://doi.org/10.1177/2158244015576550

Nyagilo, V. (2017). Financial inclusion in rural Kenya: An investigation of the role of financial technology as an instrument. *International Journal of Business Management & Finance, 1*(31), 534–553.

Panagariya, A. (2006). *Bank branch expansion and poverty reduction: A comment.* Retrieved from: www.columbia.edu/~ap2231/technical%20papers/Bank%20 Branch%20 Expansion% 20and%20Poverty.pdf. Accessed 22 Apr 2015.

Pastor, J. M., Perez, F., & Quesada, J. (1997). Efficiency analysis in banking firms: An international comparison. *European Journal of Operational Research, 98*(2), 395–407.

Pathania, A., Ali, A., & Rasool, G. (2016). Quality dimension imperative for innovative financial inclusion: A case study of select banks in J&K. *Amity Business Review, 16*(2), 115–125.

Peachey, S., & Roe, A. (2004). *Access to finance: A study for the World Savings Banks Institute.* Oxford Policy Management.

Saha, A., & Ravisankar, T. S. (2000). Rating of Indian commercial banks: A DEA approach. *European Journal of Operational Research, 124,* 187–203.

Sahu, T. N., & Maity, S. (2021). Mobile banking a new banking model: An empirical investigation of financial innovation. International Journal of Business Innovation and Research. (Accepted for publication). https://doi.org/10.1504/IJBIR.2021.10039945

Sanz, F. P., & Lima, P. D. (2013). The uptake of mobile financial services in the Middle East and North Africa region. *Enterprise Development and Microfinance, 24*(4), 295–310.

Sathye, M. (2003). Efficiency of banks in a developing economy: The case of India. *European Journal of Operational Research, 148,* 662–671.

Shafi, M., & Medabesh, A. H. (2012). Financial inclusion in developing countries: Evidences from an Indian state. *International Business Research, 5*(8), 116–122.

Singh, A. B. (2012). Mobile banking based money order for India Post: Feasible model and assessing demand potential. *Procedia – Social and Behavioral Sciences, 37,* 466–481.

Turan, M. S., & Sharma, H. (2010). Customers perspectives on E-banking services. *The Journal of Indian Management and Strategy, 15*(1), 45–54.

CHAPTER 6

Recommendations and Conclusion

6.1 SUMMARY OF THE STUDY

In this study, the roles of PSBs and Pvt. SBs in the financial inclusion have been analyzed. The present study has taken into consideration 20 banking companies, out of which 10 are from PSBs and another 10 from Pvt. SBs for the study period from 2001–2002 to 2015–2016, and the study is principally based on secondary data. The study has used several statistical and econometrical techniques and tools such as descriptive statistics, correlation coefficient, PCA, bivariate regression analysis, multiple regression analysis, stepwise regression analysis, one way ANOVA, t-test, and Tukey HSD test using SPSS and Stata for analyzing the data. To measure the performance of PSBs and Pvt. SBs in respect of financial inclusion the authors have also used DEA. With the quartile value of OTE scores, this study categorizes the inefficient banks into groups such as most inefficient, below average, above average, and marginally inefficient.

A comparative study within India and around world indicates that though India lags behind in all the financial inclusion parameters as compared to the world, numerous growth rates are found during the period of study of 15 years.

To study determinants and analyze the data according to the second objective, initially this study uses descriptive statistics to understand the basic nature of factors and correlation coefficient to check the existence of multicollinearity if any. The correlation matrix suggests that there is

© The Author(s), under exclusive license to Springer Nature
Singapore Pte Ltd. 2022
S. Maity, T. N. Sahu, *Financial Inclusion and the Role of Banking
System*, https://doi.org/10.1007/978-981-16-6085-6_6

multicollinearity between the independent variables. The study uses PCA to eliminate multicollinearity. Results of KMO and Bartlett's Test were also found appropriate to run the PCA. The multiple regression analysis with principal component scores as explanatory variables finds that there is a significant effect of APPB with off-site ATMs, population per 1000 sq. km., literacy rate, number of factories, employment, per capita NNP, bank deposits to GDP, bank credit to GDP, per capita deposits of SCBs, per capita credit of SCBs, C-D ratio, and total assets of SCBs per branch on deposit accounts and credit accounts which affect financial inclusion. The factor of gross NPA to gross advance has a significant effect on deposit accounts only. As per the results of the analysis, the other factor of GDP (percentage) considered in the study has no significant impact on financial inclusion. The APPB with ATMs has negative relation and the other factors have a positive relationship with financial inclusion. This concludes that a decrease in APPB with ATMs enhances financial inclusion or increases in other factors enhance financial inclusion. From the PCA followed by multiple regression analysis, in the Indian context the authors find 13 variables toward expansion of deposit penetration and 12 variables toward expansion of credit penetration. All these factors have a significant role in expansion of financial inclusion. All these factors influence opening a bank account to achieve the goal of financial inclusion.

From the results of ANOVA with the financial inclusion factors of bank branch per 1000 sq. km., bank branch per 1000 populations, deposits per capita, credit per capita, and C-D Ratio, the study found that there are significant disparities in financial inclusion across the six regions of CR, ER, NER, NR, SR, and WR. However, the differences between the states are not specifically identified from the ANOVA test. Hence, Tukey HSD Test (a post hoc test) has been conducted. The post hoc test revealed that in respect of bank branches per 1000 sq. km. SR, ER, and WR are comparatively in a better position than CR, NER, and NR. In respect of other parameters of bank branches per 1000 populations, deposits per capita, credit per capita, and C-D ratio, SR, WR, and NR are comparatively in a better position than CR, NER, and ER. On the basis of the results, it is concluded that CR and NER have not achieved the target of financial inclusion with respect to the national level. Again from the results of ANOVA with financial inclusion factors of deposits and credit, this study finds that there are significant disparities in financial inclusion across 35 states and union territories in India. Afterward, the study has calculated the mean, SD, and CV of deposits and credit outstanding separately for the study period. Whether there is a wide variation of deposit penetration and credit penetration across states, CV has been computed. Based on the analysis of selected parameters of branch penetration, deposit penetration, and credit penetration the authors find that there is a significant disparity in financial inclusion across regions and states. This analysis signifies that although growths of deposit and credit have taken place, they have been uneven in the states and regions over time.

From the separate bivariate regression results, the authors find that both numbers of branches with off-site ATMs and the number of mobile banking transactions have a significant role in expansion of deposit accounts and credit accounts which measures the financial inclusion status. And that is the reason regulators are taking initiatives to open more and more branches or ATMs in all locations or giving financial services through mobile. To measure the factors which influence the opening of new branches, the study uses descriptive statistics to understand the basic nature of factors and correlation coefficient to check the existence of multicollinearity, if any. The correlation coefficient ranged from 0.895 to 0.999 and found multicollinearity. Due to the existence of multicollinearity, the study uses multiple regression with the principal component score as an explanatory variable. Results of KMO and Bartlett's Test were also found appropriate to run the PCA. The results found that all the six selected variables of deposit to GDP, deposit per branch, credit to GDP, credit per branch, branch per 1000 sq. km., and APPB with their one lag values have a significant impact on opening of new branch in a location.

Banking transactions through mobile devices have been capable of making banking tasks faster, easy, anytime, and anywhere in India and abroad. It allows a customer to perform their daily banking transaction in a simple and quick manner. It increases comfort and time saving transactions which can be made any time without requiring a physical visit to a bank branch. With the rapid growth of mobile subscribers banks have been looking for an alternative channel of banking services delivery through using mobile devices. In bivariate regression analysis, the study finds that there is a significant effect on the number of banking transactions through mobile on deposit accounts and credit accounts. The stepwise regression states that internet user per capita has a significant effect on mobile banking transaction. The analysis of t-test also finds that there is no significant difference in adoption of mobile banking transactions between the two groups of PSBs and Pvt. SBs. The research work also reports the fastest growth of mobile banking technology–enabled financial information services in the banking sector of India in terms of their volume and value of mobile banking transactions. The Pvt. SBs have contributed to the overall growth of mobile banking in the banking sector of India better than the PSBs. From the analysis the authors also find that using the internet has a significant role in expansion of mobile banking transactions than other parameters of telephone line, mobile connection, literacy rate, or logarithm of GDP (NNP). Both PSBs and Pvt. SBs have played their own role toward the expansion of mobile banking transactions.

As per the results from the analysis of t-test with financial inclusion parameters of APPB, average population per ATM, deposits as percentage of GDP, credit as percentage of GDP, deposits per capita, credit per capita, C-D ratio, and assets per office, this study examines that though there is a significant difference between PSBs and Pvt. SBs, both have played a tremendous role in financial inclusion. According to the DEA, this study has found that out of 20 selected banks, 4 banks are efficient and the remaining 16 banks are inefficient. To measure efficiency the authors have considered deposits and credit as output variables and the number of branches and assets as input variables. With the quartile value of technical efficiency, this study further classified inefficient banks into groups as most inefficient, below average, above average, and marginally inefficient. Though according to the CCR model only four banks are efficient, under the BCC model ten banks are efficient. Also according to the average efficiency scores, the PSB group is more efficient than Pvt. SB group.

6.2   CONTRIBUTION OF THE STUDY

The study draws an overall picture of various factors in the Indian context which affect financial inclusion status. The study further tests the disparity of financial inclusion status between regions and states in India. The study also checks whether the number of bank branches and ATMs significantly affect financial inclusion and which factors influence the decision maker to take a decision for opening of a new branch. Due to recent improvement of technology in banking services and high cost in opening of brick-and-mortar branches, the study also checks the factors that affect mobile banking transaction and also concentrates on the comparative study between the PSBs and Pvt. SBs in implementing mobile banking. The study concluded with a comparative study of PSBs and Pvt. SBs with various financial inclusion parameters and measures the performance of the selected banks. The study is mainly based on secondary data for the period from

2001–2002 to 2015–2016 and data have been collected from various reliable sources.

In India, very little research has been done by taking into consideration the effect of a large number of factors on financial inclusion in the Indian context. The study analyzes the possible relationship between financial inclusions and various geographic, demographic, industrial growth, employment status, education level, and other factors considered in the study. To consider the macro-level data the study selected 20 largest banks which hold a 70.83 percent market share among 91 SCBs.

The study applies different modern econometric and statistical tools and techniques which may provide insight into the existing literature about the role of PSBs and Pvt. SBs in financial inclusion in India. It also extends the literature by examining the relationship between financial inclusion and factors which impact it.

The study analyzes the possible relationship and impact of the various factors on financial inclusion in the Indian context. To analyze the factors the study uses PCA. The present study uses 14 factors to measure determinants of financial inclusion while in prior studies only a few limited factors have been considered.

Findings of the study help banks and other financial institutions to make their business plan and achieve the financial inclusion target. This study will help them for selection of location of new bank branches or ATMs or expansion of business through mobile banking transaction. When a bank is not in a position to open brick-and-mortar branches in rural areas, banking services can be extended with mobile banking. "Increasing internet penetration and mobile subscribers have created a huge opportunity for banking institutions" (Boro, 2015). In this regard the government should extend their support to connect all the villages with internet facilities. "Most developed and developing countries are associated with mobile-based branchless banking" (Diniz et al., 2012). Mobile banking has been implemented to expand its banking coverage in unreached areas or excluded people. Besides the finding of factors of financial inclusion, branch expansion, and technology-based mobile banking transaction, the study also measures the performance of the selected banks. Though the major banks are inefficient under the DEA model, most of them are inefficient due to the scale size of the business rather than managerial inefficiency. With the results of DEA the study concludes that the banks have excessive scope to expand their business with the same resources or by taking full advantage of IRS.

The study also found that the growth rate of Pvt. SBs is much higher than that of PSBs in respect of various financial inclusion dimensions. Thus, entrance of Pvt. SBs in the banking industry forced greater competition on PSBs. Due to the longer presence and greater competition, the result shows that average efficiency of PSBs is higher than that of Pvt. SBs on the basis of the selected output and input variables considered in the study.

Chauvet and Jacolin (2017) in their investigation found that financial inclusion has a positive impact on the growth of firms. So ultimately while bank will take initiatives in financial inclusion, this will return them back with positive growth. This study will also help the regulators to take various initiatives of financial inclusion and direct the banks to act accordingly. This study will help to design policies in India to foster financial inclusion. Hence, this study is worth performing on emerging economies like India. Initiatives from the regulators, banks, and governments will help the unreached or non-accessible of formal financial services which ultimately help in the economic growth of our country.

6.3   POLICY RECOMMENDATION

"Financial inclusion plays an important role in the economic growth of the country" (Sharma, 2016). A large percentage of population have not been availing the formal financial services or excluded due to non-availability of banking services. So there is ample scope by the financial institutions and regulators to give an opportunity to access formal financial services to them, which will ultimately affect the economic growth of the country. During the last two decades, the authors have seen many initiatives which have been taken by regulators as well as by the financial institutions. Still, more initiatives should be required from both ends of the regulator as well as from various informal financial institutions.

- Achieving universal-level financial inclusion is the goal of government. Improvement of infrastructure like road, transport, electricity, the internet, sanitation, school, and colleges is much more important today. But at this juncture with available infrastructure, opening an account for each will pressurize the banks. In this situation, the government and banks can concentrate on opening one account to each household, which is more appropriate unless the family requires a number of accounts.

- Different school boards can insist on opening bank accounts to the children at the school level itself for every school child to make them habitual and understand the importance of bank account.
- As per the previous literature and present study, the authors find that technology can play a major role in reducing cost of financial services. Technology-driven products must be simple and user-friendly. Therefore, banks should adopt more advanced technology for banking service delivery.
- ATMs are one of the most effective instruments and cost-effective to reach rural poor. Thus, new biometric ATMs have to be reputable to assist the customers who are incapable of memorizing PIN.
- The acceptance level of mobile banking is found to be moderate among the various groups of customers in the public and Pvt. SBs. As mobile users are enormously increasing, mobile banking is the best method which has highest hidden potential to extend financial inclusion. Banks have to put extra efforts in popularizing mobile banking services among their customers. Mobile banking solutions may be explored in association with technological experts.
- As India is the country of villages, instead of opening branches which are economically not viable, more attention should be given to alternative methods like deployment of BCs, opening of ultra-small branches, mobile banking, and banking through mobile vans and kiosks depending on the requirement.
- More involvement of private sector is required to widen the scope of inclusion of an excluded section of people. To reduce the cost of services, other organizations may share the infrastructure among themselves with banks.
- Each bank should have a financial inclusion department that will try to reach the financial inclusion goal. The staff of the department will only take care of it instead of looking into daily banking service to customers. The managing director of each bank will look personally into the progress of this department.
- More interior villages in the far-flung areas should be identified under the FIP to bring effective financial inclusion. The FIP's focus is on the villages with households of more than 1000 or 2000; however, many villages in NER including Assam are of small size with even 50–100 households. So, instead of village size, RBI should take a cluster of village approach. Hence, one relook at FIP approach is

recommended to attach due importance to villages of small sizes. Pvt. SBs should be directed to enlarge this initiative.

- In order to bring the population of downtrodden sections into the fold of banking network, government should sponsor publicity campaigns through media, village panchayats, local stage shows, and so on. Special care needs to be taken for unbanked areas and rural illiterates not having any bank account or other formal financial account.

- Banking officials should encourage poor households for their development and bring them under the various government financial inclusion policies. The government and other regulatory agencies have to be engaged in substantial attempts in financing by the banks.

- Banks may appoint employees as field officers from the same state due to language barrier. The appointed field officer will personally visit the household in rural and semi-urban areas for opening bank accounts or for credit needs. In this way, banks should employ or designate a special force only to reach unreached areas.

- Since customer service is another issue that needs closer attention, staff shortage or overburdens on existing staff of banks and other institutions are a serious challenge to financial inclusion efforts. Regulators may take appropriate initiatives so that banking staff may give effort in achieving the target of financial inclusion rather than involving them only in daily routine banking transactions. Proper training also needs to be provided to the banking and other formal financial institutions' employees to meet the FIP targets.

- Proper publicity is also required in rural and semi-urban areas so that people are not attracted to the various Ponzi schemes located all over the country. The regulatory agencies should ensure that an effective regulatory mechanism is in operation to monitor the chit fund entities and private bankers in the state.

- Regulators have to plan to issue additional licenses for private banks with conditions that will force the players to have rural branches.

- The bank must create an awareness program for the people regarding banking services through advertisement and financial inclusion campaigns to encourage excluded people from the banking network. Through campaigning bank officials also can have direct contact with the excluded and underprivileged sections of the population and understand their requirements. This will not only help the government to achieve the target of financial inclusion, their long-term survival and sustenance also depend on easy access to formal financial services and products.

- To reach banking services unbanked areas should offer zero balance instead of any minimum balance limit, with no maintenance charges in order to turn un-bankable into bankable.
- It may not be possible by the government or regulators to provide one bank branch in each village or provide banking services through bank branch mode only. In these circumstances, regulators and financial institutions may expand their banking coverage through various technology-based products and services. Further, the confidence level of the customers should be enhanced by providing secure technology–based products and services. To overcome the situation banks should employ latest technology with timely up-gradation to stop fraudulent transactions.
- From time to time the government is implementing various plans and schemes for financial inclusion, social inclusion, and economic growth of the country. An appropriate check system should be kept at various levels for proper implementation and growth of the plans.
- Appropriate measures are needed to mitigate the gap in access to various financial services in real sense and financial inclusion initiatives should not remain only in paperwork but the actual outcome has to be revealed in a transparent manner and external agency should be engaged to examine the effectiveness of financial inclusion drive initiated by several banks.
- Bank account opening form should be simplified with a single page only by directly linking the database of AADHAR and PAN.
- The banks should offer all applications and forms in the regional language of the customers. Banks should provide customers access or facility of using regional language in making banking transactions.

The present study will help the financial providers and regulators to take decisions on the implementation of various financial inclusion promotion schemes from both the demand side and the supply side. Banks have a social responsibility in carrying out financial inclusion, so all bank groups should participate in achieving the target of financial inclusion.

6.4   Conclusion

In this study, an attempt has been made to check the financial inclusion status in India. The present study extensively is an evidence for the relationship between selected variables and financial inclusion in the Indian context. From the results of PCA and multiple regression analysis, it concludes that variables, mainly APPB with off-site ATMs, population per thousand sq. km., literacy rate, number of factories, employment, and so on, significantly influence the financial inclusion status in India. It has been observed that the GDP rate does not have any effect upon deposit accounts and credit accounts significantly. From the results of ANOVA, the study concludes that there is a disparity in financial inclusion across regions and states.

Access to finance is essential not only for maintaining and improving social and economic status of a person but also for meeting all needs. Without having an account people do not save for future requirements, or avoid high interest payments. Without the presence of bank branches, there can be no banking access for people. Branches are the primary interface between public and formal deposit and credit accounts. The easiest way to ensure better financial inclusion is to open more and more branches and remove various obstacles in accessing financial services from banks by very poor people. The larger the presence of bank branches, the greater is the access.

Banks will have to become more customer-centric; offering a wide range of financial products through mobile banking would bring financial inclusion. It will reduce their cost and enhance their outreach and may prove to be an effective tool for greater financial inclusion in rural areas as it has happened in other countries like Kenya. The government should work toward encouraging mobile banking and look at every technology option to enable financial empowerment of each citizen. Mobile technology could be leveraged in various ways as India is one of the largest mobile phone users with over 1000 million users in the world (data released by TRAI in May 2017). The PSBs and Pvt. SBs should encourage all customers to use mobile banking. All bank groups should take steps to implement mobile banking to low-income groups of customers and unbanked centers.

In this study, as per the bivariate regression analysis it is found that APPB and off-site ATMs have significantly influenced the financial inclusion status. When the authors applied bivariate regression analysis with another variable of banking transaction through mobile, the study finds that the same also significantly influences financial inclusion in regard to expansion of banking business through mobile, while opening of brick-and-mortar branches in rural or other areas is too costly or non-manageable due to low customer base with small business value.

In the case of measuring factors of opening new branch, this study found that deposit to GDP, deposit per branch, credit to GDP, credit per branch, branch per 1000 sq. km., and APPB have a significant impact on expansion of branches in the ensuing year. On the basis of the results of stepwise regression, it also concludes that only internet users per capita significantly influence the ICT-based mobile banking transactions, rather than other factors considered in this study in the Indian contexts like fixed telephone lines per capita, mobile connection per capita, literacy rate and logarithm value of GDP (NNP). In this study, the authors find that PSBs hold a gigantic share, and as per DEA, the authors also find that these groups of banks have high efficiency toward their role in financial inclusion.

"This research can be used as a model by other researchers, financial regulators, policymakers and government to escalate financial inclusion policy" (Maity & Sahu, 2020). The study considers 20 banking companies, 10 banks taken from PSBs group and 10 banks taken from Pvt. SB group. But in reality, there are 21 Pvt. SBs and 20 PSBs (before recent mergers) and RRBs, LABs, cooperative banks, and so on.

Their presence in rural areas has a major role in financial inclusion. Other than banks there are also India Post and other institutions which offer financial services. In this study, the authors take into consideration banking inclusion as financial inclusion. During the selection process of banks, the authors have set the basis of quantum of total income and balance sheet size as of March 2015 as selection criteria. The selected 20 banks may differ in case the study changes the selection criteria or change the selection year. The authors also concentrate on only selected banks with secondary data. The study suffers from a dearth of published information on financial inclusion.

The study paves the way for further research to examine the role of RRBs, foreign banks, co-operative banks, insurance, post offices, MFIs, SHGs, BCs, and micro-insurance on financial inclusion. The study can be extended to region-wise development, state-wise development, population group-wise development, or across other developing countries in the world and the impact of financial inclusion on economic growth. Also by not using data on the exact locations of bank branches, variations within districts or regions may be misrepresented. So, further study may be conducted by considering other variables too. Despite these limitations, this study contributes to the current knowledge of formal financial services in India.

BIBLIOGRAPHY

BOOKS, JOURNALS, WORKING PAPERS ETC.

Boro, K. (2015). Prospects and challenges of technological innovation in banking industry of North East India. *Journal of Internet Banking & Commerce, 20*(3), 1–6.

Chauvet, L., & Jacolin, L. (2017). Financial inclusion, bank concentration and firm performance. *World Development, 97*(September), 1–13.

Diniz, E., Birochi, R., & Pozzebon, M. (2012). Triggers and barriers to financial inclusion: The use of ICT-based branchless banking in an Amazon county. *Electronic Commerce Research and Applications, 11*, 484–494.

Maity, S., & Sahu, T. N. (2020). Role of public sector banks towards financial inclusion during pre and post introduction of PMJDY: A study on efficiency review. *Rajagiri Management Journal, 14*(2), 95–105.

Sharma, D. (2016). Nexus between financial inclusion and economic growth. *Journal of Financial Economic Policy, 8*(1), 13–36.

BIBLIOGRAPHY

BOOKS, JOURNALS, WORKING PAPERS ETC.

Abor, J. Y., Amidu, M., & Issahaku, H. (2017). Mobile telephony, financial inclusion and inclusive growth. *Journal of African Business*, 1–24.

Agarwal, S., Amromin, G., Ben-David, I., Chomsisengphet, S., & Evanoff, D. D. (2015). Financial literacy and financial planning: Evidence from India. *Journal of Housing Economics, 27*, 4–21.

Agarwala, V., Sahu, T. N., & Maity, S. (2021). Efficiency of public sector banks in achieving the goal of PMJDY and PMMY. *International Journal of Economics and Business Research*. (Accepted for publication). https://doi.org/10.1504/IJEBR.2022.10038248

Aggarwal, R., Kunt, A. D., & Pería, M. S. M. (2011). Do remittances promote financial development? *Journal of Development Economics, 96*, 255–264.

Ahmed, S. M., & Ansari, M. I. (1998). Financial sector development and economic growth: The south-Asian experience. *Journal of Asian Economics, 9*(3), 503–517.

Ajide, K. B. (2017). Determinants of financial inclusion in sub-Saharan Africa countries: Does institutional infrastructure matter? *CBN Journal of Applied Statistics, 8*(2), 69–89.

Alama, L., & Ausina, E. T. (2012). Bank branch geographic location patterns in Spain: Some implications for financial exclusion. *Growth and Change, 43*(3), 505–543.

Alexandre, C., Mas, I., & Radcliffe, D. (2011). Regulating new banking models to bring financial services to all. *Challenge, 54*(3), 116–134.

Amore, M., Schneider, C., & Zaldokas, A. (2013). Credit supply and corporate innovation. *Journal of Financial Economics, 109*(3), 835–855.

Ang, J. B. (2010). Finance and inequality: The case of India. *Southern Economic Journal, 76*(3), 738–761.

Annan, K. (2003). *Former UN secretary.* Retrieved from: www.wikipedia.com. Accessed 10 Apr 2016.

Ansong, D., Chowa, G., & Adjabeng, B. K. (2015). Spatial analysis of the distribution and determinants of bank branch presence in Ghana. *International Journal of Bank Marketing, 33*(3), 201–222.

Anzoategui, D., Kunt, A. D., & Peria, M. S. M. (2014). Remittances and financial inclusion: Evidence from El Salvador. *World Development, 54,* 338–349.

Appleyard, L. (2011). Community development finance institutions (CDFIs): Geographies of financial inclusion in the US and UK. *Geoforum, 42,* 250–258.

Arora, R. U. (2012). Financial inclusion and human capital in developing Asia: The Australian connection. *Third World Quarterly, 33*(1), 179–199.

Arputhamani, J. A., & Prasannakumari, K. (2011). Financial inclusion through micro finance: The way to rural development, a case study of Rajapalayan block in Virudhunagar district. *KKIMRC International Journal of Research in Finance and Accounting, 1*(1), 94–115.

Asaad, C. T. (2015). Financial literacy and financial behavior: Assessing knowledge and confidence. *Financial Services Review, 24,* 101–117.

Aysan, A. F., Dolgun, M. H., & Turhan, M. I. (2013). Assessment of the participation banks and their role in financial inclusion in Turkey. *Emerging Markets Finance & Trade, 49*(Supplement 5), 99–111.

Banerjee, S., & Francis, G. (2014). Financial inclusion and social development. *International Journal of Scientific Research and Management,* 13–18.

Banker, R. D., Charnes, A., & Cooper, W. W. (1984). Some models for estimating technical and scale inefficiencies in DEA. *Management Science, 30*(9), 1078–1092.

Bansal, S. (2014). Perspective of technology in achieving financial inclusion in rural India. *Procedia Economics and Finance, 11,* 472–480.

Barot, P. (2017). Financial inclusion in India. *Imperial Journal of Interdisciplinary Research (IJIR), 3*(4), 1098–1104.

Basak, A. (2015). The role of urban cooperative banks and non-agricultural cooperative credit societies in financial inclusion: A study in Howrah District, West Bengal. *The IUP Journal of Management Research, XIV*(3), 81–98.

Bayero, M. A. (2015). Effects of cashless economy policy on financial inclusion in Nigeria: An exploratory study. *Procedia – Social and Behavioral Sciences, 172,* 49–56.

Beck, T., Kunt, A. D., & Peria, M. S. M. (2007). Reaching out: Access to and use of banking services across countries. *Journal of Financial Economics, 85,* 234–266.

Belas, J., Koraus, M., & Gabcova, L. (2015). Electronic banking, its use and safety. Are three differences in the access of Bank customers by gender, education and age? *International Journal of Entrepreneurial Knowledge, 3*(2), 16–28.

Berger, A. N., & Deyoung, R. (2006). Technological progress and the geographic expansion of the banking industry. *Journal of Money, Credit, and Banking, 38*(6), 1485–1513.

Berger, A. N., & Humphrey, D. B. (1992). Measurement and efficiency issues in commercial banking. In Z. Griliches (Ed.), *Output measurement in services sector* (pp. 245–279). University of Chicago Press.

Berger, A. N., Leusner, J. H., & Mingo, J. J. (1997). The efficiency of bank branches. *Journal of Monetary Economics, 40*, 141–162.

Bhanot, D., Bapat, V., & Bera, S. (2012). Studying financial inclusion in North-East India. *International Journal of Bank Marketing, 30*(6), 465–484.

Bhat, A. L., & Bhat, B. J. (2013). Automated teller machines (ATMs): The changing face of banking in India. *The IUP Journal of Bank Management, XII*(4), 16–28.

Bhattacharyya, A., Lovell, C. A. K., & Sahay, P. (1997). The impact of liberalization on the productive efficiency of Indian commercial banks. *European Journal of Operational Research, 98*, 332–345.

Bihari, S. C. (2011). Growth through financial inclusion in India. *Journal of International Business Ethics, 4*(1), 28–41.

Biles, J. J. (2004). Globalization of banking and local access to financial resources: A case study from southeastern Mexico. *The Industrial Geographer, 2*(2), 159–173.

Billimoria, J., Penner, J., & Knoote, F. (2013). Developing the next generation of economic citizens: Financial inclusion and education for children and youth. *Enterprise Development and Microfinance, 24*(3), 204–217.

Birochi, R., & Pozzebon, M. (2016). Improving financial inclusion: Towards a critical financial education framework. *Sao Paulo, 56*(3), 266–287.

Boro, K. (2015). Prospects and challenges of technological innovation in banking industry of North East India. *Journal of Internet Banking & Commerce, 20*(3), 1–6.

Boufounou, P. V. (1995). Evaluating bank branch location and performance: A case study. *European Journal of Operational Research, 87*, 389–402.

Bruntha, P., & Indirapriyadharshini, B. (2015). Enquiry into financial inclusion with special reference to street hawkers of Pollachi, Tamil Nadu. *The IUP Journal of Marketing Management, XIV*(4), 56–68.

Burgess, R., & Pande, R. (2005). Do rural banks matter? Evidence from the Indian social banking experiment. *American Economic Review, 95*(3), 780–795.

Burgess, R., Wong, G., & Pande, R. (2005). Banking for the poor: Evidence from India. *Journal of the European Economic Association, 3*(2–3), 268–278.

Burgstaller, J. (2013). Bank office outreach, structure and performance in regional banking markets. *Regional Studies, 47*(7), 1131–1155.

Calcagnini, G., De, B. R., & Hester, D. D. (1999, October 29–30). *Determinants of bank branch expansion in Italy.* SIDE (Italian Economic Association), 40th Meeting.

Carbo, S., Edward, P. M. G., & Molyneux, P. (2005). *Financial exclusion.* Palgrave Macmillan.

Caskey, P. J. (2000). *Lower income Americans, higher cost financial services.* Retrieved from: http://www.filene.org. Accessed 30 May 2013.

Chakraborty, A., & Barman, S. R. (2013). Financial inclusion in Tripura: Challenges and opportunities. *Journal of Commerce & Management Thought, IV*(4), 870–879.

Chakraborty, K. C. (2012). *Financial inclusion – Issues in measurement and analysis.* Addressed at the BIS-BNM Workshop on Financial Inclusion Indicators at Kuala Lumpur on November 5.

Chakravarty, S. R., & Pal, R. (2013). Financial inclusion in India: An axiomatic approach. *Journal of Policy Modeling, 35*, 813–837.

Charnes, A., Cooper, W. W., & Rhodes, E. (1978). Measuring the efficiency of decision making units. *European Journal of Operational Research, 2*(6), 429–444.

Chattopadhyay, S. K. (2011). *Financial inclusion in India: A case study of West Bengal* (RBI Working Paper Series: 8/2011). Retrieved from: http://www.rbi.org.in/scripts/PublicationsView.aspx?id=13517. Accessed 10 June 2016.

Chauhan, S. (2015). Acceptance of mobile money by poor citizens of India: Integrating trust into the technology acceptance model. *Info., Emerald Group Publishing Limited, 17*(3), 58–68.

Chauvet, L., & Jacolin, L. (2017). Financial inclusion, bank concentration and firm performance. *World Development, 97*(September), 1–13.

Chava, S., Oetti, A., Subramanian, A., & Subramanian, K. (2013). Banking deregulation and innovation. *Journal of Financial Economics, 109*(3), 759–774.

Chen, Z., & Jin, M. (2017). Financial inclusion in China: Use of credit. *Journal of Family and Economic Issues, 38*(4), 528–540.

Chibango, C. (2014). Mobile money revolution: An opportunity for financial inclusion in Africa. *The International Journal of Humanities & Social Studies, 2*(2), 59–67.

Chibba, M. (2009). Financial inclusion, poverty reduction and the millennium development goals. *European Journal of Development Research, 21*(2), 213–230.

Chithra, N., & Selvam, M. (2013). *Determinants of financial inclusion: An empirical study on the inter-state variations in India.* Retrieved from: http://www.ssrn.com/abstract=2296096. Accessed 28 Apr 2018.

Claessens, S. (2006). A review of the issues and public policy objectives. *The World Bank Research Observer, 21*(2), 207–240.

Cnaan, R. A., Moodithaya, M. S., & Handy, F. (2012). Financial inclusion: Lessons from rural South India. *Jnl Soc. Pol., 41*(1), 183–205.

Collard, S. (2007). Toward financial inclusion in the UK: Progress and challenges. *Public Money & Management, 27*(1), 13–20.

CYFI. (2012). *Children and youth as economic citizens: Review of research on financial capability, financial inclusion and financial education.* Research working group report, Amsterdam: CYFI. Retrieved from: http://childfinanceinternational.org/index.php?option=com_mtree&task=att_download&link_id=374&cf_id=200. Accessed 19 Aug 2013.

Dangi, N., & Kumar, P. (2013). Current situation of financial inclusion in India and its future visions. *International Journal of Management and Social Sciences Research (IJMSSR), 2*(8), 155–166.

Dangi, V. (2012). Financial inclusion: A saga of Indian financial system. *Asia-Pacific Journal of Management Research and Innovation, 8*(2), 111–125.

Das, T., & Guha, P. (2015). A study on the differences in the banking parameters between pre- and post-financial inclusion periods: Some evidence for India. *The IUP Journal of Bank Management, XIV*(1), 39–56.

Dev, S. M. (2006). Financial inclusion: Issues and challenges. *Economic and Political Weekly, 41*(41), 4310–4313.

Devlin, J. F. (2005). A detailed study of financial exclusion in the UK. *Journal of Consumer Policy, 28*, 75–108.

Devlin, J. F. (2009). An analysis of influences on total financial exclusion. *The Service Industries Journal, 29*(8), 1021–1036.

Dhar, S. (2012). Banking reforms for financial inclusion: Performance of selected Indian banks. *Amity Management Review, 2*(2), 34–39.

Diniz, E., Birochi, R., & Pozzebon, M. (2012). Triggers and barriers to financial inclusion: The use of ICT-based branchless banking in an Amazon county. *Electronic Commerce Research and Applications, 11*, 484–494.

Drake, L., & Howcroft, B. (1994). Relative efficiency in the branch network of a UK bank: An empirical study. *Omega, 22*(1), 83–90.

Ergungor, O. E. (2010). Bank branch presence and access to credit in low- to moderate-income neighborhoods. *Journal of Money, Credit and Banking, 42*(7), 1321–1349.

Evanoff, D. D. (1988). Branch banking and service accessibility. *Journal of Money, Credit, and Banking, 20*(2), 191–202.

Evans, D. S., & Pirchio, A. (2014). An empirical examination of why mobile money schemes ignite in some developing countries but flounder in most. *Review of Network Economics, 13*(4), 397–451.

Federal Reserve Board. (2002). *Survey of consumer finances.* Retrieved from: http://www.federalreserve.gov/pubs/oss/oss2/scfindex.html. Accessed 28 April 2018.

Figart, D. M. (2013). Institutionalist policies for financial inclusion. *Journal of Economic Issues, XLVII*(4), 873–893.

Fisher, P. J. (2010). Black-white differences in saving behaviors. *Financial Services Review, 19*, 1–16.

Fungacova, Z., & Weill, L. (2015). Understanding financial inclusion in China. *China Economic Review, 34*, 196–206.

Gautam, T., & Garg, K. (2014). Union Bank of India: Initiatives towards IT-enabled financial inclusion. *South Asian Journal of Business and Management Cases, 3*(2), 149–156.

Ghosh, S. (2012). Determinants of banking outreach: An empirical assessment of Indian states. *The Journal of Developing Areas, 46*(2), 269–295.

Ghosh, S., & Sahu, T. N. (2021). Financial inclusion and economic status of the states of India: An empirical evidence. *Economic Notes*. https://doi.org/10.1111/ecno.12182

Giannetti, C., & Jentzsch, N. (2013). Credit reporting, financial intermediation and identification systems: International evidence. *Journal of International Money and Finance, 33*, 60–80.

Gitaharie, B. Y., Soelistianingsih, L., & Djutaharta, T. (2018). Financial inclusion: Household access to credit in Indonesia. In L. Gani, B. Y. Gitaharie, Z. A. Husodo, & A. Kuncoro (Eds.), *Competition and cooperation in economics and business*. Taylor & Francis Group.

Giuliano, P., & Ruiz-Arranz, M. (2009). Remittances, financial development, and growth. *Journal of Development Economics, 90*, 144–152.

Golany, B., & Roll, Y. (1989). An application procedure for DEA. *Omega, 17*(3), 237–250.

Goodwin, D., Adelman, L., Middleton, S., & Ashworth, K. (1999). *Debt, money management and access to financial services: Evidence from the 1999 PSE survey of Britain* (1999 PSE Survey Working Paper 8). Centre for Research in Social Policy, Loughborough University.

Government of India. (2008, January). *Report of the committee on financial inclusion* (pp. 20). Economic Advisory Council to the Prime Minister, under the Chairmanship of C. Rangarajan.

Goyal, C. (2008). Financial inclusion in the northeastern region of India with special reference to Assam. *The ICFAI Journal of Applied Finance, 14*(12), 54–64.

Gupta, N. (2014). Financial inclusion in India: The way forward. *Pezzottaite Journals, 3*(3), 1255–1264.

Gupta, P., & Singh, B. (2013). Role of literacy level in financial inclusion in India: Empirical evidence. *Journal of Economics, Business and Management, 1*(3), 272–276.

Gupte, R., Venkataramani, B., & Gupta, D. (2012). Computation of financial inclusion index for India. *Procedia – Social and Behavioral Sciences, 37*, 133–149.

Gwalani, H., & Parkhi, S. (2014). Financial inclusion – Building a success model in the Indian context. *Procedia – Social and Behavioral Sciences, 133,* 372–378.

Harimaya, K., & Kondo, K. (2012). Determinants of branch expansion by Japanese regional banks. *The IUP Journal of Bank Management, XI*(2), 7–25.

Hinson, R. E. (2011). Banking the poor: The role of mobiles. *Journal of Financial Services Marketing, 15*(4), 320–333.

Hirtle, B. (2007). The impact of network size on bank branch performance. *Journal of Banking & Finance, 31,* 3782–3805.

Hogarth, J. M., Anguelov, C. E., & Lee, J. (2003). Why households don't have checking accounts. *Economic Development Quarterly, 17*(1), 75–94.

Honohan, P. (2008). Cross-country variation in household access to financial services. *Journal of Banking & Finance, 32,* 2493–2500.

Imboden, K. (2005). Building inclusive financial sectors: The road to growth and poverty reduction. *Journal of International Affairs, 58*(2), 65–86.

Inoue, T., & Hamori, S. (2016). Financial access and economic growth: Evidence from sub-Saharan Africa. *Emerging Markets Finance & Trade, 52,* 743–753.

Iqbal, B. A., & Sami, S. (2017). Role of banks in financial inclusion in India. *Contaduría y Administración, 62,* 644–656.

Jain, S. (2015). A study of banking sector's initiatives towards financial inclusion in India. *Journal of Commerce & Management Thought, 6*(1), 55–77.

Jalaludeen, N. (2014). Is bank branch expansion driven by demand? – Some evidence from Kerala. *The IUP Journal of Bank Management, XIII*(1), 7–18.

Jones, J. H. M., Williams, M., Nilsson, E., & Thorat, Y. (2007). Training to address attitudes behaviour of rural bank managers in Madhya Pradesh, India: A programme to facilitate financial inclusion. *Journal of International Development, 19,* 841–851.

Jones, P. A. (2008). From tackling poverty to achieving financial inclusion – The changing role of British credit unions in low income communities. *The Journal of Socio-Economics, 37,* 2141–2154.

Joshi, N. C. (1998). Restructuring credit system for rural development. *Kurukshetra,* 36–38.

Joshi, V. (2014, October–December). Financial inclusion: Urban-poor in India. *SCMS Journal of Indian Management,* 29–37.

Kainth, G. S. (2013). Developing an index of financial inclusion. *Anvesha, 6*(2), 1–10.

Kamboj, S. (2014). Financial inclusion and growth of Indian economy: An empirical analysis. *The International Journal of Business & Management, 2*(9), 175–179.

Kapoor, A. (2014). Financial inclusion and the future of the Indian economy. *Futures, 56,* 35–42.

Kar, J., & Dash, P. K. (2009). Formal financial services for rural small savers: A case study of Orissa, India. *Annals of the University of Petroşani, Economics, 9*(2), 73–82.

Kasekende, L. (2014). What role does financial inclusion play in the policy agenda for inclusive growth in sub-Saharan Africa? *Development, 57*(3–4), 481–487.

Kaur, P., & Abrol, V. (2018). Measuring financial inclusion in Jammu & Kashmir state: An empirical study. *IOSR Journal of Business and Management, 20*(1), 37–44.

Kelkar, V. (2009). Financial inclusion for inclusive growth. *ASCI Journal of Management, 39*(1), 55–68.

Kempson, E., Atkinson, A., & Pilley, O. (2004). *Policy level response to financial exclusion in developed economies: Lessons for developing countries.* Report of Personal Finance Research Centre, University of Bristol.

Khan, H. R. (2011). *Financial inclusion & financial stability – Are they two sides of the same coin?* Addressed at BANCON 2011, Chennai on November 4, Organized by Indian Bankers Association and Indian Overseas Bank.

Kim, J. H. (2016). A study on the effect of financial inclusion on the relationship between income inequality and economic growth. *Emerging Markets Finance & Trade, 52*, 498–512.

King, B. (2014). *Breaking banks: The innovators, rogues, and strategists rebooting banking.* John Wiley & Sons.

King, R., & Levine, R. (1993). Finance and growth: Schumpeter might be right. *Quarterly Journal of Economics, 108*(3), 717–738.

Klapper, L. (2006). The role of factoring for financing small and medium enterprises. *Journal of Banking & Finance, 30*(11), 3111–3130.

Kodan, A. S., & Chhikara, K. S. (2011). Status of financial inclusion in Haryana: An evidence of commercial banks. *Management and Labour Studies, 36*(3), 247–267.

Kodan, A. S., Garg, N. K., & Kaidan, S. (2011). Financial inclusion: Status, issues, challenges and policy in northeastern region. *The IUP Journal of Financial Economics, IX*(2), 27–40.

Koker, L. D., & Jentzsch, N. (2013). Financial inclusion and financial integrity: Aligned incentives? *World Development, 44*, 267–280.

Koku, P. S. (2009). Doing well by doing good – Marketing strategy to help the poor: The case of commercial banks in Ghana. *Journal of Financial Services Marketing, 14*(2), 135–151.

Koku, P. S. (2015). Financial exclusion of the poor: A literature review. *International Journal of Bank Marketing, 33*(5), 654–668.

Kostov, P., Arun, T., & Annim, S. (2014). Banking the unbanked: The Mzansi intervention in South Africa. *Indian Growth and Development Review, 7*(2), 118–141.

Kozhikode, R. K., & Li, J. (2012). Political pluralism, public policies, and organizational choices: Banking branch expansion in India, 1948–2003. *Academy of Management Journal, 55*(2), 339–359.

Kulkarni, M. M., & Warke, P. (2015). The framework for assessment of ICT based financial inclusion management by nationalized banks with special reference to Marathwada region. *Journal of Commerce & Management Thought, 6*(4), 684–692.

Kumar, B., & Mohanty, B. (2011). Financial inclusion and inclusive development in SAARC countries with special reference to India. *Vilakshan, XIMB Journal of Management,* (September), 13–22.

Kumar, N. (2012a). An empirical analysis of financial inclusion across population groups in India. *The IUP Journal of Bank Management, XI*(1), 97–111.

Kumar, N. (2012b). *Financial inclusion and its determinants: Evidence from state level empirical analysis in India* (pp. 1–23). Retrieved from: https://www.researchgate.net/file.PostFileLoader.html?id...assetKey. Accessed 20 July 2016.

Kumar, N. (2013). Financial inclusion and its determinants: Evidence from India. *Journal of Financial Economic Policy, 5*(1), 4–19.

Kumar, S., & Gulati, R. (2008). An examination of technical, pure technical, and scale efficiencies in Indian public sector banks using data envelopment analysis. *Eurasian Journal of Business and Economics, 1*(2), 33–69.

Kundu, D. (2015). Addressing the demand side factors of financial inclusion. *Journal of Commerce & Management Thought, 6*(3), 397–417.

Kunt, A. D. (2014). Presidential address: Financial inclusion. *Atlantic Economic Journal, 42,* 349–356.

Kunt, A. D., Cordova, E. L., Pería, M. S. M., & Woodruff, C. (2011). Remittances and banking sector breadth and depth: Evidence from Mexico. *Journal of Development Economics, 95,* 229–241.

Kunt, A. D., & Klapper, L. (2012a, June). *Financial inclusion in Africa an overview* (Policy Research Working Paper, 6088, pp. 1–18). The World Bank Development Research Group Finance and Private Sector Development Team.

Kunt, A. D., & Klapper, L. (2012b, April). *Measuring financial inclusion* (Policy Research Working Paper, 6025). World Bank.

Kunt, A. D., & Klapper, L. (2013). Measuring financial inclusion: Explaining variation in use of financial services across and within countries. In *Brookings papers on economic activity* (pp. 279–321). Spring.

Kuri, P. K., & Laha, A. (2011). Determinants of financial inclusion: A study of some selected districts of West Bengal, India. *Indian Journal of Finance, 5,* 29–36.

Laeven, L., Levine, R., & Michalopoulos, S. (2015). Financial innovation and endogenous growth. *Journal of Financial Intermediation, 24,* 1–24.

Lanzillotti, R. F., & Saving, T. R. (1969). State branching restrictions and the availability of branching services: Comment. *Journal of Money, Credit and Banking, 1*(4), 778–788.

Leeladhar V. (2005). *Taking banking services to the common man – Financial inclusion.* Commemorative Lecture at the Fedbank Hormis Memorial Foundation at Ernakulam on December 2.

Lokhande, M. A. (2011). Financial inclusion: Options for micro, small and medium enterprises. *Synergy, IX*(I I), 39–50.

Lozano-Vivas, A., Pastor, J. T., & Pastor, J. M. (2002). An efficiency comparison of European banking systems operating under different environmental conditions. *Journal of Productivity Analysis, 18*, 59–77.

Lyons, A. C., & Scherpf, E. (2004). Moving from unbanked to banked: Evidence from the money smart program. *Financial Services Review, 13*, 215–231.

Machogu, A. M., & Okiko, L. (2015). E-banking complexities and the perpetual effect on customer satisfaction in Rwandan commercial banking industry: Gender as a moderating factor. *Journal of Internet Banking & Commerce, 20*(3), 1–8.

Mahadeva, M. (2008). Financial growth in India: Whither financial inclusion? *Margin—The Journal of Applied Economic Research, 2*(2), 177–197.

Mahadeva, M. (2009). Understanding financial abandoning from a micro perspective: Policy responses to promote inclusion in India. *Savings and Development, 33*(4), 405–430.

Mahajan, V., & Ramola, B. G. (1996). Financial services for the rural poor and women in India: Access and sustainability. *Journal of International Development, 8*(2), 211–224.

Maity, S. (2015). Financial inclusion in India: A study. In Kaushik Kundu (Ed.). Haldia Institute of Technology, School of Management and Social Science, published by *Partha Pratim Datta*, Purba Midnapore (pp. 292–304).

Maity, S. (2016a). Role of schedule commercial banks in financial inclusion: Progress and trends in India. In Nandi, J. K. & Sahu, T. N. (Eds.). Department of Commerce, Ghatal Rabindra Satabarsiki Mahavidyalaya, published by *Perfect Solution*, Kolkata (pp. 290–308).

Maity, S. (2016b). Payment bank license to India Post and its role in financial inclusion – An analysis. In Ghosh, S. & Sahu, T. N. (Eds.). Department of Commerce with Farm Management, Vidyasagar University, published by *Perfect Solution*, Kolkata (pp. 358–370).

Maity, S. (2019). Financial inclusion status in north eastern region: An evidence of commercial banks. *International Journal of Research in applied Management, Science and Technology, 4*(3), 1–11.

Maity, S. (2020). Are private sector banks really more efficient than public sector banks? – A comparative analysis using DEA. *NMIMS Management Review, 38*(2), 82–92.

Maity, S., & Ganguly, D. (2019a). SWOT analysis of India post and India post payments Bank and their role in financial inclusion. *The Management Accountant, 54*(1), 68–72.

Maity, S., & Ganguly, D. (2019b). Is demonetization really impact efficiency of banking sector – An empirical study of banks in India. *Asian Journal of Multidimensional Research, 8*(3), 315–327.

Maity, S., & Sahu, T. N. (2017). Pre-merger performance measures of state bank of India and its associate banks using data envelopment analysis. *Business Spectrum, VII*(2), 16–26.

Maity, S., & Sahu, T. N. (2018a). Bank branch expansion and financial inclusion: Evidence from selected commercial banks in India. *Al-Barkaat Journal of Finance & Management, 10*(1), 48–65.

Maity, S., & Sahu, T. N. (2018b). Role of public and private sector banks in financial inclusion in India – An empirical investigation using DEA. *SCMS Journal of Indian Management, 15*(4), 62–73.

Maity, S., & Sahu, T. N. (2019a). A study on regional disparity of Bank performance towards financial inclusion. *Management Today (International Journal of Business Studies), 9*(1), 24–31.

Maity, S., & Sahu, T. N. (2019b). Is the efficiency of banks degenerating due to the mounting of non-performing assets? An empirical investigation using DEA. *Malaysian Management Journal, 23*, 65–86.

Maity, S., & Sahu, T. N. (2020). Role of public sector banks towards financial inclusion during pre and post introduction of PMJDY: A study on efficiency review. *Rajagiri Management Journal, 14*(2), 95–105.

Maity, S., & Sahu, T. N. (2021a). How far the Indian banking sectors are efficient?: An empirical investigation. *Asian Journal of Economics and Banking.* https://doi.org/10.1108/AJEB-02-2021-0016

Maity, S., & Sahu, T. N. (2021b). Financial inclusion in north-eastern region: An investigation in the state of Assam. *VILAKSHAN – XIMB Journal of Management.* https://doi.org/10.1108/XJM-09-2020-0118

Maity, S., & Sahu, T. N. (2021). Mergers in banking industry: Some emerging issues. *International Journal of Services and Operations Management* (Accepted for publication). https://doi.org/10.1504/IJSOM.2021.10039421

Maity, S., Sahu, T. N., & Biswas, D. (2020). Assessing efficiency of private sectors banks in India: An empirical investigation using DEA. *International Journal of Financial Services Management, 10*(2), 138–155.

Malhotra, K. N., & David, F. B. (2007). *Marketing research – An applied approach* (3rd European ed.). Prentice Hall – Financial Times Publishing.

Malik, R., & Yadav, S. (2014). Financial inclusion in India: An appraisal. *International Journal of Research, 1*(4), 593–602.

Manji, A. (2010). Eliminating poverty? 'Financial Inclusion', access to land, and gender equality in international development. *The Modern Law Review, 73*(6), 985–1004.

Martínez-Campillo, A., Wijesiri, M., & Wanke, P. (2020). Evaluating the double bottom-line of social banking in an emerging country: How efficient are public banks in supporting priority and non-priority sectors in India? *Journal of Business Ethics, 162*(2), 399–420.

Mehta, I. (2011). Financial inclusion through technology for bottom of the pyramid masses with business correspondents of Mumbai area. *Aweshakar Research Journal*, 143–159.

Midgley, J. (2005). Financial inclusion, universal banking and post offices in Britain. *Area, 37*(3), 277–285.

Mishra, V., & Bisht, S. S. (2013). Mobile banking in a developing economy: A customer-centric model for policy formulation. *Telecommunications Policy, 37*, 503–514.

Mitchell, V. W. (1999). Consumer perceived risk: Conceptualizations and models. *European Journal of Marketing, 33*(1/2), 163–195.

Musau, S., Muathe, S., & Mwangi, L. (2018). Financial inclusion, GDP and credit risk of commercial banks in Kenya. *International Journal of Economics and Finance, 10*(3), 181–195.

Nice, K., & Irvine, A. (2010). Living on a low income and using banks to pay bills. *Journal of Poverty and Social Justice, 18*(1), 53–67.

Noorshella, C. N., Abdullah, A. M., & Nursalihah, A. R. (2015). Examining the key factors affecting e-service quality of small online apparel businesses in Malaysia. *SAGE Open, 5*(2). https://doi.org/10.1177/2158244015576550

Nyagilo, V. (2017). Financial inclusion in rural Kenya: An investigation of the role of financial technology as an instrument. *International Journal of Business Management & Finance, 1*(31), 534–553.

Ouma, S. A., Odongo, T. M., & Were, M. (2017). Mobile financial services and financial inclusion: Is it a boon for savings mobilization? *Review of Development Finance, 7*, 29–35.

Padmanbhan, & Sumam. (2014). Financial inclusion: A study of Union Bank. *Indian Research Journal, 1*(March), 1–7.

Panagariya, A. (2006). *Bank branch expansion and poverty reduction: A comment.* Retrieved from: www.columbia.edu/~ap2231/technical%20papers/Bank%20 Branch%20 Expansion% 20and%20Poverty.pdf. Accessed 22 Apr 2015.

Pandey, T., Krishna, N., Vickers, V., Menezes, A., & Raghavendra, M. (2010). Innovative payment solutions in agricultural value chain as a means for greater financial inclusion. *Agricultural Economics Research Review, 23*(Conference Number), 527–534.

Pastor, J. M., Perez, F., & Quesada, J. (1997). Efficiency analysis in banking firms: An international comparison. *European Journal of Operational Research, 98*(2), 395–407.

Pathania, A., Ali, A., & Rasool, G. (2016). Quality dimension imperative for innovative financial inclusion: A case study of select banks in J&K. *Amity Business Review, 16*(2), 115–125.

Paul, A. J. (2001). *Access to credit on a low income: A study into how people on low incomes in Liverpool access and use consumer credit.* Retrieved from: http://creditunionresearch.com. Accessed 13 Apr 2017.

Peachey, S., & Roe, A. (2004). *Access to finance: A study for the World Savings Banks Institute.* Oxford Policy Management.

Planning Commission. (2008). *Hundred Small Steps: Report of the Committee on Financial Sector Reforms.* SAGE India.

Prina, S. (2015). Banking the poor via savings accounts: Evidence from a field experiment. *Journal of Development Economics, 115,* 16–31.

Raichoudhury, A. (2020). Major determinants of financial inclusion: State-level evidences from India. *Vision, 24*(2), 151–159.

Raina, N. (2014). An analytical study: Inclusive approach to banking by scheduled commercial banks as a key driver for inclusive growth. *Journal for Contemporary Research in Management,* 1–8.

Rajan, R. G. (2008). A hundred small steps: Report of the committee on financial sector reforms. In *Planning commission.* Government of India.

Ramji, M. (2009). *Financial inclusion in Gulbarga: Finding usage in access* (Institute for Financial Management and Research Centre for Micro Finance Working Paper Series No. 26, pp. 1–37).

Ranjani, K. S., & Bapat, V. (2015). Deepening financial inclusion beyond account opening: Road ahead for banks. *Business Perspectives and Research, 3*(1), 52–65.

Rao, K. G. K. S. (2007). Financial inclusion: An introspection. *Economic and Political Weekly, 42*(5), 355–360.

Reynolds, F. (2003). Promoting financial inclusion. *Poverty, 114,* 1–7.

Rhine, S. L. W., & Greene, W. H. (2006). The determinants of being unbanked for U.S. immigrants. *The Journal of Consumer Affairs, 40*(1), 21–40.

Rose, J. T. (1993). Commercial banks as financial intermediaries and current trends in banking: A pedagogical framework. *Financial Practice and Education – FALL,* 113–118.

Russell, R., Brooks, R., Nair, A., & Fredline, L. (2006). The initial impacts of a matched savings program: The saver plus program. *Economic Papers, 25*(1), 32–40.

Sachan, A., & Ali, A. (2006). Competing in the age of information technology in a developing economy: Experiences of an Indian bank. *Journal of Cases on Information Technology, 8*(2), 62–76.

Saha, A., & Ravisankar, T. S. (2000). Rating of Indian commercial banks: A DEA approach. *European Journal of Operational Research, 124*, 187–203.

Sahu, T. N., Agarwala, V., & Maity, S. (2020). Social welfare through Mudra Yojana: How did the public sector banks perform in realizing the dream? *International Journal of Business Excellence.* (Accepted for publication).

Sahu, T. N., & Maity, S. (2021). Mobile banking a new banking model: An empirical investigation of financial innovation. *International Journal of Business Innovation and Research.* (Accepted for publication). https://doi.org/10.1504/IJBIR.2021.10039945

Sajuyigbe, A. S. (2017). Influence of financial inclusion and social inclusion on the performance of women owned business in Lagos state, Nigeria. *Scholedge International Journal of Management & Development, 4*(3), 18–27.

Sakaria, S. (2013). Evaluation of financial inclusion strategy components: Reflections from India. *Journal of International Management Studies, 13*(1), 83–92.

Sanz, F. P., & Lima, P. D. (2013). The uptake of mobile financial services in the Middle East and North Africa region. *Enterprise Development and Microfinance, 24*(4), 295–310.

Sarker, S., Ghosh, S. K., & Palit, M. (2015). Role of banking – Sector to inclusive through inclusive finance in Bangladesh. *Studies in Business and Economics, 10*(2), 145–156.

Sarma, M., & Pais, J. (2008, September). *Financial inclusion and development: A cross country analysis* (pp. 1–28). Paper presented at the annual conference of the human development and capability association, New Delhi. Retrieved from: www.icrier.org/pdf/6nov08/Mandira%20Sarma-Paper.pdf. Accessed 20 July 2016.

Sathye, M. (2003). Efficiency of banks in a developing economy: The case of India. *European Journal of Operational Research, 148*, 662–671.

Savitha, B. (2014). Performance of cooperative banks in the delivery of micro-credit in Andhra Pradesh. *Research Journal of Social Science & Management, 4*(8), 92–101.

Seaver, W. L., & Fraser, D. R. (1979). Branch banking and the availability of banking services in metropolitan areas. *Journal of Financial and Quantitative Analysis, XIV*(1), 153–160.

Sehrawat, M., & Giri, A. K. (2016). Financial development and poverty reduction in India: An empirical investigation. *International Journal of Social Economics, 43*(2), 106–122.

Sen, A. (2000). *Development as freedom.* Anchor Books.

Shafi, M., & Medabesh, A. H. (2012). Financial inclusion in developing countries: Evidences from an Indian state. *International Business Research, 5*(8), 116–122.

Sharma, D. (2016). Nexus between financial inclusion and economic growth. *Journal of Financial Economic Policy, 8*(1), 13–36.

Sharma, N., & Goyal, R. (2017). Pradhan Mantri Jan Dhan Yojana (PMJDY) – A conceptual study. *International Journal of Research-Granthaalayah*, 5(4), 143–152.

Sharma, R., & Sharma, S. (2014). Banking sector in India: An overview. *Global Journal of Commerce and Management Perspective*, 3(3), 37–39.

Siddik, M. N. A., Ahsan, T., & Kabiraj, S. (2019). Does financial permeation promote economic growth? Some econometric evidence from Asian countries. *SAGE Open*, 9(3). https://doi.org/10.1177/2158244019865811

Simkhada, N. R. (2013). Problems and prospects of the cooperative sector in Nepal for promoting financial inclusion. *Enterprise Development and Microfinance*, 24(2), 146–159.

Sinclair, S. (2013). Financial inclusion and social financialisation: Britain in a European context. *International Journal of Sociology and Social Policy*, 33(11/12), 658–676.

Singh, A. B. (2012). Mobile banking based money order for India Post: Feasible model and assessing demand potential. *Procedia – Social and Behavioral Sciences*, 37, 466–481.

Singh, C., Mittal, A., Garg, R., Goenka, A., Goud, R., Ram, K., ... & Kumar, U. (2014). *Financial inclusion in India: Select issues*. IIM Bangalore research paper (474).

Singh, U. (2014). Financial literacy and financial stability are two aspects of efficient economy. *Journal of Finance, Accounting and Management*, 5(2), 59–76.

Stephen, N., & Tom, T. R. (2015). The role of cooperative banks in financial inclusion. *The IUP Journal of Bank Management*, XIV(3), 55–64.

Stephens, M. C. (2012). *Promoting responsible financial inclusion: A risk-based approach to supporting mobile financial services expansion* (pp. 329–343). Retrieved from: https://www.ftc.gov/sites/default/files/documents/public_comments/ftc-host-workshop-mobile-payments-and-their-impact-consumers-project-no.124808-561018-00012%C2%A0/561018-00012-82712.pdf. Accessed 5 May 2017.

Subrahmanyam, G. (1993). Productivity growth in India's public sector banks: 1970-89. *Journal of Quantitative Economics*, 9, 209–223.

Sukumaran, K. (2015). Financial literacy – Concept and practice. *Journal for Contemporary Research in Management*, 59–65.

Swamy, V. (2011a). Financial inclusion in India: An evaluation of the coverage, progress and trends. *The IUP Journal of Financial Economics*, IX(2), 7–26.

Swamy, V. (2011b). Does government intervention in credit deployment cause inclusive growth? – An evidence from Indian banking. *International Journal of Business Insights & Transformation*, 4(1), 35–45.

Swamy, V. (2013). Institutional reforms in finance to the poor. *ASCI Journal of Management*, 43(1), 39–66.

Swamy, V. (2014). Financial inclusion, gender dimension, and economic impact on poor households. *World Development, 56*, 1–15.

Thakur, S. (1990). *Two decades of Indian banking: The service sector scenario.* Chanakya Publications.

Thorat, U. (2007). *Financial inclusion – The Indian experience.* Speech at the HMT-DFID financial inclusion conference 2007, Whitehall Place, London, UK on June 19.

Thyagarajan, S., & Venkatesan, J. (2008). *Cost-benefit and usage behaviour analysis of no frills accounts: A study report on Cuddalore district* (IFMR/CMF Working Paper). IFMR/CMF, Chennai.

Treasury, H. M. (2007). *Financial inclusion: The way forward.* The report of the financial inclusion task force. United Kingdom, Retrieved from: www.bris.ac.uk/poverty/downloads/keyofficialdocuments/Financ. Accessed 10 Apr 2016.

Turan, M. S., & Sharma, H. (2010). Customers perspectives on E-banking services. *The Journal of Indian Management and Strategy, 15*(1), 45–54.

United Nations. (2006). *Building inclusive financial sectors for development.* Retrieved from: http://www.un.org/esa/ffd/msc/bluebook/Blue%20Book%20Overview%202005%20-E.pdf. Accessed 26 Apr 2018.

Unnikrishnan, R., & Jagannathan, L. (2015). Unearthing global financial inclusion levels and analysis of financial inclusion as a mediating factor in global human development. *Serbian Journal of Management, 10*(1), 19–32.

Wentzel, J. P., Diatha, K. S., & Yadavalli, V. S. S. (2013). An application of the extended technology acceptance model in understanding technology-enabled financial service adoption in South Africa. *Development Southern Africa, 30*(4–5), 659–673.

Worthington, A. C. (2007). Personal bank account access and awareness: An analysis of the technological and informational constraints of Australian consumers. *International Journal of Consumer Studies, 31*, 443–452.

Yan Yuan, L. X. (2015). Are poor able to access the informal credit market? Evidence from rural households in China. *China Economic Review, 33*, 232–246.

Yorulmaz, R. (2013). *Construction of a regional financial inclusion index in Turkey.* Retrieved from: http://www.bddk.org.tr/websites/turkce/raporlar/bddkdergi/12252makale4.pdf. Accessed 5 Oct 2014.

Zardkoohi, A., & Fraser, D. R. (1988). Geographical deregulation and competition in U.S. banking markets. *The Financial Review, 33*, 85–98.

Zhan, M., Anderson, S. G., & Zhang, S. (2012). Utilization of formal and informal financial services among immigrants in the United States. *Social Development Issues, 34*(3), 1–17.

Zins, A., & Weill, L. (2016). The determinants of financial inclusion in Africa. *Review of Development Finance, 6*, 46–57.

WEBSITES

Annual Survey of Industries: http://www.csoisw.gov.in/CMS/cms/Home.aspx
Census of India: http://censusindia.gov.in
Database of Indian Economy: https://dbie.rbi.org.in/DBIE/dbie.rbi?site=home
Department for International Development: https://www.gov.uk/government/
    organisations/department-for-international-development
International Monetary Fund: http://www.imf.org
Ministry of Statistics and Programme Implementation: http://www.mospi.gov.in
National Bank for Agriculture and Rural Development: https://www.nabard.org
Open Government Data Platform of India: https://data.gov.in
Reserve Bank of India: https://www.rbi.org.in
Telecom Regulatory Authority of India: http://www.trai.gov.in
World Bank: http://www.worldbank.org

INDEX

© The Author(s), under exclusive license to Springer Nature Singapore Pte Ltd. 2022
S. Maity, T. N. Sahu, *Financial Inclusion and the Role of Banking System*, https://doi.org/10.1007/978-981-16-6085-6

Printed by Printforce, the Netherlands